J Ruskin.

SELECTIONS FROM THE WRITINGS

OF

JOHN RUSKIN,

D.C.L., LL.D.,

HONORARY STUDENT OF CHRIST CHURCH, HONORARY FELLOW OF CORPUS
CHRISTI COLLEGE, AND SOMETIME SLADE PROFESSOR OF
FINE ART IN THE UNIVERSITY OF OXFORD.

FIRST SERIES

1843—1860.

WITH A PORTRAIT.

FOURTH EDITION.

GEORGE ALLEN, SUNNYSIDE, ORPINGTON,

AND

156, CHARING CROSS ROAD, LONDON.

1899.

The Fourth Edition of these " Selections," in two volumes, was printed in June 1899.

Printed by BALLANTYNE, HANSON & CO.
At the Ballantyne Press

To the original "Selections from Ruskin" the following "Advertisement" was prefixed :—

"The Publishers beg to state that this volume has originated in suggestions, from numerous quarters, that a book of the kind would be acceptable to a large circle of readers, to whom, from various and obvious causes, the principal works whence it is derived are not easily accessible.

"The Publishers think it right to add that Mr. Ruskin, though tacitly consenting to this publication, has taken no part in making the selections, and is in no way responsible for the appearance of the volume."

This new volume is based upon the old favourite. Passages printed in *Frondes Agrestes*, and a few others, have been replaced by new selections from the same works; some parts have been rearranged, and the whole has been revised; but the work has been kept within the same limits; that is to say, it includes only the earlier publications of Mr. Ruskin,—*Modern Painters*, and associated writings, up to the year 1860.

A companion volume contains a series of selections from the later writings of Mr. Ruskin.

THE selections are from the following works:—

Modern Painters—"M. P."—reference figures denoting volume, part, section—when the part is so divided, chapter and paragraph.

The Seven Lamps of Architecture—"S. L. A."—references to chapter and paragraph.

The Stones of Venice—"S. V."—references to volume, chapter and paragraph.

Lectures on Architecture and Painting, delivered at Edinburgh—"L. A. P."

The Elements of Drawing—"E. D."

The Political Economy of Art, now published under the title of *A Joy for Ever, and its Price in the Market*—"J. E."

The Two Paths—"T. P." In the last four books, references are to chapter or lecture, and paragraph.

Arrows of the Chace, a collection of letters to newspapers, &c.—"A. C."—references to volume and page.

On the Old Road, a collection of magazine articles, &c.—"O. R."—references to volume and paragraph.

Notes on the principal Pictures at the Royal Academy. Catalogue of Turner's Works at Marlborough House. Inaugural Address. Cambridge School of Art—also reprinted in "On the Old Road."

CONTENTS OF FIRST SERIES.

I. SCENES OF TRAVEL.

II. CHARACTERISTICS OF NATURE.

III. PAINTING AND POETRY.

IV. PAINTERS AND PICTURES.

V. ARCHITECTURE AND SCULPTURE.

VI. ETHICAL AND DIDACTIC.

SELECTIONS FROM RUSKIN.

I. SCENES OF TRAVEL.

1. FRENCH AND ENGLISH.—Once on coming from the Continent, almost the first inscription I saw in my native English was this:

"To Let, a Genteel House, up this road."

And it struck me forcibly, for I had not come across the idea of gentility, among the upper limestones of the Alps, for seven months; nor do I think that the Continental nations in general *have* the idea. They would have advertised a "pretty" house, or a "large" one, or a "convenient" one; but they could not, by any use of the terms afforded by their several languages, have got at the English "genteel." Consider, a little, all the meanness that there is in that epithet, and then see, when next you cross the Channel, how scornful of it that Calais spire will look.

Of which spire the largeness and age are also opposed exactly to the chief appearances of modern England, as one feels them on first returning to it; that marvellous smallness both of houses and scenery, so that a ploughman in the valley has his head on a level with the tops of all the hills in the neighbourhood; and a house is organised into complete establishment, —parlour, kitchen, and all, with a knocker to its door, and a garret window to its roof, and a bow to its second story, on a scale of 12 feet wide by 15 high, so that three such at least would go into the granary of an ordinary Swiss cottage: and also our serenity of perfection, our peace of conceit, everything being done that vulgar minds can conceive as wanting to be done; the spirit of well-principled housemaids everywhere, exerting itself for perpetual propriety and renovation, so that nothing is old, but only "old-fashioned," and contemporary, as it were, in date and impressiveness only with last year's bonnets. Abroad, a building of the eighth or tenth century stands ruinous in the open street; the children play round it, the peasants heap their corn in it, the buildings of yesterday nestle about it, and fit their new stones into its rents, and tremble in sympathy as it trembles. No one wonders at it, or thinks of it as separate, and of another time; we feel the ancient world to be a real thing, and one with the new: antiquity is no dream; it is rather the children playing about the old stones that are the dream. But all is

continuous; and the words, "from generation
to generation," understandable there. Whereas
here we have a living present, consisting merely
of what is "fashionable" and "old-fashioned;"
and a past, of which there are no vestiges;
a past which peasant or citizen can no more
conceive; all equally far away; Queen Elizabeth
as old as Queen Boadicea, and both incredible.
At Verona we look out of Can Grande's window
to his tomb; and if he does not stand beside us,
we feel only that he is in the grave instead of
the chamber,—not that he is *old*, but that he
might have been beside us last night. But in
England the dead are dead to purpose. One
cannot believe they ever were alive, or anything
else than what they are now—names in school-
books.

Then that spirit of trimness. The smooth
paving stones; the scraped, hard, even, rutless
roads; the neat gates and plates, and essence
of border and order, and spikiness and spruce-
ness. Abroad, a country-house has some confession of human weakness and human fates
about it. There are the old grand gates still,
which the mob pressed sore against at the
Revolution, and the strained hinges have never
gone so well since; and the broken greyhound
on the pillar—still broken—better so: but the
long avenue is gracefully pale with fresh green,
and the courtyard bright with orange-trees; the

garden is a little run to waste—since Mademoiselle was married nobody cares much about it; and one range of apartments is shut up—nobody goes into them since Madame died. But with us, let who will be married or die, we neglect nothing. All is polished and precise again next morning; and whether people are happy or miserable, poor or prosperous, still we sweep the stairs of a Saturday.—*M. P.*, IV. v. 1, § 4–6.

2. ROUEN IN PROUT'S TIME.—Rouen was, of all the cities of France, the richest in those objects with which the painter's mind had the profoundest sympathy. It was other than it is now; revolutionary fury had indeed spent itself upon many of its noblest monuments, but the interference of modern restoration or improvement was unknown. Better the unloosed rage of the fiend than the scrabble of self-complacent idiocy. The façade of the cathedral was as yet unencumbered by the blocks of new stonework, never to be carved, by which it is now defaced; the Church of St. Nicholas existed (the last fragments of the niches of its gateway were seen by the writer dashed upon the pavement in 1840 to make room for the new "Hôtel St. Nicholas"); the Gothic turret had not vanished from the angle of the Place de la Pucelle; the Palais de Justice remained in its grey antiquity, and the Norman houses still lifted their fantastic ridges of gable

along the busy quay (now fronted by as formal a range of hotels and offices as that of the West Cliff of Brighton). All was at unity with itself, and the city lay, under its guarding hills, one labyrinth of delight, its grey and fretted towers, misty in their magnificence of height, letting the sky like blue enamel through the foiled spaces of their crowns of open work; the walls and gates of its countless churches wardered by saintly groups of solemn statuary, clasped about by wandering stems of sculptured leafage, and crowned by fretted niche and fairy pediment— meshed like gossamer with inextricable tracery: many a quaint monument of past times standing to tell its far-off tale in the place from which it has since perished—in the midst of the throng and murmur of those shadowy streets—all grim with jutting props of ebon woodwork, lightened only here and there by a sunbeam glancing down from the scaly backs, and points, and pyramids of the Norman roofs, or carried out of its narrow range by the gay progress of some snowy cap or scarlet camisole.—*Art Journal*, March 1849 (*O. R.*, I. § 144).

3. NUREMBERG is gathered at the base of a sandstone rock, rising in the midst of a dry but fertile plain. The rock forms a prolonged and curved ridge, of which the concave side, at the highest point, is precipitous; the other

slopes gradually to the plain. Fortified with wall and tower along its whole crest, and crowned with a stately castle, it defends the city—not with its precipitous side—but with its slope. The precipice is turned to the town. It wears no aspect of hostility towards the surrounding fields; the roads lead down into them by gentle descents from the gates. To the south and east the walls are on the level of the plain; within them, the city itself stands on two swells of hill, divided by a winding river. Its architecture has, however, been much overrated. The effect of the streets, so delightful to the eye of the passing traveller, depends chiefly on one appendage of the roof, namely, its warehouse windows. Every house, almost without exception, has at least one boldly opening dormer window, the roof of which sustains a pulley for raising goods; and the under part of this strong overhanging roof is always carved with a rich pattern, not of refined design, but effective.* Among these comparatively modern structures are mingled, however, not unfrequently, others, turreted at the angles, which are true Gothic of the fifteenth, some of the fourteenth, century; and the principal churches remain nearly as in Dürer's time. Their Gothic is none

---

* To obtain room for the goods, the roofs slope steeply, and their other dormer windows are richly carved—but all are of wood; and, for the most part, I think, some hundred years later than Dürer's time. A large number of the oriel and bow windows on the façades are wooden also, and of recent date.

of it good, nor even rich (though the façades have their ornament so distributed as to give them a sufficiently elaborate effect at a distance); their size is diminutive; their interiors mean, rude, and ill-proportioned, wholly dependent for their interest on ingenious stone-cutting in corners, and finely twisted ironwork; of these the mason's exercises are in the worst possible taste, possessing not even the merit of delicate execution; but the designs in metal are usually meritorious, and Fischer's shrine of St. Sebald is good, and may rank with Italian work.

Though, however, not comparable for an instant to any great Italian or French city, Nuremberg possesses one character peculiar to itself, that of a self-restrained, contented, quaint domesticity. It would have been vain to expèct any first-rate painting, sculpture, or poetry, from the well-regulated community of merchants of small ware. But it is evident they were affectionate and trustworthy—that they had playful fancy and honourable pride. There is no exalted grandeur in their city, nor any deep beauty; but an imaginative homeliness, mingled with some elements of melancholy and power, and a few even of grace.

This homeliness, among many other causes, arises out of one in chief. The richness of the houses depends, as I just said, on the dormer windows; but their deeper character on the pitch and space of roofs. . . . In Dürer's own engraving, "The Cannon," the distance is an actual portrait of part of the landscape seen from those castle ramparts, looking towards Franconian Switzerland.

If the reader will be at the pains to turn to it, he will see at a glance the elements of the Nuremberg country, as they still exist. Wooden cottages, thickly grouped, enormously high in the roofs; the sharp church spire, small and slightly grotesque, surmounting them; beyond, a richly cultivated, healthy plain, bounded by woody hills. By a strange coincidence the very plant which constitutes the staple produce of those fields, is in almost ludicrous harmony with the grotesqueness and neatness of the architecture around; and one may almost fancy that the builders of the little knotted spires and turrets of the town, and workers of its dark iron flowers, are in spiritual presence, watching and guiding the produce of the field,—when one finds the footpaths bordered, everywhere, by the bossy spires and lustrous jetty flowers of the black hollyhock.—*M. P.*, V. IX. 4, § 6-8.

4. PINE FOREST IN THE JURA.—Among the hours of his life to which the writer looks back with peculiar gratitude, as having been marked by more than ordinary fulness of joy or clearness of teaching, is one passed, now some years ago,

near time of sunset, among the broken masses of
pine forest which skirt the course of the Ain,
above the village of Champagnole, in the Jura.
It is a spot which has all the solemnity, with
none of the savageness, of the Alps; where
there is a sense of a great power beginning
to be manifested in the earth, and of a deep and
majestic concord in the rise of the long low lines
of piny hills; the first utterance of those mighty
mountain symphonies, soon to be more loudly
lifted and wildly broken along the battlements
of the Alps. But their strength is as yet restrained; and the far-reaching ridges of pastoral
mountain succeed each other, like the long and
sighing swell which moves over quiet waters
from some far-off stormy sea. And there is a
deep tenderness pervading that vast monotony.
The destructive forces and the stern expression
of the central ranges are alike withdrawn. No
frost-ploughed, dust-encumbered paths of ancient
glacier fret the soft Jura pastures; no splintered
heaps of ruin break the fair ranks of her forests;
no pale, defiled, or furious rivers rend their rude
and changeful ways among her rocks. Patiently,
eddy by eddy, the clear green streams wind along
their well-known beds; and under the dark
quietness of the undisturbed pines, there spring
up, year by year, such company of joyful flowers
as I know not the like of among all the blessings
of the earth. It was Spring time, too; and all

were coming forth in clusters crowded for very
love; there was room enough for all, but they
crushed their leaves into all manner of strange
shapes only to be nearer each other.   There was
the wood anemone, star after star, closing every
now and then into nebulæ; and there was the
oxalis, troop by troop, like virginal processions
of the Mois de Marie, the dark vertical clefts in
the limestone choked up with them as with heavy
snow, and touched with ivy on the edges—ivy as
light and lovely as the vine; and, ever and anon,
a blue gush of violets, and cowslip bells in sunny
places; and in the more open ground, the vetch,
and comfrey, and mezereon, and the small
sapphire buds of the Polygala Alpina, and the
wild strawberry, just a blossom or two, all
showered amidst the golden softness of deep,
warm, amber-coloured moss.   I came out presently on the edge of the ravine: the solemn
murmur of its waters rose suddenly from beneath, mixed with the singing of the thrushes
among the pine boughs; and, on the opposite
side of the valley, walled all along as it was by
grey cliffs of limestone, there was a hawk sailing
slowly off their brow, touching them nearly with
his wings, and with the shadows of the pines
flickering upon his plumage from above; but
with a fall of a hundred fathoms under his
breast, and the curling pools of the green river
gliding and glittering dizzily beneath him, their

foam globes moving with him as he flew. It would be difficult to conceive a scene less dependent upon any other interest than that of its own secluded and serious beauty; but the writer well remembers the sudden blankness and chill which were cast upon it when he endeavoured, in order more strictly to arrive at the sources of its impressiveness, to imagine it, for a moment, a scene in some aboriginal forest of the New Continent. The flowers in an instant lost their light, the river its music; the hills became oppressively desolate; a heaviness in the boughs of the darkened forest showed how much of their former power had been dependent upon a life which was not theirs, how much of the glory of the imperishable, or continually renewed, creation is reflected from things more precious in their memories than it, in its renewing. Those ever springing flowers and ever flowing streams had been dyed by the deep colours of human endurance, valour, and virtue; and the crests of the sable hills that rose against the evening sky received a deeper worship, because their far shadows fell eastward over the iron wall of Joux, and the four-square keep of Granson.— *S. L. A.*, VI. § I.

5. THE MOUNTAIN GLOOM.—The unhappy alterations which have lately taken place in the town of Lucerne have still spared two of its

ancient bridges; both of which, being long
covered walks, appear, in past times, to have
been to the population of the town what the Mall
was to London, or the Gardens of the Tuileries
are to Paris. For the continual contemplation of
those who sauntered from pier to pier, pictures
were painted on the woodwork of the roof.
These pictures, in the one bridge, represent all
the important Swiss battles and victories; in the
other they are the well-known series of which
Longfellow has made so beautiful a use in the
Golden Legend, the *Dance of Death.*

Imagine the countenances with which a com-
mittee, appointed for the establishment of a
new "promenade" in some flourishing modern
town, would receive a proposal to adorn such
promenade with pictures of the Dance of Death!

Now just so far as the old bridge at Lucerne,
with the pure deep, and blue water of the Reuss
eddying down between its piers, and with the
sweet darkness of green hills, and far-away
gleaming of lake and Alps alternating upon the
eye on either side; and the gloomy lesson
frowning in the shadow, as if the deep tone of
a passing bell, overhead, were mingling for ever
with the plashing of the river as it glides by
beneath: just so far, I say, as this differs from
the straight and smooth strip of level dust,
between two rows of round-topped acacia trees,
wherein the inhabitants of an English watering-

place or French fortified town take their delight,
—so far I believe the life of the old Lucernois,
with all its happy waves of light, and mountain
strength of will, and solemn expectation of
eternity, to have differed from the generality of
the lives of those who saunter for their habitual
hour up and down the modern promenade. But
the gloom is not always of this noble kind. As
we penetrate farther among the hills we shall
find it becoming very painful. We are walking,
perhaps, in a summer afternoon, up the valley of
Zermatt (a German valley), the sun shining
brightly on grassy knolls and through fringes
of pines, the goats leaping happily, and the cattle
bells ringing sweetly, and the snowy mountains
shining like heavenly castles far above. We see,
a little way off, a small white chapel, sheltered
behind one of the flowery hillocks of mountain
turf; and we approach its little window, thinking
to look through it into some quiet home of
prayer; but the window is grated with iron, and
open to the winds, and when we look through it,
behold—a heap of white human bones mouldering into whiter dust!

So also in that sweet valley of Trient, between
Chamouni and the Valais, at every turn of the
pleasant pathway, where the scent of the thyme
lies richest upon its rocks, we shall see a little
cross and shrine set under one of them; and go
up to it, hoping to receive some happy thought

of the Redeemer, by whom all these lovely things were made, and still consist. But when we come near—behold, beneath the cross, a rude picture of souls tormented in red tongues of hell fire, and pierced by demons.

As we pass towards Italy the appearance of this gloom deepens; and when we descend the southern slope of the Alps we shall find this bringing forward of the image of Death associated with an endurance of the most painful aspects of disease; so that conditions of human suffering, which in any other country would be confined in hospitals, are permitted to be openly exhibited by the wayside; and with this exposure of the degraded human form is farther connected an insensibility to ugliness and imperfection in other things; so that the ruined wall, neglected garden, and uncleansed chamber, seem to unite in expressing a gloom of spirit possessing the inhabitants of the whole land. It does not appear to arise from poverty, nor careless contentment with little: there is here nothing of Irish recklessness or humour; but there seems a settled obscurity in the soul,—a chill and plague, as if risen out of a sepulchre, which partly deadens, partly darkens, the eyes and hearts of men, and breathes a leprosy of decay through every breeze, and every stone. "Instead of well-set hair, baldness, and burning instead of beauty."

Nor are definite proofs wanting that the feeling is independent of mere poverty or indolence. In the most gorgeous and costly palace garden the statues will be found green with moss, the terraces defaced or broken; the palace itself, partly coated with marble, is left in other places rough with cementless and jagged brick, its iron balconies bent and rusted, its pavements overgrown with grass. The more energetic the effort has been to recover from this state, and to shake off all appearance of poverty, the more assuredly the curse seems to fasten on the scene, and the unslaked mortar, and unfinished wall, and ghastly desolation of incompleteness entangled in decay, strike a deeper despondency into the beholder.

The feeling would be also more easily accounted for if it appeared inconsistent in its regardlessness of beauty,—if what was *done* were altogether as inefficient as what was deserted. But the balcony, though rusty and broken, is delicate in design, and supported on a nobly carved slab of marble; the window, though a mere black rent in ragged plaster, is encircled by a garland of vine and fronted by a thicket of the sharp leaves and aurora-coloured flowers of the oleander; the courtyard, overgrown by mournful grass, is terminated by a bright fresco of gardens and fountains; the corpse, borne with the bare face to heaven, is

strewn with flowers; beauty is continually
mingled with the shadow of death.—*M. P.*, IV.
V. 19, § 10–13.

6. ALPINE PRECIPICES.—The most frightful
and most characteristic cliff in the whole group
is the range of the Rochers des Fys, above the
Col d'Anterne. It happens to have a bed of
harder limestone at the top than in any other part
of its mass; and this bed, protecting its summit,
enables it to form itself into the most ghastly
ranges of pinnacle which I know among mountains. In one spot the upper ledge of limestone
has formed a complete cornice, or rather bracket
—for it is not extended enough to constitute a
cornice, which projects far into the air over the
wall of ashy rock, and is seen against the clouds,
when they pass into the chasm beyond, like the
nodding coping-stones of a castle—only the wall
below is not less than 2500 feet in height,—not
vertical, but steep enough to seem so to the imagination.

Such precipices are among the most impressive
as well as the most really dangerous of mountain
ranges; in many spots inaccessible with safety
either from below or from above; dark in colour,
robed with everlasting mourning, for ever tottering like a great fortress shaken by war, fearful as
much in their weakness as in their strength, and
yet gathered after every fall into darker frowns

and unhumiliated threatening; for ever incapable of comfort or of healing from herb or flower, nourishing no root in their crevices, touched by no hue of life on buttress or ledge, but, to the utmost, desolate; knowing no shaking of leaves in the wind, nor of grass beside the stream,—no motion but their own mortal shivering, the dreadful crumbling of atom from atom in their corrupting stones; knowing no sound of living voice or living tread, cheered neither by the kid's bleat nor the marmot's cry; haunted only by uninterpreted echoes from far off, wandering hither and thither, among their walls, unable to escape, and by the hiss of angry torrents, and sometimes the shriek of a bird that flits near the face of them, and sweeps frightened back from under their shadow into the gulph of air; and, sometimes, when the echo has fainted, and the wind has carried the sound of the torrent away, and the bird has vanished, and the mouldering stones are still for a little time,—a brown moth, opening and shutting its wings upon a grain of dust, may be the only thing that moves, or feels, in all the waste of weary precipice, darkening five thousand feet of the blue depth of heaven.

It will not be thought that there is nothing in a scene such as this deserving our contemplation, or capable of conveying useful lessons, if it were fitly rendered by art. . . .

A new world of sublimity might be opened to

us, if any painter of power and feeling would
devote himself, for a few months, to these solemn
cliffs of the dark limestone Alps, and would only
paint one of them as it truly stands, not in rain
nor storm, but in its own eternal sadness : perhaps
best on some fair summer evening, when its
fearful veil of immeasurable rock is breathed upon
by warm air, and touched with fading rays of
purple ; and all that it has of the melancholy of
ruin, mingled with the might of endurance, and
the foreboding of danger, rises in its grey gloom
against the gentle sky ; the soft wreaths of the
evening clouds expiring along its ridges one by
one, and leaving it, at last, with no light but that
of its own cascades, standing like white pillars
here and there along its sides, motionless and
soundless in their distance. . . .

I commend, therefore, in conclusion, the
precipice to the artist's *patience ;* to which there
is this farther and final encouragement, that,
though one of the most difficult of subjects, it is
one of the kindest of sitters. A group of trees
changes the colour of its leafage from week to
week, and its position from day to day ; it is sometimes languid with heat, and sometimes heavy
with rain ; the torrent swells or falls in shower
or sun ; the best leaves of the foreground may be
dined upon by cattle, or trampled by unwelcome
investigators of the chosen scene. But the cliff
can neither be eaten, nor trampled down ; neither

bowed by the shower, nor withered by the heat : it is always ready for us when we are inclined to labour ; will always wait for us when we would rest ; and, what is best of all, will always talk to us when we are inclined to converse. With its own patient and victorious presence, cleaving daily through cloud after cloud, and reappearing still through the tempest drift, lofty and serene amidst the passing rents of blue, it seems partly to rebuke, and partly to guard, and partly to calm and chasten, the agitations of the feeble human soul that watches it ; and that must be indeed a dark perplexity, or a grievous pain, which will not be in some degree enlightened or relieved by the vision of it, when the evening shadows are blue on its foundation, and the last rays of the sunset resting on the fair height of its golden fortitude.—*M. P.*, IV. v. 16, § 20–22, 24, 43.

7. SAVOYARD PEASANTS.—No contrast can be more painful than that between the dwelling of any well-conducted English cottager, and that of the equally honest Savoyard. The one, set in the midst of its dull flat fields and uninteresting hedgerows, shows in itself the love of brightness and beauty ; its daisy-studded garden-beds, its smoothly swept brick path to the threshold, its freshly sanded floor and orderly shelves of household furniture, all testify to energy of heart, and

happiness in the simple course and simple possessions of daily life. The other cottage, in the midst of an inconceivable, inexpressible beauty, set on some sloping bank of golden sward, with clear fountains flowing beside it, and wild flowers, and noble trees, and goodly rocks gathered round into a perfection as of Paradise, is itself a dark and plague-like stain in the midst of the gentle landscape. Within a certain distance of its threshold the ground is foul and cattle-trampled; its timbers are black with smoke, its garden choked with weeds and nameless refuse, its chambers empty and joyless, the light and wind gleaming and filtering through the crannies of their stones. All testifies that to its inhabitant the world is labour and vanity; that for him neither flowers bloom, nor birds sing, nor fountains glisten; and that his soul hardly differs from the grey cloud that coils and dies upon his hills, except in having no fold of it touched by the sunbeams.

Is it not strange to reflect, that hardly an evening passes in London or Paris, but one of those cottages is painted for the better amusement of the fair and idle, and shaded with pasteboard pines by the scene-shifter; and that good and kind people,— poetically-minded,— delight themselves in imagining the happy life led by peasants who dwell by Alpine fountains, and kneel to crosses upon peaks of rock? that nightly we lay down our gold, to fashion forth simulacra of peasants, in gay ribands and white bodices, singing sweet songs, and bowing gracefully to the picturesque crosses : and all the while the veritable peasants are kneeling, songlessly, to veritable crosses, in another temper than the kind and fair audiences deem of, and assuredly with another kind of answer than is got out of the opera catastrophe ; an answer having reference, it may be in dim futurity, to those very audiences themselves ?   If all the gold that has gone to paint the simulacra of the cottages, and to put new songs in the mouths of the simulacra of the peasants, had gone to brighten the existent cottages, and to put new songs in the mouths of the existent peasants, it might in the end, perhaps, have turned out better so, not only for the peasant, but for even the audience.   For that form of the False Ideal has also its correspondent True Ideal,—consisting not in the naked beauty of statues, nor in the gauze flowers and crackling tinsel of theatres, but in the clothed and fed beauty of living men, and in the lights and laughs of happy homes.   Night after night, the desire of such an ideal springs up in every idle human heart ; and night after night, as far as idleness can, we work out this desire in costly lies.   We paint the faded actress, build the lath landscape, feed our benevolence with fallacies of felicity, and satisfy our righteousness with poetry of justice. The time will come when, as the heavy-folded curtain falls upon our own stage of life, we shall begin to comprehend that the justice we loved was intended to have been done in fact, and not in poetry, and the felicity we sympathised in, to have been bestowed and not feigned. We talk much of money's worth, yet perhaps may one day be surprised to find that what the wise and charitable European public gave to one night's rehearsal of hypocrisy—to one hour's pleasant warbling of Linda or Lucia—would have filled a whole Alpine valley with happiness, and poured the waves of harvest over the famine of many a Lammermoor. —*M. P.*, IV. V. 19, § 5, 6.

8. SION IN THE VALAIS.—Sion is in the midst of a marshy valley, pregnant with various disease; the water either stagnant, or disgorged in wild torrents charged with earth; the air, in the morning, stagnant also, hot, close, and infected; in the afternoon, rushing up from the outlet at Martigny in fitful and fierce whirlwind; one side of the valley in almost continual shade, the other (it running east and west) scorched by southern sun, and sending streams of heat into the air all night long from its torrid limestones; while less traceable plagues than any of these bring on the inhabitants, at a certain time of life, violent affections of goître, and often, in infancy, cretinism.

Agriculture is attended with the greatest difficulties and dependencies; the land which the
labour of a life has just rendered fruitful, is often
buried in an hour; and the carriage of materials,
as well as the traversing of land on the steep hill
sides, attended with extraordinary fatigue.

Owing to these various influences, Sion, the
capital of the district, presents one of the most
remarkable scenes for the study of the particular
condition of human feeling at present under consideration that I know among mountains. It
consists of little more than one main street, winding round the roots of two ridges of crag, and
branching, on the side towards the rocks, into
a few narrow lanes, on the other, into spaces of
waste ground, of which part serve for military
exercises, part are enclosed in an uncertain and
vague way; a ditch half-filled up, or wall half-
broken down, seeming to indicate their belonging,
or having been intended to belong, to some of
the unfinished houses which are springing up
amidst their weeds. But it is difficult to say, in
any part of the town, what is garden ground and
what is waste; still more, what is new building
and what old. The houses have been for the
most part built roughly of the coarse limestone
of the neighbouring hills, then coated with plaster,
and painted, in imitation of Palladian palaces,
with grey architraves and pilasters, having
draperies from capital to capital. With this

false decoration is curiously contrasted a great
deal of graceful, honest, and original ironwork,
in bulging balconies, and floreted gratings of
huge windows, and branching sprays, for any
and every purpose of support or guard. The
plaster, with its fresco, has in most instances
dropped away, leaving the houses peeled and
scarred; daubed into uncertain restoration with
new mortar, and in the best cases thus left; but
commonly fallen also, more or less, into ruin,
and either roofed over at the first story when
the second has fallen, or hopelessly abandoned;
—not pulled down, but left in white and ghastly
shells to crumble into heaps of limestone and
dust, a pauper or two still inhabiting where
inhabitation is possible. The lanes wind among
these ruins; the blue sky and mountain grass
are seen through the windows of their rooms
and over their partitions, on which old gaudy
papers flaunt in rags: the weeds gather, and the
dogs scratch about their foundations; yet there
are no luxuriant weeds, for their ragged leaves
are blanched with lime, crushed under perpetually
falling fragments, and worn away by listless
standing of idle feet. There is always mason's
work doing, always some fresh patching and
whitening; a dull smell of mortar, mixed with
that of stale foulness of every kind, rises with
the dust, and defiles every current of air; the
corners are filled with accumulations of stones,

partly broken, with crusts of cement sticking to them, and blotches of nitre oozing out of their pores. The lichenous rocks and sunburnt slopes of grass stretch themselves hither and thither among the wreck, curiously traversed by stairs and walls and half-cut paths, that disappear below starkly black arches, and cannot be followed, or rise in windings round the angles, and in unfenced slopes along the fronts, of the two masses of rock which bear, one the dark castle, the other the old church and convent of Sion; beneath, in a rudely inclosed square at the outskirts of the town, a still more ancient Lombardic church raises its grey tower, a kind of esplanade extending between it and the Episcopal palace, and laid out as a plot of grass, intersected by gravel walks; but the grass, in strange sympathy with the inhabitants, will not grow *as* grass, but chokes itself with a network of grey weeds, quite wonderful in its various expression of thorny discontent and savageness; the blue flower of the borage, which mingles with it in quantities, hardly interrupting its character, for the violent black spot in the centre of its blue takes away the tenderness of the flower, and it seems to have grown there in some supernatural mockery of its old renown of being good against melancholy. The rest of the herbage is chiefly composed of the dwarf mallow, the wild succory, the wall-rocket, goosefoot, and milfoil; plants, nearly all of them, jagged in the leaf, broken and dimly clustered in flower, haunters of waste ground and places of outcast refuse.

Beyond this plot of ground the Episcopal palace, a half-deserted, barrack-like building, overlooks a *neglected vineyard*, of which the clusters, black on the under side, snow-white on the other with lime-dust, gather around them a melancholy hum of flies. Through the arches of this trellis-work the avenue of the great valley is seen in descending distance, enlarged with line beyond line of tufted foliage, languid and rich, degenerating at last into leagues of grey Maremma, wild with the thorn and the willow; on each side of it, sustaining themselves in mighty slopes and unbroken reaches of colossal promontory, the great mountains secede into supremacy through rosy depths of burning air, and the crescents of snow gleam over their dim summits, as—if there could be Mourning, as once there was War, in Heaven—a line of waning moons might be set for lamps along the sides of some sepulchral chamber in the Infinite.—*M. P.*, IV. v. 19, § 30, 31.

9. THE Z'MUTT GLACIER.—The whole surface of it is covered with blocks of reddish gneiss, or other slaty crystalline rocks, some fallen from the Cervin, some from the Weisshorn, some brought from the Stockje and Dent

d'Erin, but little rolled or ground down in the transit, and covering the ice, often four or five feet deep, with a species of macadamization on a large scale (each stone being usually some foot or foot and a half in diameter), anything but convenient to a traveller in haste. Higher up, the ice opens into broad white fields and furrows, hard and dry, scarcely fissured at all, except just under the Cervin, and forming a silent and solemn causeway, paved, as it seems, with white marble from side to side; broad enough for the march of an army in line of battle, but quiet as a street of tombs in a buried city, and bordered on each hand by ghostly cliffs of that faint granite purple which seems, in its far-away height, as unsubstantial as the dark blue that bounds it;—the whole scene so changeless and soundless; so removed, not merely from the presence of men, but even from their thoughts; so destitute of all life of tree or herb, and so immeasurable in its lonely brightness of majestic death, that it looks like a world from which not only the human, but the spiritual, presences had perished, and the last of its archangels, building the great mountains for their monuments, had laid themselves down in the sunlight to an eternal rest, each in his white shroud.—*M. P.*, IV. v. 16, § 13.

10. AT SALLENCHE.—The imagination is

eminently a *weariable* faculty, eminently delicate, and incapable of bearing fatigue; so that
if we give it too many objects at a time to employ
itself upon, or very grand ones for a long time
together, it fails under the effort, becomes jaded,
exactly as the limbs do by bodily fatigue, and
incapable of answering any farther appeal till
it has had rest. And this is the real nature
of the weariness which is so often felt in
travelling, from seeing too much. It is not
that the monotony and number of the beautiful
things seen have made them valueless, but that
the imaginative power has been overtaxed; and,
instead of letting it rest, the traveller, wondering
to find himself dull, and incapable of admiration,
seeks for something more admirable, excites and
torments, and drags the poor fainting imagination up by the shoulders: "Look at this, and
look at that, and this more wonderful still!"—
until the imaginative faculty faints utterly away,
beyond all farther torment, or pleasure, dead
for many a day to come; and the despairing
prodigal takes to horse-racing in the Campagna,
good now for nothing else than that; whereas,
if the imagination had only been laid down on
the grass, among simple things, and left quiet
for a little while, it would have come to itself
gradually, recovered its strength and colour, and
soon been fit for work again. So that, whenever
the imagination is tired, it is necessary to find

for it something, not *more* admirable but *less* admirable; such as in that weak state it can deal with; then give it peace, and it will recover.

I well recollect the walk on which I first found out this; it was on the winding road from Sallenche, sloping up the hills towards St. Gervais, one cloudless Sunday afternoon. The road circles softly between bits of rocky bank and mounded pasture; little cottages and chapels gleaming out from among the trees at every turn. Behind me, some leagues in length, rose the jagged range of the mountains of the Réposoir; on the other side of the valley, the mass of the Aiguille de Varens, heaving its seven thousand feet of cliff into the air at a single effort, its gentle gift of waterfall, the Nant d'Arpenaz, like a pillar of cloud at its feet; Mont Blanc and all its aiguilles, one silver flame, in front of me; marvellous blocks of mossy granite and dark glades of pine around me; but I could enjoy nothing, and could not for a long while make out what was the matter with me, until at last I discovered that if I confined myself to one thing,—and that a little thing,—a tuft of moss or a single crag at the top of the Varens, or a wreath or two of foam at the bottom of the Nant d'Arpenaz, I began to enjoy it directly, because then I had mind enough to put into the thing, and the enjoyment arose from the quantity of the imaginative energy I could bring to bear upon it; but when I looked at or thought of all together, moss, stones, Varens, Nant d'Arpenaz, and Mont Blanc, I had not mind enough to give to all, and none were of any value. The conclusion which would have been formed, upon this, by a German philosopher, would have been that the Mont Blanc *was* of no value; that he and his imagination only were of value; that the Mont Blanc, in fact, except so far as he was able to look at it, could not be considered as having any existence. But the only conclusion which occurred to me as reasonable under the circumstances (I have seen no ground for altering it since) was, that I was an exceedingly small creature, much tired, and, at the moment, not a little stupid; for whom a blade of grass, or a wreath of foam, was quite food enough and to spare, and that if I tried to take any more, I should make myself ill. Whereupon, associating myself fraternally with some ants, who were deeply interested in the conveyance of some small sticks over the road, and rather, as I think they generally are, in too great a hurry about it, I returned home in a little while with great contentment; thinking how well it was ordered that, as Mont Blanc and his pine forests could not be everywhere, nor all the world come to see them, the human mind, on the whole, should enjoy itself most surely, in an ant-like

manner, and be happy and busy with the bits
of sticks and grains of crystal that fall in its
way to be handled, in daily duty.—*M. P.*, III. IV.
10, § 14, 15.

11. THE VILLA OF CARDINAL MAURICE OF
SAVOY: TURIN.—If you glance at the map, you
will observe that Turin is placed in the centre of
the crescent which the Alps form, round the
basin of Piedmont; it is within ten miles of the
foot of the mountains at the nearest point, and
from that point the chain extends half round the
city in one unbroken Moorish crescent, forming
three-fourths of a circle from the Col de Tende to
the St. Gothard; that is to say, just two hundred
miles of Alps, as the bird flies. . . .

You see, then, from this spot, the plain of
Piedmont, on the north and south, literally as far
as the eye can reach; so that the plain terminates
as the sea does, with a level blue line, only tufted
with woods instead of waves, and crowded with
towers of cities instead of ships. Then, in the
luminous air beyond and behind this blue horizon-
line, stand, as it were, the shadows of mountains,
they themselves dark, for the southern slopes of
the Alps of the Lago Maggiore and Bellinzona
are all without snow; but the light of the unseen
snowfields, lying level behind the visible peaks, is
sent up with strange reflection upon the clouds;
an everlasting light of calm Aurora in the north.

Then, higher and higher around the approaching darkness of the plain, rise the central chains, not as on the Switzer's side, a recognizable group and following of successive and separate hills, but a wilderness of jagged peaks, cast in passionate and fierce profusion along the circumference of heaven; precipice behind precipice, and gulf beyond gulf, filled with the flaming of the sunset, and forming mighty channels for the flowings of the clouds, which roll up against them out of the vast Italian plain, forced together by the narrowing crescent, and breaking up at last against the Alpine wall in towers of spectral spray, or sweeping up its ravines with long moans of complaining thunder. Out from between the cloudy pillars, as they pass, emerge for ever the great battlements of the memorable and perpetual hills: Viso, with her shepherd-witnesses to ancient faith; Rocca-Melone, the highest place of Alpine pilgrimage; Iseran, who shed her burial sheets of snow about the march of Hannibal; Cenis, who shone with her glacier light on the descent of Charlemagne; Paradiso, who watched with her opposite crest the stoop of the French eagle to Marengo; and underneath all these, lying in her soft languor, this tender Italy, lapped in dews of sleep, or more than sleep—one knows not if it is trance, from which morning shall yet roll the blinding mists away, or if the fair shadows of her quietude are indeed the shades of purple death.   And, lifted a

little above this solemn plain, and looking beyond
it to its snowy ramparts, vainly guardian, stands
this palace dedicate to pleasure, the whole legend
of Italy's past history written before it by the
finger of God, written as with an iron pen upon
the rock for ever, on all those fronting walls of re-
proachful Alp; blazoned in gold of lightning upon
the clouds that still open and close their unsealed
scrolls in heaven; painted in purple and scarlet
upon the mighty missal pages of sunset after
sunset, spread vainly before a nation's eyes for a
nation's prayer. So stands this palace of pleasure;
desolate as it deserves—desolate in smooth corridor
and glittering chamber—desolate in pleached walk
and planted bower—desolate in that worst and
bitterest abandonment which leaves no light of
memory. No ruins are here of walls rent by war,
and falling above their defenders into mounds of
graves: no remnants are here of chapel-altar, or
temple-porch, left shattered or silent by the power
of some purer worship: no vestiges are here of
sacred hearth and sweet homestead, left lonely
through vicissitudes of fate, and heaven-sent
sorrow. Nothing is here but the vain apparellings
of pride sunk into dishonour, and vain appanages
of delight now no more delightsome. The hill-
waters, that once flowed and plashed in the
garden fountains, now trickle sadly through the
weeds that encumber their basins, with a sound
as of tears: the creeping, insidious, neglected

flowers weave their burning nets about the white marble of the balustrades, and rend them slowly, block from block, and stone from stone: the thin sweet-scented leaves tremble along the old masonry joints as if with palsy at every breeze; and the dark lichens, golden and grey, make the foot-fall silent in the path's centre.

And day by day as I walked there, the same sentence seemed whispered by every shaking leaf, and every dying echo, of garden and chamber:—

" Thus end all the arts of life, only in death; and thus issue all the gifts of man, only in his dishonour, when they are pursued or possessed in the service of pleasure only."

This then is the great enigma of Art History,— you must not follow Art without pleasure, nor must you follow it for the sake of pleasure. And the solution of that enigma is simply this fact; that wherever Art has been followed *only* for the sake of luxury or delight, it has contributed, and largely contributed, to bring about the destruction of the nation practising it: but wherever Art has been used *also* to teach any truth, or supposed truth—religious, moral, or natural—there it has elevated the nation practising it, and itself with the nation.—*Inaugural Address, Cambridge.*

12. CAN GRANDE'S TOMB.—So early as about the year 1335, the consummate form of the Gothic

tomb occurs in the monument of Can Grande della Scala at Verona. It is set over the portal of the chapel anciently belonging to the family. The sarcophagus is sculptured with shallow bas-reliefs, representing (which is rare in the tombs with which I am acquainted in Italy, unless they are those of saints) the principal achievements of the warrior's life, especially the siege of Vicenza and battle of Placenza; these sculptures, however, form little more than a chased and roughened groundwork for the fully relieved statues representing the Annunciation, project-ing boldly from the front of the sarcophagus. Above, the Lord of Verona is laid in his long robe of civil dignity, wearing the simple bonnet, consisting merely of a fillet bound round the brow, knotted and falling on the shoulder. He is laid as asleep; his arms crossed upon his body, and his sword by his side. Above him, a bold arched canopy is sustained by two pro-jecting shafts, and on the pinnacle of its roof is the statue of the knight on his war-horse; his helmet, dragon-winged and crested with the dog's head, tossed back behind his shoulders, and the broad and blazoned drapery floating back from his horse's breast,—so truly drawn by the old workman from the life, that it seems to wave in the wind, and the knight's spear to shake, and his marble horse to be evermore quickening its pace, and starting into heavier and hastier charge,

as the silver clouds float past behind it in the
sky.—*S. V.*, III. II., § 53.

13. FROM PADUA TO VENICE.—Come with
me, on an autumnal morning, through the dark
gates of Padua, and let us take the broad road
leading towards the East.

It lies level, for a league or two, between its
elms, and vine festoons full laden, their thin
leaves veined into scarlet hectic, and their clusters
deepened into gloomy blue; then mounts an
embankment above the Brenta, and runs between
the river and the broad plain, which stretches
to the north in endless lines of mulberry and
maize. The Brenta flows slowly, but strongly;
a muddy volume of yellowish-grey water, that
neither hastens nor slackens, but glides heavily
between its monotonous banks, with here and
there a short, babbling eddy twisted for an
instant into its opaque surface, and vanishing,
as if something had been dragged into it and
gone down. Dusty and shadeless, the road fares
along the dyke on its northern side; and the tall
white tower of Dolo is seen trembling in the
heat-mist far away, and never seems nearer than
it did at first. Presently, you pass one of the
much-vaunted " villas on the Brenta: " a glaring,
spectral shell of brick and stucco, its windows
with painted architraves like picture-frames, and
a courtyard paved with pebbles in front of it,

all burning in the thick glow of the feverish sunshine, but fenced from the high road, for magnificence' sake, with goodly posts and chains ; then
another, of Kew Gothic, with Chinese variations,
painted red and green ; a third, composed for the
greater part of dead wall, with fictitious windows
painted upon it, each with a pea-green blind, and
a classical architrave in bad perspective; and a
fourth, with stucco figures set on the top of its
garden-wall : some antique, like the kind to be
seen at the corner of the New Road, and some
of clumsy grotesque dwarfs, with fat bodies and
large boots. This is the architecture to which
her studies of the Renaissance have conducted
modern Italy.

The sun climbs steadily, and warms into intense
white the walls of the little piazza of Dolo, where
we change horses. Another dreary stage among
the now divided branches of the Brenta, forming
irregular and half-stagnant canals ; with one or
two more villas on the other side of them, but
these of the old Venetian type, which we may
have recognised before at Padua, and sinking
fast into utter ruin, black, and rent, and lonely,
set close to the edge of the dull water, with what
were once small gardens beside them, kneaded
into mud, and with blighted fragments of gnarled
hedges and broken stakes for their fencing ; and
here and there a few fragments of marble steps,
which have once given them graceful access

from the water's edge, now settling into the mud in broken joints, all aslope, and slippery with green weed. At last the road turns sharply to the north, and there is an open space, covered with bent grass, on the right of it: but do not look that way.

Five minutes more, and we are in the upper room of the little inn at Mestre, glad of a moment's rest in shade. The table is (always, I think) covered with a cloth of nominal white and perennial grey, with plates and glasses at due intervals, and small loaves of a peculiar white bread, made with oil, and more like knots of flour than bread. The view from its balcony is not cheerful: a narrow street, with a solitary brick church and barren campanile on the other side of it; and some conventual buildings, with a few crimson remnants of fresco about their windows: and, between them and the street, a ditch with some slow current in it, and one or two small houses beside it, one with an arbour of roses at its door, as in an English tea-garden; the air, however, about us having in it nothing of roses, but a close smell of garlic and crabs, warmed by the smoke of various stands of hot chestnuts. There is much vociferation also going on beneath the window respecting certain wheel-barrows which are in rivalry for our baggage; we appease their rivalry with our best patience, and follow them down the narrow street.

We have but walked some two hundred yards
when we come to a low wharf or quay, at the
extremity of a canal, with long steps on each
side down to the water, which latter we fancy
for an instant has become black with stagnation;
another glance undeceives us,—it is covered with
the black boats of Venice. We enter one of
them, rather to try if they be real boats or not,
than with any definite purpose, and glide away;
at first feeling as if the water were yielding continually beneath the boat and letting her sink
into soft vacancy. It is something clearer than
any water we have seen lately, and of a pale
green; the banks only two or three feet above it,
of mud and rank grass, with here and there a
stunted tree; gliding swiftly past the small casement of the gondola, as if they were dragged by
upon a painted scene.

Stroke by stroke, we count the plunges of
the oar, each heaving up the side of the boat
slightly as her silver beak shoots forward. We
lose patience, and extricate ourselves from the
cushions: the sea air blows keenly by, as we
stand leaning on the roof of the floating cell. In
front, nothing to be seen but long canal and level
bank; to the west, the tower of Mestre is lowering
fast, and behind it there have risen purple shapes,
of the colour of dead rose-leaves, all round the
horizon, feebly defined against the afternoon
sky,—the Alps of Bassano. Forward still: the

endless canal bends at last, and then breaks into
intricate angles about some low bastions, now torn
to pieces and staggering in ugly rents towards the
water,—the bastions of the fort of Malghera.
Another turn, and another perspective of canal;
but not interminable. The silver beak cleaves it
fast,—it widens: the rank grass of the banks sinks
lower, and lower, and at last dies in tawny knots
along an expanse of weedy shore. Over it, on
the right, but a few years back, we might have
seen the lagoon stretching to the horizon, and the
warm southern sky bending over Malamocco to
the sea. Now we can see nothing but what seems
a low and monotonous dockyard wall, with flat
arches to let the tide through it;—this is the railroad bridge, conspicuous above all things. But
at the end of those dismal arches there rises, out
of the wide water, a straggling line of low and
confused brick buildings, which, but for the
many towers which are mingled among them,
might be the suburbs of an English manufacturing town. Four or five domes, pale, and
apparently at a greater distance, rise over the
centre of the line; but the object which first
catches the eye is a sullen cloud of black smoke
brooding over the northern half of it, and which
issues from the belfry of a church.

It is Venice.—*S. V.*, I. xxx., § 7-10.

14. THE APPROACH TO VENICE.—In the

olden days of travelling, now to return no more, in which distance could not be vanquished without toil, but in which that toil was rewarded, partly by the power of deliberate survey of the countries through which the journey lay, and partly by the happiness of the evening hours, when, from the top of the last hill he had surmounted, the traveller beheld the quiet village where he was to rest, scattered among the meadows beside its valley stream; or, from the long hoped-for turn in the dusty perspective of the causeway, saw, for the first time, the towers of some famed city, faint in the rays of sunset—hours of peaceful and thoughtful pleasure, for which the rush of the arrival in the railway station is perhaps not always, or to all men, an equivalent,—in those days, I say, when there was something more to be anticipated and remembered in the first aspect of each successive halting-place, than a new arrangement of glass roofing and iron girder, there were few moments of which the recollection was more fondly cherished by the traveller, than that which, as I endeavoured to describe in the close of the last chapter, brought him within sight of Venice, as his gondola shot into the open lagoon from the canal of Mestre. Not but that the aspect of the city itself was generally the source of some slight disappointment, for, seen in this direction, its buildings are far less characteristic than those of the other great towns of Italy; but this inferiority was partly disguised by distance, and more than atoned for by the strange rising of its walls and towers out of the midst, as it seemed, of the deep sea; for it was impossible that the mind or the eye could at once comprehend the shallowness of the vast sheet of water which stretched away in leagues of rippling lustre to the north and south, or trace the narrow line of islets bounding it to the east. The salt breeze, the white moaning sea-birds, the masses of black weed separating and disappearing gradually, in knots of heaving shoal, under the advance of the steady tide, all proclaimed it to be indeed the ocean on whose bosom the great city rested so calmly; not such blue, soft, lake-like ocean as bathes the Neapolitan promontories, or sleeps beneath the marble rocks of Genoa; but a sea with the bleak power of our own northern waves, yet subdued into a strange spacious rest, and changed from its angry pallor into a field of burnished gold, as the sun declined behind the belfry tower of the lonely island church, fitly named "St. George of the Seaweed." As the boat drew nearer to the city, the coast which the traveller had just left sank behind him into one long, low, sad-coloured line, tufted irregularly with brushwood and willows: but, at what seemed its northern extremity, the hills of Arqua rose in a dark cluster of purple pyramids, balanced on the bright mirage of the lagoon; two or three smooth surges of inferior hill extended themselves about their roots, and beyond these, beginning with the craggy peaks above Vicenza, the chain of the Alps girded the whole horizon to the north —a wall of jagged blue, here and there showing through its clefts a wilderness of misty precipices, fading far back into the recesses of Cadore, and itself rising and breaking away eastward, where the sun struck opposite upon its snow, into mighty fragments of peaked light, standing up behind the barred clouds of evening, one after another, countless, the crown of the Adrian Sea, until the eye turned back from pursuing them, to rest upon the nearer burning of the campaniles of Murano, and on the great city, where it magnified itself along the waves, as the quick silent pacing of the gondola drew nearer and nearer. And at last, when its walls were reached, and the outmost of its untrodden streets was entered, not through towered gate or guarded rampart, but as a deep inlet between two rocks of coral in the Indian Sea; when first upon the traveller's sight opened the long ranges of columned palaces,—each with its black boat moored at the portal,—each with its image cast down, beneath its feet, upon that green pavement which every breeze broke into new fantasies of rich tessellation; when first, at the extremity of the bright vista, the shadowy Rialto threw its colossal curve slowly forth from behind the palace of the Camerlenghi; that strange curve, so delicate, so adamantine, strong as a mountain cavern, graceful as a bow just bent; when first, before its moonlike circumference was all risen, the gondolier's cry, "Ah! Stalì," struck sharp upon the ear, and the prow turned aside under the mighty cornices that half met over the narrow canal, where the plash of the water followed close and loud, ringing along the marble by the boat's side; and when at last that boat darted forth upon the breadth of silver sea, across which the front of the Ducal Palace, flushed with its sanguine veins, looks to the snowy palace of Our Lady of Salvation, it was no marvel that the mind should be so deeply entranced by the visionary charm of a scene so beautiful and so strange, as to forget the darker truths of its history and its being. Well might it seem that such a city had owed her existence rather to the rod of the enchanter, than the fear of the fugitive; that the waters which encircled her had been chosen for the mirror of her state, rather than the shelter of her nakedness; and that all which in nature was wild or merciless,—Time and Decay, as well as the waves and tempests,—had been won to adorn her instead of to destroy, and might still spare, for ages to come, that beauty which seemed to have fixed for its throne the sands of the hour-glass as well as of the sea.

And although the last few eventful years, fraught with change to the face of the whole

earth, have been more fatal in their influence on
Venice than the five hundred that preceded them;
though the noble landscape of approach to her can
now be seen no more, or seen only by a glance,
as the engine slackens its rushing on the iron
line; and though many of her palaces are for ever
defaced, and many in desecrated ruins, there is
still so much of magic in her aspect, that the
hurried traveller, who must leave her before the
wonder of that first aspect has been worn away,
may still be led to forget the humility of her origin,
and to shut his eyes to the depth of her desolation.   They, at least, are little to be envied, in
whose hearts the great charities of the imagination
lie dead, and for whom the fancy has no power to
repress the importunity of painful impressions,
or to raise what is ignoble, and disguise what is
discordant, in a scene so rich in its remembrances,
so surpassing in its beauty.—*S. V.*, II. I., § 1, 2.

15. AN ENGLISH CATHEDRAL AND ST.
MARK'S.—I wish that the reader, before I bring
him into St. Mark's Place, would imagine himself
for a little time in a quiet English cathedral
town, and walk with me to the west front of
its cathedral.   Let us go together up the more
retired street, at the end of which we can see
the pinnacles of one of the towers, and then
through the low grey gateway, with its battle-
mented top and small latticed window in the

centre, into the inner private-looking road or close, where nothing goes in but the carts of the tradesmen who supply the bishop and the chapter, and where there are little shaven grass-plots, fenced in by neat rails, before old-fashioned groups of somewhat diminutive and excessively trim houses, with little oriel and bay windows jutting out here and there, and deep wooden cornices and eaves painted cream colour and white, and small porches to their doors in the shape of cockle-shells, or little, crooked, thick, indescribable wooden gables warped a little on one side; and so forward till we come to larger houses, also old-fashioned, but of red brick, and with gardens behind them, and fruit walls, which show here and there, among the nectarines, the vestiges of an old cloister arch or shaft, and looking in front on the cathedral square itself, laid out in rigid divisions of smooth grass and gravel walk, yet not uncheerful, especially on the sunny side where the canons' children are walking with their nurserymaids. And so, taking care not to tread on the grass, we will go along the straight walk to the west front, and there stand for a time, looking up at its deep-pointed porches and the dark places between their pillars where there were statues once, and where the frag-ments, here and there, of a stately figure are still left, which has in it the likeness of a king, perhaps indeed a king on earth, perhaps a saintly king long ago in heaven; and so higher and higher up to the great mouldering wall of rugged sculpture and confused arcades, shattered and grey, and grisly with heads of dragons and mocking fiends, worn by the rain and swirling winds into yet unseemlier shape, and coloured on their stony scales by the deep russet-orange lichen, melancholy gold; and so, higher still, to the bleak towers, so far above that the eye loses itself among the bosses of their traceries, though they are rude and strong, and only sees like a drift of eddying black points, now closing, now scattering, and now settling suddenly into invisible places among the bosses and flowers, the crowd of restless birds that fill the whole square with that strange clangour of theirs, so harsh and yet so soothing, like the cries of birds on a solitary coast between the cliffs and the sea.

Think for a little while of that scene, and the meaning of all its small formalisms, mixed with its serene sublimity. Estimate its secluded, continuous, drowsy felicities, and its evidence of the sense and steady performance of such kind of duties as can be regulated by the cathedral clock; and weigh the influence of those dark towers on all who have passed through the lonely square at their feet for centuries, and on all who have seen them rising far away over the wooded plain, or

catching on their square masses the last rays
of the sunset, when the city at their feet was
indicated only by the mist at the bend of the
river.   And then let us quickly recollect that
we are in Venice, and land at the extremity of
the Calle Lunga San Moisè, which may be
considered as there answering to the secluded
street that led us to our English cathedral
gateway.

We find ourselves in a paved alley,* some
seven feet wide where it is widest, full of
people, and resonant with cries of itinerant
salesmen,—a shriek in their beginning, and
dying away into a kind of brazen ringing, all
the worse for its confinement between the high
houses of the passage along which we have to
make our way.   Overhead an inextricable confusion of rugged shutters, and iron balconies
and chimney flues pushed out on brackets to
save room, and arched windows with projecting
sills of Istrian stone, and gleams of green leaves
here and there where a fig-tree branch escapes
over a lower wall from some inner cortile,
leading the eye up to the narrow stream of
blue sky high over all.   On each side, a row of
shops, as densely set as may be, occupying, in
fact, intervals between the square stone shafts,
about eight feet high, which carry the first
floors : intervals of which one is narrow and

[* Now widened and modernised.]

serves as a door; the other is, in the more respectable shops, wainscoted to the height of the counter and glazed above, but in those of the poorer tradesmen left open to the ground, and the wares laid on benches and tables in the open air, the light in all cases entering at the front only, and fading away in a few feet from the threshold into a gloom which the eye from without cannot penetrate, but which is generally broken by a ray or two from a feeble lamp at the back of the shop, suspended before a print of the Virgin. The less pious shopkeeper sometimes leaves his lamp unlighted, and is contented with a penny print; the more religious one has his print coloured and set in a little shrine with a gilded or figured fringe, with perhaps a faded flower or two on each side, and his lamp burning brilliantly. Here, at the fruiterer's, where the dark-green watermelons are heaped upon the counter like cannonballs, the Madonna has a tabernacle of fresh laurel leaves; but the pewterer next door has let his lamp out, and there is nothing to be seen in his shop but the dull gleam of the studded patterns on the copper pans, hanging from his roof in the darkness. Next comes a "Vendita Frittole e Liquori," where the Virgin, enthroned in a very humble manner beside a tallow candle on a back shelf, presides over certain ambrosial morsels of a nature too ambiguous to be defined

I.   D

or enumerated. But a few steps farther on, at
the regular wine-shop of the calle, where we are
offered "Vino Nostrani a Soldi 28·32," the
Madonna is in great glory, enthroned above
ten or a dozen large red casks of three-
year-old vintage, and flanked by goodly ranks
of bottles of Maraschino, and two crimson
lamps ; and for the evening, when the gondoliers
will come to drink out, under her auspices, the
money they have gained during the day, she
will have a whole chandelier.

A yard or two farther, we pass the hostelry of
the Black Eagle, and glancing as we pass through
the square door of marble, deeply moulded, in the
outer wall, we see the shadows of its pergola of
vines resting on an ancient well, with a pointed
shield carved on its side ; and so presently emerge
on the bridge and Campo San Moisè, whence to
the entrance into St. Mark's Place, called the
Bocca di Piazza (mouth of the square), the Venetian character is nearly destroyed, first by the
frightful façade of San Moisè, which we will
pause at another time to examine, and then by the
modernising of the shops as they near the piazza,
and the mingling with the lower Venetian populace of lounging groups of English and Austrians.
We will push fast through them into the shadow
of the pillars at the end of the "Bocca di Piazza,"
and then we forget them all; for between those
pillars there opens a great light, and, in the midst

of it, as we advance slowly, the vast tower of St. Mark seems to lift itself visibly forth from the level field of chequered stones ; and, on each side, the countless arches prolong themselves into ranged symmetry, as if the rugged and irregular houses that pressed together above us in the dark alley had been struck back into sudden obedience and lovely order, and all their rude casements and broken walls had been transformed into arches charged with goodly sculpture, and fluted shafts of delicate stone.

And well may they fall back, for beyond those troops of ordered arches there rises a vision out of the earth, and all the great square seems to have opened from it in a kind of awe, that we may see it far away ;—a multitude of pillars and white domes, clustered into a long low pyramid of coloured light ; a treasure-heap, it seems, partly of gold, and partly of opal and mother-of-pearl, hollowed beneath into five great vaulted porches, ceiled with fair mosaic, and beset with sculpture of alabaster, clear as amber and delicate as ivory, sculpture fantastic and involved, of palm leaves and lilies, and grapes and pomegranates, and birds clinging and fluttering among the branches, all twined together into an endless network of buds and plumes ; and, in the midst of it, the solemn forms of angels, sceptred, and robed to the feet, and leaning to each other across the gates, their figures indistinct among the gleaming

of the golden ground through the leaves beside
them, interrupted and dim, like the morning light
as it faded back among the branches of Eden,
when first its gates were angel-guarded long ago.
And round the walls of the porches there are set
pillars of variegated stones, jasper and porphyry,
and deep-green serpentine spotted with flakes of
snow, and marbles, that half refuse and half yield
to the sunshine, Cleopatra-like, "their bluest
veins to kiss"—the shadow, as it steals back
from them, revealing line after line of azure undulation, as a receding tide leaves the waved
sand ; their capitals rich with interwoven tracery,
rooted knots of herbage, and drifting leaves of
acanthus and vine, and mystical signs, all
beginning and ending in the Cross; and above
them, in the broad archivolts, a continuous chain
of language and of life—angels, and the signs of
heaven and the labours of men, each in its appointed season upon the earth ; and above these
another range of glittering pinnacles, mixed with
white arches edged with scarlet flowers,—a confusion of delight, amidst which the breasts of the
Greek horses are seen blazing in their breadth of
golden strength, and the St. Mark's Lion, lifted
on a blue field covered with stars, until at last,
as if in ecstacy, the crests of the arches break
into a marble foam, and toss themselves far
into the blue sky in flashes and wreaths of
sculptured spray, as if the breakers on the Lido

shore had been frost-bound before they fell, and the sea-nymphs had inlaid them with coral and amethyst.

Between that grim cathedral of England and this, what an interval! There is a type of it in the very birds that haunt them; for, instead of the restless crowd, hoarse-voiced and sable-winged, drifting on the bleak upper air, the St. Mark's porches are full of doves, that nestle among the marble foliage, and mingle the soft iridescence of their living plumes, changing at every motion, with the tints, hardly less lovely, that have stood unchanged for seven hundred years.—*S. V.*, II. IV., § 10–14.

16. INTERIOR OF ST. MARK'S.—Through the heavy door whose bronze network closes the place of his rest,* let us enter the church itself. It is lost in still deeper twilight, to which the eye must be accustomed for some moments before the form of the building can be traced; and then there opens before us a vast cave, hewn out into the form of a Cross, and divided into shadowy aisles by many pillars. Round the domes of its roof the light enters only through narrow apertures like large stars; and here and there a ray or two from some far-away casement wanders into the darkness, and casts a narrow

---

* The Doge Andrea Dandolo.

phosphoric stream upon the waves of marble that
heave and fall in a thousand colours along the
floor.   What else there is of light is from torches,
or silver lamps, burning ceaselessly in the recesses of the chapels; the roof sheeted with gold,
and the polished walls covered with alabaster,
give back, at every curve and angle, some feeble
gleaming to the flames; and the glories round
the heads of the sculptured saints flash out upon
us as we pass them, and sink again into the
gloom.   Under foot and over head, a continual
succession of crowded imagery, one picture passing into another, as in a dream; forms beautiful
and terrible mixed together; dragons and serpents, and ravening beasts of prey, and graceful
birds that in the midst of them drink from running
fountains and feed from vases of crystal; the
passions and the pleasures of human life symbolised together, and the mystery of its redemption; for the mazes of interwoven lines and
changeful pictures lead always at last to the
Cross, lifted and carved in every place and upon
every stone; sometimes with the serpent of
eternity wrapt round it, sometimes with doves
beneath its arms, and sweet herbage growing
forth from its feet; but conspicuous most of all
on the great rood that crosses the church before
the altar, raised in bright blazonry against the
shadow of the apse.   And although in the
recesses of the aisles and chapels, when the

mist of the incense hangs heavily, we may see continually a figure traced in faint lines upon their marble, a woman standing with her eyes raised to heaven, and the inscription above her, "Mother of God," she is not here the presiding deity. It is the Cross that is first seen, and always, burning in the centre of the temple; and every dome and hollow of its roof has the figure of Christ in the utmost height of it, raised in power, or returning in judgment.

Nor is this interior without effect on the minds of the people. At every hour of the day there are groups collected before the various shrines, and solitary worshippers scattered through the darker places of the church, evidently in prayer both deep and reverent, and, for the most part, profoundly sorrowful. The devotees at the greater number of the renowned shrines of Romanism may be seen murmuring their appointed prayers with wandering eyes and unengaged gestures; but the step of the stranger does not disturb those who kneel on the pavement of St. Mark's; and hardly a moment passes, from early morning to sunset, in which we may not see some half-veiled figure enter beneath the Arabian porch, cast itself into long abasement on the floor of the temple, and then rising slowly with more confirmed step, and with a passionate kiss and clasp of the arms given to the feet of the crucifix, by which the lamps burn always in the northern aisle, leave the church, as if comforted.—*S. V.*, II. IV., § 18, 19.

17. TOMB OF THE DOGE ANDREA DAN-DOLO.—We are in a low vaulted room;* vaulted, not with arches, but with small cupolas starred with gold, and chequered with gloomy figures: in the centre is a bronze font charged with rich bas-reliefs, a small figure of the Baptist standing above it in a single ray of light that glances across the narrow room, dying as it falls from a window high in the wall, and the first thing that it strikes, and the only thing that it strikes brightly, is a tomb. We hardly know if it be a tomb indeed; for it is like a narrow couch set beside the window, low-roofed and curtained, so that it might seem, but that it is some height above the pavement, to have been drawn towards the window, that the sleeper might be wakened early;—Only there are two angels who have drawn the curtain back, and are looking down upon him. Let us look also, and thank that gentle light that rests upon his forehead for ever, and dies away upon his breast.

The face is of a man in middle life, but there are two deep furrows right across the forehead, dividing it like the foundations of a tower: the height of it above is bound by the fillet of the

* The Baptistery of St. Mark's.

ducal cap. The rest of the features are singularly small and delicate, the lips sharp, perhaps the sharpness of death being added to that of the natural lines; but there is a sweet smile upon them, and a deep serenity upon the whole countenance. The roof of the canopy above has been blue, filled with stars; beneath, in the centre of the tomb on which the figure rests, is a seated figure of the Virgin, and the border of it all around is of flowers and soft leaves, growing rich and deep, as if in a field in summer.

It is the Doge Andrea Dandolo, a man early great among the great of Venice; and early lost. She chose him for her king in his 36th year; he died ten years later, leaving behind him that history to which we owe half of what we know of her former fortunes.

Look round at the room in which he lies. The floor of it is of rich mosaic, encompassed by a low seat of red marble, and its walls are of alabaster, but worn and shattered, and darkly stained with age, almost a ruin,—in places the slabs of marble have fallen away altogether, and the rugged brickwork is seen through the rents, but all beautiful; the ravaging fissures fretting their way among the islands and channelled zones of the alabaster, and the time-stains on its translucent masses darkened into fields of rich golden brown, like the colour of seaweed

when the sun strikes on it through deep sea.
The light fades away into the recess of the
chamber towards the altar, and the eye can
hardly trace the lines of the bas-relief behind
it of the baptism of Christ: but on the vaulting
of the roof the figures are distinct, and there are
seen upon it two great circles, one surrounded
by the "Principalities and powers in heavenly
places," of which Milton has expressed the
ancient division in a single massy line,

"Thrones, Dominations, Princedoms, Virtues, Powers,"

and around the other, the Apostles; Christ the
centre of both: and upon the walls, again and
again repeated, the gaunt figure of the Baptist,
in every circumstance of his life and death; and
the streams of the Jordan running down between
their cloven rocks; the axe laid to the root of
a fruitless tree that springs upon their shore.
"Every tree that bringeth not forth good fruit
shall be hewn down, and cast into the fire."
Yes, verily: to be baptized with fire, or to be
cast therein; it is the choice set before all men.
The march-notes still murmur through the grated
window, and mingle with the sounding in our
ears of the sentence of judgment, which the
old Greek has written on that Baptistery wall.
Venice has made her choice.

He who lies under that stony canopy would
have taught her another choice, in his day, if

she would have listened to him: but he and his counsels have long been forgotten by her, and the dust lies upon his lips.—*S. V.*, II. IV., § 16–18.

18. THE DUCAL PALACE.—Sometimes, when walking at evening on the Lido, whence the great chain of the Alps, crested with silver clouds, might be seen rising above the front of the Ducal Palace, I used to feel as much awe in gazing on the building as on the hills, and could believe that God had done a greater work in breathing into the narrowness of dust the mighty spirits by whom its haughty walls had been raised, and its burning legends written, than in lifting the rocks of granite higher than the clouds of heaven, and veiling them with their various mantle of purple flower and shadowy pine.—*S. V.*, II. VIII., § 140.

19. SOUTH ITALY.—We are accustomed to hear the south of Italy spoken of as a beautiful country. Its mountain forms are graceful above others, its sea bays exquisite in outline and hue; but it is only beautiful in superficial aspect. In closer detail it is wild and melancholy. Its forests are sombre-leaved, labyrinth-stemmed; the ca-rubbe, the olive, laurel, and ilex, are alike in that strange feverish twisting of their branches, as if in spasms of half human pain:—Avernus forests;

one fears to break their boughs, lest they should
cry to us from the rents; the rocks they shade
are of ashes, or thrice-molten lava; iron sponge
whose every pore has been filled with fire.   Silent
villages, earthquake shaken, without commerce,
without industry, without knowledge, without hope,
gleam in white ruin from hillside to hillside;
far-winding wrecks of immemorial walls surround
the dust of cities long forsaken : the mountain
streams moan through the cold arches of their
foundations, green with weed, and rage over the
heaps of their fallen towers.   Far above, in
thunder-blue serration, stand the eternal edges of
the angry Apennine, dark with rolling impendence
of volcanic cloud.—*M. P.*, V. IX. 4, § 12.

20. NORTH AND SOUTH.—The charts of the
world which have been drawn up by modern
science have thrown into a narrow space the
expression of a vast amount of knowledge ; but
I have never yet seen any one pictorial enough
to enable the spectator to imagine the kind of
contrast in physical character which exists between Northern and Southern countries.   We
know the differences in detail, but we have not
that broad glance and grasp which would enable
us to feel them in their fulness.   We know that
gentians grow on the Alps, and olives on the
Apennines ; but we do not enough conceive for
ourselves that variegated mosaic of the world's

surface which a bird sees in its migration, that
difference between the districts of the gentian
and of the olive which the stork and the swallow
see far off, as they lean upon the sirocco wind.
Let us, for a moment, try to raise ourselves
even above the level of their flight, and imagine
the Mediterranean lying beneath us like an
irregular lake, and all its ancient promontories
sleeping in the sun : here and there an angry
spot of thunder, a grey stain of storm, moving
upon the burning field; and here and there
a fixed wreath of white volcano smoke, surrounded by its circle of ashes ; but for the most
part a great peacefulness of light, Syria and
Greece, Italy and Spain, laid like pieces of a
golden pavement into the sea-blue, chased, as we
stoop nearer to them, with bossy beaten work
of mountain chains, and glowing softly with
terraced gardens, and flowers heavy with frankincense, mixed among masses of laurel and orange,
and plumy palm, that abate with their grey-green
shadows the burning of the marble rocks, and
of the ledges of porphyry sloping under lucent
sand. Then let us pass farther towards the
north, until we see the orient colours change
gradually into a vast belt of rainy green, where
the pastures of Switzerland, and poplar valleys
of France, and dark forests of the Danube and
Carpathians stretch from the mouths of the Loire
to those of the Volga, seen through clefts in grey

swirls of rain-cloud and flaky veils of the mist
of the brooks, spreading low along the pasture
lands: and then, farther north still, to see the
earth heave into mighty masses of leaden rock
and heathy moor, bordering with a broad waste
of gloomy purple that belt of field and wood,
and splintering into irregular and grisly islands
amidst the northern seas, beaten by storm, and
chilled by ice-drift, and tormented by furious
pulses of contending tide, until the roots of the
last forests fail from among the hill ravines, and
the hunger of the north wind bites their peaks
into barrenness; and, at last, the wall of ice,
durable like iron, sets, deathlike, its white teeth
against us out of the polar twilight. And, having
once traversed in thought this gradation of the
zoned iris of the earth in all its material vastness,
let us go down nearer to it, and watch the
parallel change in the belt of animal life: the
multitudes of swift and brilliant creatures that
glance in the air and sea, or tread the sands of
the southern zone; striped zebras and spotted
leopards, glistening serpents, and birds arrayed
in purple and scarlet. Let us contrast their
delicacy and brilliancy of colour, and swiftness
of motion, with the frost-cramped strength, and
shaggy covering, and dusky plumage of the
northern tribes; contrast the Arabian horse with
the Shetland, the tiger and leopard with the
wolf and bear, the antelope with the elk, the

bird of paradise with the osprey: and then, sub-
missively acknowledging the great laws by which
the earth and all that it bears are ruled throughout their being, let us not condemn, but rejoice
in the expression by man of his own rest in the
statutes of the lands that gave him birth. Let
us watch him with reverence as he sets side by
side the burning gems, and smooths with soft
sculpture the jasper pillars, that are to reflect
a ceaseless sunshine, and rise into a cloudless
sky: but not with less reverence let us stand
by him, when, with rough strength and hurried
stroke, he smites an uncouth animation out of
the rocks which he has torn from among the
moss of the moorland, and heaves into the
darkened air the pile of iron buttress and rugged
wall, instinct with a work of an imagination as
wild and wayward as the northern sea; creations
of ungainly shape and rigid limb, but full of
wolfish life; fierce as the winds that beat, and
changeful as the clouds that shade them.—
S. V., II. vi., § 8.

II.

CHARACTERISTICS OF NATURE.

21. THE DISTANT GLEAM.—I suppose there are few among those who love Nature otherwise than by profession and at second-hand, who look not back to their youngest and least-learned days as those of the most intense, superstitious, insatiable, and beatific perception of her splendours. And if it were possible for us to recollect all the unaccountable and happy instincts of the careless time, and to reason upon them with the maturer judgment, we might arrive at more rapid and right results than either the philosophy or the sophisticated practice of art has yet attained. But we lose the perceptions before we are capable of methodising or comparing them.

One, however, of these child instincts, I believe that few forget, the emotion, namely, caused by all open ground, or lines of any spacious kind against the sky, behind which there might be conceived the Sea. It is an emotion more pure than that caused by the sea itself, for I recollect distinctly running down behind the banks of a high beach to get their land line cutting against the sky, and receiving a more strange delight from this than from the sight of the ocean. I am not sure that this feeling is common to all children, (or would be common, if they were all in circumstances admitting it,) but I have ascertained it to be frequent among those who possess the most vivid sensibilities for nature; and I am certain that the modification of it which belongs to our after years is common to all, the love, namely, of a light distance appearing over a comparatively dark horizon. This I have tested too frequently to be mistaken, by offering to indifferent spectators forms of equal abstract beauty in half tint, relieved, the one against dark sky, the other against a bright distance. The preference is invariably given to the latter; and it is very certain that this preference arises not from any supposition of there being greater truth in this than the other, for the same preference is unhesitatingly accorded to the same effect in Nature herself. Whatever beauty there may result from effects of light on foreground objects, —from the dew of the grass, the flash of the cascade, the glitter of the birch trunk, or the fair daylight hues of darker things (and joyfulness there is in all of them), there is yet a light which the eye invariably seeks with a deeper feeling of the beautiful,—the light of the declining or breaking day, and the flakes of scarlet cloud burning like watch-fires in the green sky of the horizon; a deeper feeling, I say, not perhaps more acute, but having more of spiritual hope and longing, less of animal and present life, more manifest, invariably, in those of more serious and determined mind, (I use the word serious, not as being opposed to cheerful, but to trivial and volatile,) but I think, marked and unfailing even in those of the least thoughtful dispositions. I am willing to let it rest on the determination of every reader, whether the pleasure which he has received from these effects of calm and luminous distance be not the most singular and memorable of which he has been conscious; whether all that is dazzling in colour, perfect in form, gladdening in expression, be not of evanescent and shallow appealing, when compared with the still small voice of the level twilight behind purple hills, or the scarlet arch of dawn over the dark troublous-edged sea.—*M. P.*, II. III. i. 5, § 2–4.

22. SPLENDOURS OF SUNSET.—Nature has a thousand ways and means of rising above herself, but incomparably the noblest manifesta-tions of her capability of colour are in these sunsets among the high clouds. I speak espe-cially of the moment before the sun sinks, when his light turns pure rose-colour, and when this light falls upon a zenith covered with countless cloud-forms of inconceivable delicacy, threads and flakes of vapour, which would in common

daylight be pure snow-white, and which give, therefore, fair field to the tone of light. There is, then, no limit to the multitude, and no check to the intensity, of the hues assumed. The whole sky from the zenith to the horizon becomes one molten mantling sea of colour and fire; every black bar turns into massy gold, every ripple and wave into unsullied shadowless crimson, and purple, and scarlet, and colours for which there are no words in language, and no ideas in the mind—things which can only be conceived while they are visible; the intense hollow blue of the upper sky melting through it all, showing here deep, and pure, and lightless; there, modulated by the filmy formless body of the transparent vapour, till it is lost imperceptibly in its crimson and gold.

The concurrence of circumstances necessary to produce the sunsets of which I speak does not take place above five or six times in a summer, and then only for a space of from five to ten minutes, just as the sun reaches the horizon. Considering how seldom people think of looking for a sunset at all, and how seldom, if they do, they are in a position from which it can be fully seen, the chances that their attention should be awake, and their position favourable, during these few flying instants of the year, are almost as nothing. What can the citizen, who can see only the red light on the canvas of the waggon

at the end of the street, and the crimson colour
of the bricks of his neighbour's chimney, know
of the flood of fire which deluges the sky from
the horizon to the zenith? What can even the
quiet inhabitant of the English lowlands, whose
scene for the manifestation of the fire of heaven
is limited to the tops of hayricks, and the rooks'
nests in the old elm trees, know of the mighty
passages of splendour which are tossed from Alp
to Alp over the azure of a thousand miles of
champaign? Even granting the constant vigour
of observation, and supposing the possession of
such impossible knowledge, it needs but a
moment's reflection to prove how incapable the
memory is of retaining for any time the distinct
image of the sources even of its most vivid
impressions. What recollection have we of the
sunsets which delighted us last year? We may
know that they were magnificent, or glowing, but
no distinct image of colour or form is retained—
nothing of whose *degree* (for the great difficulty
with the memory is to retain, not facts, but
degrees of fact) we could be so certain as to say
of anything now presented to us, that it is like it.
If we did say so, we should be wrong; for we
may be quite certain that the energy of an
impression fades from the memory, and becomes
more and more indistinct every day; and thus
we compare a faded and indistinct image with
the decision and certainty of one present to the

senses. How constantly do we affirm that the thunderstorm of last week was the most terrible one we ever saw in our lives, because we compare it, not with the thunderstorm of last year, but with the faded and feeble recollection of it.— *M. P.*, I. II. ii. 2, § 7, 8.

23. A THUNDERSTORM.—Two great and principal passions are evidently appointed by the Deity to rule the life of man; namely, the love of God, and the fear of sin, and of its companion—Death. How many motives we have for Love, how much there is in the universe to kindle our admiration and to claim our gratitude, there are, happily, multitudes among us who both feel and teach. But it has not, I think, been sufficiently considered how evident, throughout the system of creation, is the purpose of God that we should often be affected by Fear; not the sudden, selfish, and contemptible fear of immediate danger, but the fear which arises out of the contemplation of great powers in destructive operation, and generally from the perception of the presence of death. Nothing appears to me more remarkable than the array of scenic magnificence by which the imagination is appalled, in myriads of instances, when the actual danger is comparatively small; so that the utmost possible impression of awe shall be produced upon the minds of all, though direct suffering is inflicted

upon few. Consider, for instance, the moral effect of a single thunderstorm. Perhaps two or three persons may be struck dead within a space of a hundred square miles; and their deaths, unaccompanied by the scenery of the storm, would produce little more than a momentary sadness in the busy hearts of living men. But the preparation for the judgment, by all that mighty gathering of the clouds; by the questioning of the forest leaves, in their terrified stillness, which way the winds shall go forth; by the murmuring to each other, deep in the distance, of the destroying angels before they draw forth their swords of fire; by the march of the funeral darkness in the midst of the noonday, and the rattling of the dome of heaven beneath the chariot-wheels of death;—on how many minds do not these produce an impression almost as great as the actual witnessing of the fatal issue! and how strangely are the expressions of the threatening elements fitted to the apprehension of the human soul! The lurid colour, the long, irregular, convulsive sound, the ghastly shapes of flaming and heaving cloud, are all as true and faithful in their appeal to our instinct of danger, as the moaning or wailing of the human voice itself is to our instinct of pity. It is not a reasonable calculating terror which they awake in us; it is no matter that we count distance by seconds, and measure probability by averages.

That shadow of the thundercloud will still do its work upon our hearts, and we shall watch it passing away as if we stood upon the threshing-floor of Araunah.—*S. V.*, III. III., § 41.

24. THE ANGEL OF THE SEA.—But the Angel of the Sea has also another message,—in the "great rain of his strength," rain of trial, sweeping away ill-set foundations. Then, his robe is not spread softly over the whole heaven, as a veil, but sweeps back from his shoulders, ponderous, oblique, terrible—leaving his sword-arm free.

The approach of trial-storm, hurricane-storm, is indeed in its vastness as the clouds of the softer rain. But it is not slow nor horizontal, but swift and steep : swift with passion of raven-ous winds ; steep as slope of some dark, hollowed hill. The fronting clouds come leaning forward, one thrusting the other aside, or on ; impatient, ponderous, impendent, like globes of rock tossed of Titans—Ossa on Olympus—but hurled forward all, in one wave of cloud-lava—cloud whose throat is as a sepulchre. Fierce behind them rages the oblique wrath of the rain, white as ashes, dense as showers of driven steel ; the pillars of it full of ghastly life ; Rain-Furies, shrieking as they fly ;—scourging, as with whips of scorpions ;— the earth ringing and trembling under them, heaven wailing wildly, the trees stooped blindly down, covering their faces, quivering in every leaf with horror, ruin of their branches flying by them like black stubble.—*M. P.*, V. VII. 4, § 8.

25. THE MYSTERIES OF NATURE.—In general, active men, of strong sense and stern principle, do not care to see anything in a leaf, but vegetable tissue, and are so well convinced of useful moral truth, that it does not strike them as a new or notable thing when they find it in any way symbolised by material nature; hence there is a strong presumption, when first we perceive a tendency in any one to regard trees as living, and enunciate moral aphorisms over every pebble they stumble against, that such tendency proceeds from a morbid temperament, like Shelley's, or an inconsistent one, like Jaques's. But when the active life is nobly fulfilled, and the mind is then raised beyond it into clear and calm beholding of the world around us, the same tendency again manifests itself in the most sacred way: the simplest forms of nature are strangely animated by the sense of the Divine presence; the trees and flowers seem all, in a sort, children of God; and we ourselves, their fellows, made out of the same dust, and greater than they only in having a greater portion of the Divine power exerted on our frame, and all the common uses and palpably visible forms of things, become subordinate in our minds to their inner glory,—to the mysterious

voices in which they talk to us about God, and the changeful and typical aspects by which they witness to us of holy truth, and fill us with obedient, joyful, and thankful emotion.

It is in raising us from the first state of inactive reverie to the second of useful thought, that scientific pursuits are to be chiefly praised. But in restraining us at this second stage, and checking the impulses towards higher contemplation, they are to be feared or blamed. They may in certain minds be consistent with such contemplation; but only by an effort: in their nature they are always adverse to it, having a tendency to chill and subdue the feelings, and to resolve all things into atoms and numbers. For most men, an ignorant enjoyment is better than an informed one; it is better to conceive the sky as a blue dome than a dark cavity, and the cloud as a golden throne than a sleety mist. I much question whether any one who knows optics, however religious he may be, can feel in equal degree the pleasure or reverence which an unlettered peasant may feel at the sight of a rainbow. And it is mercifully thus ordained, since the law of life, for a finite being, with respect to the works of an infinite one, must be always an infinite ignorance. We cannot fathom the mystery of a single flower, nor is it intended that we should; but that the pursuit of science should constantly be stayed by the love of beauty, and accuracy of knowledge by tenderness of emotion.—*M. P.*, III. IV. 17, § 41, 42.

26. VEGETATION.—What infinite wonderfulness there is in this vegetation, considered, as indeed it is, the means by which the earth becomes the companion of man—his friend and his teacher! In the conditions which we have traced in its rocks, there could only be seen preparation for his existence;—the characters which enable him to live on it safely, and to work with it easily—in all these it has been inanimate and passive; but vegetation is to it as an imperfect soul, given to meet the soul of man. The earth in its depths must remain dead and cold, incapable except of slow crystalline change; but at its surface, which human beings look upon and deal with, it ministers to them through a veil of strange intermediate being; which breathes, but has no voice; moves, but cannot leave its appointed place; passes through life without consciousness, to death without bitterness; wears the beauty of youth, without its passion; and declines to the weakness of age, without its regret.—*M. P.*, V. VI. 1, § 2.

27. LEAFAGE OF TREES.—One of the most remarkable characters of natural leafage is the constancy with which, while the leaves are arranged on the spray with exquisite regularity,

that regularity is modified in their actual effect. For as in every group of leaves some are seen sideways, forming merely long lines, some fore-shortened, some crossing each other, every one differently turned and placed from all the others, the forms of the leaves, though in themselves similar, give rise to a thousand strange and differing forms in the group; and the shadows of some, passing over the others, still farther disguise and confuse the mass, until the eye can distinguish nothing but a graceful and flexible disorder of innumerable forms, with here and there a perfect leaf on the extremity, or a sym-metrical association of one or two, just enough to mark the specific character and to give unity and grace, but never enough to repeat in one group what was done in another, never enough to prevent the eye from feeling that, however regular and mathematical may be the structure of parts, what is composed out of them is as various and infinite as any other part of nature. Nor does this take place in general effect only. Break off an elm bough three feet long, in full leaf, and lay it on the table before you, and try to draw it, leaf for leaf. It is ten to one if in the whole bough (provided you do not twist it about as you work) you find one form of a leaf exactly like another; perhaps you will not even have *one* complete. Every leaf will be oblique, or foreshortened, or curled, or crossed by another, or shaded by another, or have something or other the matter with it; and though the whole bough will look graceful and symmetrical, you will scarcely be able to tell how or why it does so, since there is not one line of it like another. . . .

But if Nature is so various when you have a bough on the table before you, what must she be when she retires from you, and gives you her whole mass and multitude? The leaves then at the extremities become as fine as dust, a mere confusion of points and lines between you and the sky, a confusion which, you might as well hope to draw sea-sand particle by particle, as to imitate leaf for leaf. This, as it comes down into the body of the tree, gets closer, but never opaque; it is always transparent, with crumbling lights in it letting you through to the sky: then, out of this, come, heavier and heavier, the masses of illumined foliage, all dazzling and inextricable, save here and there a single leaf on the extremities: then, under these, you get deep passages of broken irregular gloom, passing into transparent, green-lighted, misty hollows; the twisted stems glancing through them in their pale and entangled infinity, and the shafted sunbeams, rained from above, running along the lustrous leaves for an instant; then lost, then caught again on some emerald bank or knotted root, to be sent up again with a faint reflex on the white under-sides of dim groups of drooping foliage, the shadows of the upper boughs running in grey network down the glossy stems, and resting in quiet chequers upon the glittering earth ; but all penetrable and transparent, and, in proportion, inextricable and incomprehensible, except where across the labyrinth and the mystery of the dazzling light and dream-like shadow, falls, close to us, some solitary spray, some wreath of two or three motionless large leaves, the type and embodying of all that in the rest we feel and imagine, but can never see.—*M. P.*, I. II. vi. 1, § 16–18.

28. THE PINE.—Of the many marked adaptations of nature to the mind of man, it seems one of the most singular, that trees intended especially for the adornment of the wildest mountains should be, in broad outline, the most formal of trees. The vine, which is to be the companion of man, is waywardly docile in its growth, falling into festoons beside his cornfields, or roofing his garden-walks, or casting its shadow all summer upon his door. Associated always with the trimness of cultivation, it introduces all possible elements of sweet wildness. The pine, placed nearly always among scenes disordered and desolate, brings into them all possible elements of order and precision. Lowland trees may lean to this side and that, though it is but a meadow breeze that bends them, or a bank of cowslips from which their trunks lean aslope.

But let storm and avalanche do their worst, and let the pine find only a ledge of vertical precipice to cling to, it will nevertheless grow straight. Thrust a rod from its last shoot down the stem; it shall point to the centre of the earth as long as the tree lives.

Also it may be well for lowland branches to reach hither and thither for what they need, and to take all kinds of irregular shape and extension. But the pine is trained to need nothing, and to endure everything. It is resolvedly whole, self-contained, desiring nothing but rightness, content with restricted completion. Tall or short, it will be straight. Small or large, it will be round. It may be permitted also to these soft lowland trees that they should make themselves gay with show of blossom, and glad with pretty charities of fruitfulness. We builders with the sword have harder work to do for man, and must do it in close-set troops. To stay the sliding of the mountain snows, which would bury him; to hold in divided drops, at our sword-points, the rain which would sweep away him and his treasure-fields; to nurse in shade among our brown fallen leaves the tricklings that feed the brooks in drought; to give massive shield against the winter wind, which shrieks through the bare branches of the plain :—such service must we do him stedfastly while we live. Our bodies, also, are at his service : softer than the bodies of other trees,

though our toil is harder than theirs. Let him
take them as pleases him, for his houses and
ships. So also it may be well for these timid
lowland trees to tremble with all their leaves,
or turn their paleness to the sky, if but a rush
of rain passes by them ; or to let fall their leaves
at last, sick and sere. But we pines must live
carelessly amidst the wrath of clouds. We only
wave our branches to and fro when the storm
pleads with us, as men toss their arms in a
dream.

And finally, these weak lowland trees may
struggle fondly for the last remnants of life, and
send up feeble saplings again from their roots
when they are cut down. But we builders with
the sword perish boldly ; our dying shall be
perfect and solemn, as our warring ; we give up
our lives without reluctance, and for ever.

I wish the reader to fix his attention for a
moment on these two great characters of the
pine, its straightness and rounded perfectness ;
both wonderful, and in their issue lovely, though
they have hitherto prevented the tree from being
drawn. I say, first, its straightness. Because
we constantly see it in the wildest scenery, we
are apt to remember only as characteristic examples of it those which have been disturbed
by violent accident or disease. Of course such
instances are frequent. The soil of the pine is
subject to continual change ; perhaps the rock

in which it is rooted splits in frost and falls
forward, throwing the young stems aslope, or
the whole mass of earth round it is undermined
by rain, or a huge boulder falls on its stem from
above, and forces it for twenty years to grow
with weight of a couple of tons leaning on its
side.   Hence, especially at edges of loose cliffs,
about waterfalls, or at glacier banks, and in other
places liable to disturbance, the pine may be
seen distorted and oblique; and in Turner's
"Source of the Arveron," he has, with his usual
unerring perception of the main point in any
matter, fastened on this means of relating the
glacier's history.   The glacier cannot explain
its own motion; and ordinary observers saw in
it only its rigidity; but Turner saw that the
wonderful thing was its non-rigidity.   Other ice
is fixed, only this ice stirs.   All the banks are
staggering beneath its waves, crumbling and
withered as by the blast of a perpetual storm.
He made the rocks of his foreground loose—
rolling and tottering down together; the pines
smitten aside by them, their tops dead, bared by
the ice wind. . .

Yet I have been more struck by their character
of finished delicacy at a distance from the central
Alps, among the pastoral hills of the Emmenthal,
or lowland districts of Berne, where they are set
in groups between the cottages, whose shingle
roofs (they also of pine) of deep grey blue, and

lightly carved fronts, golden and orange in the autumn sunshine, gleam on the banks and lawns of hill-side,—endless lawns, mounded, and studded, and bossed all over with deeper green hay-heaps, orderly set, like jewellery (the mountain hay, when the pastures are full of springs, being strangely dark and fresh in verdure for a whole day after it is cut). And amidst this delicate delight of cottage and field, the young pines stand delicatest of all, scented as with frankincense, their slender stems straight as arrows, and crystal white, looking as if they would break with a touch like needles; and their arabesques of dark leaf pierced through and through by the pale radiance of clear sky, opal blue, where they follow each other along the soft hill-ridges, up and down.

I have watched them in such scenes with the deeper interest, because of all trees they have hitherto had most influence on human character. The effect of other vegetation, however great, has been divided by mingled species; elm and oak in England, poplar in France, birch in Scotland, olive in Italy and Spain, share their power with inferior trees, and with all the changing charm of successive agriculture. But the tremendous unity of the pine absorbs and moulds the life of a race. The pine shadows rest upon a nation. The Northern peoples, century after century, lived under one or other

I.   F

of the two great powers of the Pine and the Sea, both infinite. They dwelt amidst the forests, as they wandered on the waves, and saw no end, nor any other horizon; still the dark green trees, or the dark green waters, jagged the dawn with their fringe or their foam. And whatever elements of imagination or of warrior strength, or of domestic justice, were brought down by the Norwegian and the Goth against the dissoluteness or degradation of the South of Europe, were taught them under the green roofs and wild penetralia of the pine.—*M. P.*, IV. V. 9, § 4–6, 10–11.

29. PINES AT SUNRISE.—When the sun rises behind a ridge of pines, and those pines are seen from a distance of a mile or two, against his light, the whole form of the tree, trunk, branches, and all, becomes one frostwork of intensely brilliant silver, which is relieved against the clear sky like a burning fringe, for some distance on either side of the sun. Now suppose that a person who had never seen pines were, for the first time in his life, to see them under this strange aspect, and, reasoning as to the means by which such effect could be produced, laboriously to approach the eastern ridge, how would he be amazed to find that the fiery spectres had been produced by trees with swarthy and grey trunks, and dark green leaves! We, in our simplicity, if we had

been required to produce such an appearance, should have built up trees of chased silver, with trunks of glass, and then been grievously amazed to find that, at two miles off, neither silver nor glass were any more visible; but Nature knew better, and prepared for her fairy work with the strong branches and dark leaves, in her own mysterious way.—*S. V.*, I. XXI., § 18.

30. NATURE NEGLECTED. — Being thus prepared for us in all ways, and made beautiful, and good for food, and for building, and for instruments of our hands, this race of plants, deserving boundless affection and admiration from us, becomes, in proportion to their obtaining it, a nearly perfect test of our being in right temper of mind and way of life; so that no one can be far wrong in either who loves the trees enough, and every one is assuredly wrong in both who does not love them, if his life has brought them in his way. It is clearly possible to do without them, for the great companionship of the sea and sky are all that sailors need; and many a noble heart has been taught the best it had to learn between dark stone walls. Still if human life be cast among trees at all, the love borne to them is a sure test of its purity. And it is a sorrowful proof of the mistaken ways of the world that the " country," in the simple sense of a place of fields and trees, has hitherto been the source of reproach to its inhabitants,

and that the words " countryman, rustic, clown, paysan, villager," still signify a rude and untaught person, as opposed to the words " townsman " and " citizen." We accept this usage of words, or the evil which it signifies, somewhat too quietly; as if it were quite necessary and natural that country-people should be rude, and townspeople gentle. Whereas I believe that the result of each mode of life may, in some stages of the world's progress, be the exact reverse ; and that another use of words may be forced upon us by a new aspect of facts, so that we may find ourselves saying : " Such and such a person is very gentle and kind—he is quite rustic ; and such and such another person is very rude and ill-taught—he is quite urbane."

At all events, cities have hitherto gained the better part of their good report through our evil ways of going on in the world generally : chiefly and eminently through our bad habit of fighting with each other. No field, in the middle ages, being safe from devastation, and every country lane yielding easier passage to the marauders, peacefully-minded men necessarily congregated in cities, and walled themselves in, making as few cross-country roads as possible : while the men who sowed and reaped the harvest of Europe were only the servants or slaves of the barons. The disdain of all agricultural pursuits by the nobility, and of all plain facts by the monks, kept educated Europe in a state of mind over which natural phenomena could have no power; body and intellect being lost in the practice of war without purpose, and the meditation of words without meaning. Men learned the dexterity with sword and syllogism, which they mistook for education, within cloister and tilt-yard; and looked on all the broad space of the world of God mainly as a place for exercise of horses, or for growth of food.

There is a beautiful type of this neglect of the perfectness of the Earth's beauty, by reason of the passions of men, in that picture of Paul Uccello's of the battle of Sant' Egidio, in which the armies meet on a country road beside a hedge of wild roses; the tender red flowers tossing above the helmets, and glowing between the lowered lances. For in like manner the whole of Nature only shone hitherto for man between the tossing of helmet-crests; and sometimes I cannot but think of the trees of the earth as capable of a kind of sorrow, in that imperfect life of theirs, as they opened their innocent leaves in the warm spring-time, in vain for men; and all along the dells of England her beeches cast their dappled shade only where the outlaw drew his bow, and the king rode his careless chase; and by the sweet French rivers their long ranks of poplar waved in the twilight, only to show the flames of burning cities on the horizon, through the tracery

of their stems; amidst the fair defiles of the
Apennines, the twisted olive-trunks hid the
ambushes of treachery; and on their valley
meadows, day by day, the lilies which were
white at the dawn were washed with crimson at
sunset.—*M. P.*, V. VI. I, § 4–6.

31. THE EARTHLY PARADISE.—"To dress it
and to keep it."

That, then, was to be our work. Alas! what
work have we set ourselves upon instead! How
have we ravaged the garden instead of kept it—
feeding our war-horses with its flowers, and
splintering its trees into spear-shafts!

"And at the East a flaming sword."

Is its flame quenchless? and are those gates
that keep the way indeed passable no more? or
is it not rather that we no more desire to enter?
For what can we conceive of that first Eden
which we might not yet win back, if we chose?
It was a place full of flowers, we say. Well:
the flowers are always striving to grow wherever
we suffer them; and the fairer, the closer. There
may, indeed, have been a Fall of Flowers, as a
Fall of Man; but assuredly creatures such as we
are can now fancy nothing lovelier than roses
and lilies, which would grow for us side by side,
leaf overlapping leaf, till the Earth was white and
red with them, if we cared to have it so. And
Paradise was full of pleasant shades and fruitful

avenues. Well: what hinders us from covering as much of the world as we like with pleasant shade, and pure blossom, and goodly fruit? Who forbids its valleys to be covered over with corn till they laugh and sing? Who prevents its dark forests, ghostly and uninhabitable, from being changed into infinite orchards, wreathing the hills with frail-floreted snow, far away to the half-lighted horizon of April, and flushing the face of all the autumnal earth with glow of clustered food? But Paradise was a place of peace, we say, and all the animals were gentle servants to us. Well: the world would yet be a place of peace if we were all peacemakers, and gentle service should we have of its creatures if we gave them gentle mastery. But so long as we make sport of slaying bird and beast, so long as we choose to contend rather with our fellows than with our faults, and make battlefield of our meadows instead of pasture—so long, truly, the Flaming Sword will still turn every way, and the gates of Eden remain barred close enough, till we have sheathed the sharper flame of our own passions, and broken down the closer gates of our own hearts.—*M. P.*, V. VI. 1, § 1.

32. MOUNTAIN GLORIES.— . . . The best image which the world can give of Paradise is in the slope of the meadows, orchards, and corn-fields on the sides of a great Alp, with its purple

rocks and eternal snows above; this excellence not being in any wise a matter referable to feeling, or individual preferences, but demonstrable by calm enumeration of the number of lovely colours on the rocks, the varied grouping of the trees, and quantity of noble incidents in stream, crag, or cloud, presented to the eye at any given moment.

For consider, first, the difference produced in the whole tone of landscape colour by the introduction of purple, violet, and deep ultramarine blue, which we owe to mountains. In an ordinary lowland landscape we have the blue of the sky; the green of grass, which I will suppose (and this is an unnecessary concession to the lowlands) entirely fresh and bright; the green of trees; and certain elements of purple, far more rich and beautiful than we generally should think, in their bark and shadows (bare hedges and thickets, or tops of trees, in subdued afternoon sunshine, are nearly perfect purple, and of an exquisite tone), as well as in ploughed fields, and dark ground in general. But among mountains, in *addition* to all this, large unbroken spaces of pure violet and purple are introduced in their distances; and even near, by films of cloud passing over the darkness of ravines or forests, blues are produced of the most subtle tenderness; these azures and purples passing into rose-colour of otherwise wholly unattainable delicacy among the upper summits, the blue of the sky being at the same time purer and deeper than in the plains. Nay, in some sense, a person who has never seen the rose-colour of the rays of dawn crossing a blue mountain twelve or fifteen miles away, can hardly be said to know what *tenderness* in colour means at all; *bright* tenderness he may, indeed, see in the sky or in a flower, but this grave tenderness of the far-away hill-purples he cannot conceive.

Together with this great source of pre-eminence in *mass* of colour, we have to estimate the influence of the finished inlaying and enamel-work of the colour-jewellery on every stone; and that of the continual variety in species of flower; most of the mountain flowers being, besides, separately lovelier than the lowland ones. The wood hyacinth and wild rose are, indeed, the only *supreme* flowers that the lowlands can generally show; and the wild rose is also a mountaineer, and more fragrant in the hills, while the wood hyacinth, or grape hyacinth, at its best, cannot match even the dark bell-gentian, leaving the light-blue star-gentian in its uncontested queenliness, and the Alpine rose and Highland heather wholly without similitude. The violet, lily of the valley, crocus, and wood anemone are, I suppose, claimable partly by the plains as well as the hills; but the large orange lily and narcissus I have never seen but on hill pastures, and the exquisite oxalis is pre-eminently a mountaineer.

To this supremacy in mosses and flowers we have next to add an inestimable gain in the continual presence and power of water. Neither in its clearness, its colour, its fantasy of motion, its calmness of space, depth, and reflection, or its wrath, can water be conceived by a lowlander, out of sight of sea. A sea wave is far grander than any torrent—but of the sea and its influences we are not now speaking; and the sea itself, though it *can* be clear, is never calm, among our shores, in the sense that a mountain lake can be calm. The sea seems only to pause; the mountain lake to sleep, and to dream. Out of sight of the ocean a lowlander cannot be considered ever to have seen water at all. The mantling of the pools in the rock shadows, with the golden flakes of light sinking down through them like falling leaves, the ringing of the thin currents among the shallows, the flash and the cloud of the cascade, the earthquake and foam-fire of the cataract, the long lines of alternate mirror and mist that lull the imagery of the hills reversed in the blue of morning,—all these things belong to those hills as their undivided inheritance.

To this supremacy in wave and stream is joined a no less manifest pre-eminence in the character of trees. It is possible among plains, in the species of trees which properly belong to them, the poplars of Amiens, for instance, to obtain a serene simplicity of grace, which, as I said, is a better help to the study of gracefulness, as such, than any of the wilder groupings of the hills; so, also, there are certain conditions of symmetrical luxuriance developed in the park and avenue, rarely rivalled in their way among mountains; and yet the mountain superiority in foliage is, on the whole, nearly as complete as it is in water: for exactly as there are some expressions in the broad reaches of a navigable lowland river, such as the Loire or Thames, not, in their way, to be matched among the rock rivers, and yet for all that a lowlander cannot be said to have truly seen the element of water at all; so even in the richest parks and avenues he cannot be said to have truly seen trees. For the resources of trees are not developed until they have difficulty to contend with; neither their tenderness of brotherly love and harmony, till they are forced to choose their ways of various life where there is contracted room for them, talking to each other with their restrained branches. The various action of trees rooting themselves in inhospitable rocks, stooping to look into ravines, hiding from the search of glacier winds, reaching forth to the rays of rare sunshine, crowding down together to drink at sweetest streams, climbing hand in hand among the difficult slopes, opening in sudden dances round the mossy knolls, gathering into companies at rest among the fragrant fields, gliding in grave procession over the heavenward ridges—nothing of this can be conceived among the unvexed and unvaried felicities of the lowland forest: while to all these direct sources of greater beauty are added, first the power of redundance,—the mere quantity of foliage visible in the folds and on the promontories of a single Alp being greater than that of an entire lowland landscape (unless a view from some cathedral tower); and to this charm of redundance, that of clearer *visibility*,—tree after tree being constantly shown in successive height, one behind another, instead of the mere tops and flanks of masses, as in the plains; and the forms of multitudes of them continually defined against the clear sky, near and above, or against white clouds entangled among their branches, instead of being confused in dimness of distance.

Finally, to this supremacy in foliage we have to add the still less questionable supremacy in clouds. There is no effect of sky possible in the lowlands which may not in equal perfection be seen among the hills; but there are effects by tens of thousands, for ever invisible and inconceivable to the inhabitant of the plains, manifested among the hills in the course of one day. The mere power of familiarity with the clouds, of walking with them and above them, alters and renders clear our whole conception of the base-less architecture of the sky; and for the beauty of it, there is more in a single wreath of early cloud, pacing its way up an avenue of pines, or pausing among the points of their fringes, than in all the white heaps that fill the arched sky of the plains from one horizon to the other. And of the nobler cloud manifestations,—the breaking of their troublous seas against the crags, their black spray sparkling with lightning; or the going forth of the morning along their pavements of moving marble, level-laid between dome and dome of snow;—of these things there can be as little imagination or understanding in an inhabitant of the plains as of the scenery of another planet than his own.

And, observe, all these superiorities are matters plainly measurable and calculable, not in any wise to be referred to estimate of *sensation*. Of the grandeur or expression of the hills I have not spoken; how far they are great, or strong, or terrible, I do not for the moment consider, because vastness, and strength, and terror, are not to all minds subjects of desired contemplation. It may make no difference to some men whether a natural object be large or small, whether it be strong or feeble. But loveliness of colour, perfectness of form, endlessness of change, wonderfulness of structure, are precious to all

undiseased human minds; and the superiority
of the mountains in all these things to the lowland is, I repeat, as measurable as the richness
of a painted window matched with a white one,
or the wealth of a museum compared with that
of a simply furnished chamber. They seem to
have been built for the human race, as at once
their schools and cathedrals; full of treasures
of illuminated manuscript for the scholar, kindly
in simple lessons to the worker, quiet in pale
cloisters for the thinker, glorious in holiness for
the worshipper. And of these great cathedrals
of the earth, with their gates of rock, pavements
of cloud, choirs of stream and stone, altars of
snow, and vaults of purple traversed by the
continual stars,—of these, as we have seen, it
was written, nor long ago, by one of the best of
the poor human race for whom they were built,
wondering in himself for whom their Creator
could have made them, and thinking to have
entirely discerned the Divine intent in them—
"They are inhabited by the Beasts."

Was it then indeed thus with us, and so lately?
Had mankind offered no worship in their mountain churches? Was all that granite sculpture
and floral painting done by the angels in vain?—
M. P., IV. V. 20, § 3–10.

33. THE INFLUENCE OF MOUNTAINS.—The
palace of a Greek leader in early times might

have gardens, fields, and farms around it, but was sure to be near some busy city or sea-port: in later times, the city itself became the principal dwelling-place, and the country was visited only to see how the farm went on, or traversed in a line of march. Far other was the life of the mediæval baron, nested on his solitary jut of crag; entering into cities only occasionally for some grave political or warrior's purpose, and, for the most part, passing the years of his life in lion-like isolation; the village inhabited by his retainers straggling indeed about the slopes of the rocks at his feet, but his own dwelling standing gloomily apart, between them and the uncompanionable clouds, commanding, from sunset to sunrise, the flowing flame of some calm unvoyaged river, and the endless undulation of the untraversable hills. How different must the thoughts about nature have been, of the noble who lived among the bright marble porticoes of the Greek groups of temple or palace,—in the midst of a plain covered with corn and olives, and by the shore of a sparkling and freighted sea,—from those of the master of some mountain promontory in the green recesses of Northern Europe, watching night by night, from amongst his heaps of storm-broken stone, rounded into towers, the lightning of the lonely sea flash round the sands of Harlech, or the mists changing their shapes for ever, among the changeless pines, that fringe the crests of Jura.

Nor was it without similar effect on the minds of men that their journeyings and pilgrimages became more frequent than those of the Greek, the extent of ground traversed in the course of them larger, and the mode of travel more companionless. To the Greek a voyage to Egypt, or the Hellespont, was the subject of lasting fame and fable, and the forests of the Danube and the rocks of Sicily closed for him the gates of the intelligible world. What parts of that narrow world he crossed were crossed with fleets or armies; the camp always populous on the plain, and the ships drawn in cautious symmetry around the shore. But to the mediæval knight, from Scottish moor to Syrian sand, the world was one great exercise ground, or field of adventure; the staunch pacing of his charger penetrated the pathlessness of outmost forest, and sustained the sultriness of the most secret desert. Frequently alone,—or, if accompanied, for the most part only by retainers of lower rank, incapable of entering into complete sympathy with any of his thoughts, he must have been compelled often to enter into dim companionship with the silent nature around him, and must assuredly sometimes have talked to the wayside flowers of his love, and to the fading clouds of his ambition.

But, on the other hand, the idea of retirement from the world for the sake of self-mortification, of combat with demons, or communion with angels, and with their King,—authoritatively commended as it was to all men by the continual practice of Christ Himself,—gave to all mountain solitude at once a sanctity and a terror, in the mediæval mind, which were altogether different from anything that it had possessed in the un-Christian periods.   On the one side, there was an idea of sanctity attached to rocky wilderness, because it had always been among hills that the Deity had manifested Himself most intimately to men, and to the hills that His saints had nearly always retired for meditation, for especial communion with Him, and to prepare for death.   Men acquainted with the history of Moses, alone at Horeb, or with Israel at Sinai,—of Elijah by the brook Cherith, and in the Horeb cave; of the deaths of Moses and Aaron on Hor and Nebo; of the preparation of Jephthah's daughter for her death among the Judæa mountains; of the continual retirement of Christ Himself to the mountains for prayer, His temptation in the desert of the Dead Sea, His sermon on the hills of Capernaum, His transfiguration on Mount Hermon, and His evening and morning walks over Olivet for the four or five days preceding His crucifixion,—were not likely to look with irreverent or unloving eyes upon the blue

I.   G

hills that girded their golden horizon, or drew down upon them the mysterious clouds out of the height of the darker heaven. But with this impression of their greater sanctity was involved also that of a peculiar terror. In all this,—their haunting by the memories of prophets, the presences of angels, and the everlasting thoughts and words of the Redeemer,—the mountain ranges seemed separated from the active world, and only to be fitly approached by hearts which were condemnatory of it. Just in so much as it appeared necessary for the noblest men to retire to the hill-recesses before their missions could be accomplished, or their spirits perfected, in so far did the daily world seem by comparison to be pronounced profane and dangerous; and to those who loved that world, and its work, the mountains were thus voiceful with perpetual rebuke, and necessarily contemplated with a kind of pain and fear, such as a man engrossed by vanity feels at being by some accident forced to hear a startling sermon, or to assist at a funeral service. Every association of this kind was deepened by the practice and the precept of the time; and thousands of hearts, which might otherwise have felt that there was loveliness in the wild landscape, shrank from it in dread, because they knew that the monk retired to it for penance, and the hermit for contemplation. The horror which the Greek had felt for hills only when they were uninhabitable and barren, attached itself now to many of the sweetest spots of earth; the feeling was conquered by political interests, but never by admiration; military ambition seized the frontier rock, or maintained itself in the unassailable pass; but it was only for their punishment, or in their despair, that men consented to tread the crocused slopes of the Chartreuse, or the soft glades and dewy pastures of Vallombrosa.—*M. P.*, III. IV. 14, § 8–10.

34. THE BEAUTY OF AIGUILLES.—A rose is rounded by its own soft ways of growth, a reed is bowed into tender curvature by the pressure of the breeze; but we could not, from these, have proved any resolved preference, by Nature, of curved lines to others, inasmuch as it might always have been answered that the curves were produced, not for beauty's sake, but infallibly by the laws of vegetable existence; and, looking at broken flints or rugged banks afterwards, we might have thought that we only liked the curved lines because associated with life and organism, and disliked the angular ones, because associated with inaction and disorder. But Nature gives us in these mountains a more clear demonstration of her will. She is here driven to make fracture the law of being. She cannot tuft the rock-edges with moss, or round them by water, or hide them with leaves and

roots. She is bound to produce a form, admirable to human beings, by continual breaking away of substance. And behold—so soon as she is compelled to do this—she changes the law of fracture itself. "Growth," she seems to say, "is not essential to my work, nor concealment, nor softness; but curvature is: and if I must produce my forms by breaking them, the fracture itself shall be in curves. If, instead of dew and sunshine, the only instruments I am to use are the lightning and the frost, then their forked tongues and crystal wedges shall still work out my laws of tender line. Devastation instead of nurture may be the task of all my elements, and age after age may only prolong the unrenovated ruin; but the appointments of typical beauty which have been made over all creatures shall not therefore be abandoned; and the rocks shall be ruled, in their perpetual perishing, by the same ordinances that direct the bending of the reed and the blush of the rose."—*M. P.*, IV. v. 14, § 25.

35. MOUNTAIN SCULPTURE.—But what, then, has given rise to all those coiled plungings of the crest hither and thither, yet with such strange unity of motion?

Yes. There is the cloud. How the top of the hill was first shaped so as to let the currents of water act upon it in so varied a way we know not, but I think that the appearance of *interior* force of elevation is for the most part deceptive. The series of beds would be found, if examined in section, very uniform in their arrangement, only a little harder in one place, and more delicate in another. A stream receives a slight impulse this way or that, at the top of the hill, but increases in energy and sweep as it descends, gathering into itself others from its sides, and uniting their power with its own. A single knot of quartz occurring in a flake of slate at the crest of the ridge may alter the entire destinies of the mountain form. It may turn the little rivulet of water to the right or left, and that little turn will be to the future direction of the gathering stream what the touch of a finger on the barrel of a rifle would be to the direction of the bullet. Each succeeding year increases the importance of every determined form, and arranges in masses yet more and more harmonious, the pro- montories shaped by the sweeping of the eternal waterfalls.

The importance of the results thus obtained by the slightest change of direction in the infant streamlets, furnishes an interesting type of the formation of human characters by habit. Every one of those notable ravines and crags is the expression, not of any sudden violence done to the mountain, but of its little *habits*, persisted in continually. It was created with one ruling instinct; but its destiny depended, nevertheless, for effective result, on the direction of the small and all but invisible tricklings of water, in which the first shower of rain found its way down its sides. The feeblest, most insensible oozings of the drops of dew among its dust were in reality arbiters of its eternal form; commissioned, with a touch more tender than that of a child's finger, —as silent and slight as the fall of a half-checked tear on a maiden's cheek,—to fix for ever the forms of peak and precipice, and hew those leagues of lifted granite into the shapes that were to divide the earth and its kingdoms. Once the little stone evaded,—once the dim furrow traced,—and the peak was for ever invested with its majesty, the ravine for ever doomed to its degradation. Thenceforward, day by day, the subtle habit gained in power; the evaded stone was left with wider basement; the chosen furrow deepened with swifter-sliding wave; repentance and arrest were alike impossible, and hour after hour saw written in larger and rockier characters upon the sky, the history of the choice that had been directed by a drop of rain, and of the balance that had been turned by a grain of sand.—*M. P.*, IV. V. 15, § 22, 23.

36. NATURAL OBJECTS AT A DISTANCE.— Are not all natural things, it may be asked, as lovely near, as far away? Nay, not so. Look at

the clouds, and watch the delicate sculpture of their alabaster sides, and the rounded lustre of their magnificent rolling. They were meant to be beheld far away; they were shaped for their place, high above your head; approach them, and they fuse into vague mists, or whirl away in fierce fragments of thunderous vapour. Look at the crest of the Alp, from the far-away plains over which its light is cast, whence human souls have communion with it by their myriads. The child looks up to it in the dawn, and the husbandman in the burden and heat of the day, and the old man in the going down of the sun, and it is to them all as the celestial city on the world's horizon; dyed with the depth of heaven, and clothed with the calm of eternity. There was it set, for holy dominion, by Him who marked for the sun his journey, and bade the moon know her going down. It was built for its place in the far-off sky; approach it, and, as the sound of the voice of man dies away about its foundation, and the tide of human life, shallowed upon the vast aërial shore, is at last met by the Eternal " Here shall thy waves be stayed," the glory of its aspect fades into blanched fearfulness : its purple walls are rent into grisly rocks, its silver fretwork saddened into wasting snow : the storm-brands of ages are on its breast, the ashes of its own ruin lie solemnly on its white raiment.

Nor in such instances as these alone, though, strangely enough, the discrepancy between apparent and actual beauty is greater in proportion to the unapproachableness of the object, is the law observed. For every distance from the eye there is a peculiar kind of beauty, or a different system of lines of form; the sight of that beauty is reserved for that distance, and for that alone. If you approach nearer, that kind of beauty is lost, and another succeeds, to be disorganised and reduced to strange and incomprehensible means and appliances in its turn. If you desire to perceive the great harmonies of the form of a rocky mountain, you must not ascend upon its sides. All is there disorder and accident, or seems so; sudden starts of its shattered beds hither and thither; ugly struggles of unexpected strength from under the ground; fallen fragments, toppling one over another into more helpless fall. Retire from it, and, as your eye commands it more and more, as you see the ruined mountain world with a wider glance, behold! dim sympathies begin to busy themselves in the disjointed mass; line binds itself into stealthy fellowship with line; group by group, the helpless fragments gather themselves into ordered companies; new captains of hosts and masses of battalion become visible, one by one, and far away answers of foot to foot, and of bone to bone, until the powerless chaos is seen risen up with girded loins, and not one piece of all the unregarded heap could now be spared from the mystic whole.—*S. V.*, I. XXI., § 17.

37. ALPINE SNOW.—In the range of inorganic nature, I doubt if any object can be found more perfectly beautiful than a fresh, deep, snow drift, seen under warm light. Its curves are of inconceivable perfection and changefulness; its surface and transparency alike exquisite; its light and shade of inexhaustible variety and inimitable finish, the shadows sharp, pale, and of heavenly colour, the reflected lights intense and multitudinous, and mingled with the sweet occurrences of transmitted light. No mortal hand can approach the majesty or loveliness of it, yet it is possible, by care and skill, at least to suggest the preciousness of its forms and intimate the nature of its light and shade; but this has never been attempted; it could not be done except by artists of a rank exceedingly high, and there is something about the feeling of snow in ordinary scenery which such men do not like. But when the same qualities are exhibited on a magnificent Alpine scale, and in a position where they interfere with no feeling of life, I see not why they should be neglected, as they have hitherto been, unless that the difficulty of reconciling the brilliancy of snow with a picturesque light and shade is so great that most good artists disguise or avoid the greater part of upper Alpine

scenery, and hint at the glacier so slightly that they do not feel the necessity of careful study of its forms. . . .

Every high Alp has as much snow upon it as it can carry. It is not, observe, a mere coating of snow of given depth throughout, but it is snow loaded on until the rocks can hold no more. The surplus does not fall in the winter, because, fastened by continual frost, the quantity of snow which an Alp can carry is greater than each single winter can bestow; it falls in the first mild day of spring in enormous avalanches. Afterwards the melting continues, gradually removing from all the steep rocks the small quantity of snow which was all they could hold, and leaving them black and bare among the accumulated fields of unknown depth, which occupy the capacious valleys and less inclined superficies of the mountain.

Hence it follows that the deepest snow does not take, nor indicate, the actual forms of the rocks on which it lies, but it hangs from peak to peak in unbroken and sweeping festoons, or covers whole groups of peaks, which afford it sufficient hold, with vast and unbroken domes: these festoons and domes being guided in their curves, and modified in size, by the violence and prevalent direction of the winter winds.

We have, therefore, every variety of indication of the under mountain form: first the mere coating which is soon to be withdrawn, and which shows as a mere sprinkling or powdering, after a storm on the higher peaks; then the shallow incrustation on the steep sides, glazed by the running down of its frequent meltings, frozen again in the night; then the deeper snow, more or less cramped or modified by sudden eminences of emergent rock, or hanging in fractured festoons and huge blue irregular cliffs on the mountain flanks, and over the edges and summits of their precipices in nodding drifts, far overhanging, like a cornice (perilous things to approach the edge of, from above); finally, the pure accumulation of overwhelming depth, smooth, sweeping, and almost cleftless, and modified only by its lines of drifting. Countless phenomena of exquisite beauty belong to each of these conditions, not to speak of the transition of the snow into ice at lower levels; but all on which I shall at present insist is, that the artist should not think of his Alp merely as a white mountain, but conceive it as a group of peaks loaded with an accumulation of snow, and that especially he should avail himself of the exquisite curvatures, never failing, by which the snow unites and opposes the harsh and broken lines of the rock. —*M. P.*, I. II. iv. 2, § 19, 20.

38. A MOUNTAIN TORRENT.—When water, not in very great body, runs in a rocky bed

much interrupted by hollows, so that it can rest every now and then in a pool as it goes along, it does not acquire a continuous velocity of motion. It pauses after every leap, and curdles about, and rests a little and then goes on again; and if in this comparatively tranquil and rational state of mind it meets with any obstacle, as a rock or stone, it parts on each side of it with a little bubbling foam, and goes round; if it comes to a step in its bed, it leaps it lightly, and then after a little splashing at the bottom, stops again to take breath. But if its bed be on a continuous slope, not much interrupted by hollows, so that it cannot rest, or if its own mass be so increased by flood that its usual resting-places are not sufficient for it, but that it is perpetually pushed out of them by the following current, before it has had time to tranquillise itself, it of course gains velocity with every yard that it runs; the impetus got at one leap is carried to the credit of the next, until the whole stream becomes one mass of unchecked accelerating motion. Now when water in this state comes to an obstacle, it does not part at it, but clears it, like a race-horse; and when it comes to a hollow, it does not fill it up and run out leisurely at the other side, but it rushes down into it and comes up again on the other side, as a ship into the hollow of the sea. Hence the whole appearance of the bed of the stream is

changed, and all the lines of the water altered in
their nature.   The quiet stream is a succession
of leaps and pools; the leaps are light and
springy, and parabolic, and make a great deal
of splashing when they tumble into the pool;
then we have a space of quiet curdling water
and another similar leap below.   But the stream
when it has gained an impetus, *takes the shape*
of its bed, goes down into every hollow, not with
a leap, but with a swing, not foaming, nor splashing, but in the bending line of a strong sea-wave,
and comes up again on the other side, over rock
and ridge, with the ease of a bounding leopard;
if it meet a rock three or four feet above the
level of its bed, it will often neither part nor
foam, nor express any concern about the matter,
but clear it in a smooth dome of water, without
apparent exertion, the whole surface of the surge
being drawn into parallel lines by its extreme
velocity, so that the whole river has the appearance of a deep and raging sea, with this only
difference, that the torrent-waves always break
backwards, and sea-waves forwards.   Thus, then,
in the water which has gained an impetus, we
have the most exquisite arrangements of curved
lines, perpetually changing from convex to concave, and *vice versâ*, following every swell and
hollow of the bed with their modulating grace,
and all in unison of motion, presenting perhaps
the most beautiful series of inorganic forms which

nature can possibly produce; for the sea runs too much into similar and concave curves with sharp edges, but every motion of the torrent is united, and all its curves are modifications of beautiful line.—*M. P.*, I. II. v. 3, § 22–24.

39. THE UNRULY BREAKERS.—Let us go down and stand by the beach of it,—of the great irregular sea, and count whether the thunder of it is not out of time.   One,—two:—here comes a well-formed wave at last, trembling a little at the top, but, on the whole, orderly.   So, crash among the shingle, and up as far as this grey pebble; now stand by and watch!   Another:— Ah, careless wave! why couldn't you have kept your crest on? it is all gone away into spray, striking up against the cliffs there—I thought as much—missed the mark by a couple of feet! Another;—How now, impatient one! couldn't you have waited till your friend's reflux was done with, instead of rolling yourself up with it in that unseemly manner?   You go for nothing. A fourth, and a goodly one at last.   What think we of yonder slow rise, and crystalline hollow, without a flaw?   Steady, good wave; not so fast, not so fast; where are you coming to?— By our architectural word, this is too bad; two yards over the mark, and ever so much of you in our face besides; and a wave which we had some hope of, behind there, broken all to pieces

out at sea, and laying a great white tablecloth of foam all the way to the shore, as if the marine gods were to dine off it! Alas, for these unhappy arrow shots of Nature; she will never hit her mark with those unruly waves of hers, nor get one of them into the ideal shape, if we wait for her a thousand years.—*S. V.*, I. XXX., § 3.

40. SEA WAVES.—Afloat even twenty yards from the shore, we receive a totally different impression. Every wave around us appears vast, every one different from all the rest; and the breakers present, now that we see them with their backs towards us, the grand, extended, and varied lines of long curvature which are peculiarly expressive both of velocity and power. Recklessness, before unfelt, is manifested in the mad, perpetual, changeful, undirected motion, not of wave after wave, as it appears from the shore, but of the very same water rising and falling. Of waves that successively approach and break, each appears to the mind a separate individual, whose part being performed, it perishes, and is succeeded by another; and there is nothing in this to impress us with the idea of restlessness, any more than in any successive and continuous functions of life and death. But it is when we perceive that it is no succession of wave, but the same water, constantly rising, and crashing,

and recoiling, and rolling in again in new forms and with fresh fury, that we perceive the perturbed spirit, and feel the intensity of its unwearied rage. The sensation of power is also trebled; for not only is the vastness of apparent size much increased, but the whole action is different; it is not a passive wave, rolling sleepily forward until it tumbles heavily, prostrated upon the beach; but a sweeping exertion of tremendous and living strength, which does not now appear to *fall*, but to *burst* upon the shore; which never perishes, but recoils and recovers.—*M. P.*, I. II. v. 3, § 31.

41. THE LAW OF HELP.—The highest and first law of the universe — and the other name of life is, therefore, "help." The other name of death is "separation." Government and cooperation are in all things and eternally the laws of life. Anarchy and competition, eternally, and in all things, the laws of death.

Perhaps the best, though the most familiar example we could take of the nature and power of consistence, will be that of the possible changes in the dust we tread on.

Exclusive of animal decay, we can hardly arrive at a more absolute type of impurity than the mud or slime of a damp, over-trodden path, in the outskirts of a manufacturing town. I do not say mud of the road, because that is mixed with animal refuse; but take merely an ounce or two of the blackest slime of a beaten footpath on a rainy day, near a large manufacturing town.

That slime we shall find in most cases composed of clay (or brickdust, which is burnt clay) mixed with soot, a little sand, and water. All these elements are at helpless war with each other, and destroy reciprocally each other's nature and power, competing and fighting for place at every tread of your foot;—sand squeezing out clay, and clay squeezing out water, and soot meddling everywhere and defiling the whole. Let us suppose that this ounce of mud is left in perfect rest, and that its elements gather together, like to like, so that their atoms may get into the closest relations possible.

Let the clay begin. Ridding itself of all foreign substance, it gradually becomes a white earth, already very beautiful; and fit, with help of congealing fire, to be made into finest porcelain, and painted on, and be kept in king's palaces. But such artificial consistence is not its best. Leave it still quiet to follow its own instinct of unity, and it becomes not only white, but clear; not only clear, but hard; nor only clear and hard, but so set that it can deal with light in a wonderful way, and gather out of it the loveliest blue rays only, refusing the rest. We call it then a sapphire.

Such being the consummation of the clay, we

I.   H

give similar permission of quiet to the sand. It also becomes, first, a white earth, then proceeds to grow clear and hard, and at last arranges itself in mysterious, infinitely fine, parallel lines, which have the power of reflecting not merely the blue rays, but the blue, green, purple, and red rays in the greatest beauty in which they can be seen through any hard material whatsoever. We call it then an opal.

In next order the soot sets to work; it cannot make itself white at first, but instead of being discouraged, tries harder and harder, and comes out clear at last, and the hardest thing in the world; and for the blackness that it had, obtains in exchange the power of reflecting all the rays of the sun at once in the vividest blaze that any solid thing can shoot. We call it then a diamond.

Last of all the water purifies or unites itself, contented enough if it only reach the form of a dew-drop; but if we insist on its proceeding to a more perfect consistence, it crystallises into the shape of a star.

And for the ounce of slime which we had by political economy of competition, we have, by political economy of co-operation, a sapphire, an opal, and a diamond, set in the midst of a star of snow.—*M. P.*, V. VIII. 1, § 6–9.

42. THE BEAUTIFUL ALONE NOT GOOD FOR MAN.—I believe that it is not good for man to

live among what is most beautiful;—that he is a creature incapable of satisfaction by anything upon earth; and that to allow him habitually to possess, in any kind whatsoever, the utmost that earth can give, is the surest way to cast him into lassitude or discontent.

If the most exquisite orchestral music could be continued without a pause for a series of years, and children were brought up and educated in the room in which it was perpetually resounding, I believe their enjoyment of music, or understanding of it, would be very small. And an accurately parallel effect seems to be produced upon the powers of contemplation, by the redundant and ceaseless loveliness of the high mountain districts. The faculties are paralyzed by the abundance, and cease, as we before noticed of the imagination, to be capable of excitement, except by other subjects of interest than those which present themselves to the eye. So that it is, in reality, better for mankind that the forms of their common landscape should offer no violent stimulus to the emotions,—that the gentle upland, browned by the bending furrows of the plough, and the fresh sweep of the chalk down, and the narrow winding of the copse-clad dingle, should be more frequent scenes of human life than the Arcadias of cloud-capped mountain or luxuriant vale; and that, while humbler (though always infinite) sources of interest are given to each of us around the homes to which we are restrained for the greater part of our lives, these mightier and stranger glories should become the objects of adventure,—at once the cynosures of the fancies of childhood, and themes of the happy memory, and the winter's tale of age.—*M. P.*, IV. V. 11, § 7.

43. NATURE'S BEAUTY.—Now, therefore, I think that, without the risk of any farther serious objection occurring to you, I may state what I believe to be the truth,—that beauty has been appointed by the Deity to be one of the elements by which the human soul is continually sustained; it is therefore to be found more or less in all natural objects, but in order that we may not satiate ourselves with it, and weary of it, it is rarely granted to us in its utmost degrees. When we see it in those utmost degrees, we are attracted to it strongly, and remember it long, as in the case of singularly beautiful scenery, or a beautiful countenance. On the other hand, absolute ugliness is admitted as rarely as perfect beauty; but degrees of it more or less distinct are associated with whatever has the nature of death and sin, just as beauty is associated with what has the nature of virtue and of life.—*L. A. P.*, I., § 11.

44. NATURE'S INFINITY.—One lesson, however, we are invariably taught by all, however

approached or viewed, that the work of the Great Spirit of nature is as deep and unapproachable in the lowest as in the noblest objects; that the Divine mind is as visible in its full energy of operation on every lowly bank and mouldering stone, as in the lifting of the pillars of heaven, and settling the foundation of the earth; and that to the rightly perceiving mind, there is the same infinity, the same majesty, the same power, the same unity, and the same perfection, manifest in the casting of the clay as in the scattering of the cloud, in the mouldering of the dust as in the kindling of the day-star.—*M. P.*, I. II. iv. 4, § 30.

III.

PAINTING AND POETRY.

45. THE PURPOSE OF ART.—Although with respect to many important scenes, it might be one of the most precious gifts that could be given us to see them with *our own eyes*, yet also in many things it is more desirable to be permitted to see them with the eyes of others; and although, to the small, conceited, and affected painter displaying his narrow knowledge and tiny dexterities, our only word may be, "Stand aside from between that nature and me:" yet to the great imaginative painter—greater a million times in every faculty of soul than we—our word may wisely be, "Come between this nature and me—this nature which is too great and too wonderful for me; temper it for me, interpret it to me; let me see with your eyes, and hear with your ears, and have help and strength from your great spirit."

All the noblest pictures have this character. They are true or inspired ideals, seen in a moment to *be* ideal; that is to say, the result of all the highest powers of the imagination, engaged in the discovery and apprehension of the purest truths, and having so arranged them as best to show their preciousness and exalt their clearness. They are always orderly, always one, ruled by one great purpose throughout, in the fulfilment of which every atom of the detail is called to help, and would be missed if removed; this peculiar oneness being the result, not of obedience to any teachable law, but of the magnificence of tone in the perfect mind, which accepts only what is good for its great purposes, rejects whatever is foreign or redundant, and instinctively and instantaneously ranges whatever it accepts, in sublime subordination and helpful brotherhood.—*M. P.*, III. IV. 10, § 19.

46. THE PROPER STUDY OF MANKIND.— The power of thus fully *perceiving* any natural object depends on our being able to group and fasten all our fancies about it as a centre, making a garland of thoughts for it, in which each separate thought is subdued and shortened of its own strength, in order to fit it for harmony with others; the intensity of our enjoyment of the object depending, first, on its own beauty, and then on the richness of the garland. And men who have this habit of clustering and harmonising their thoughts are a little too apt to look scornfully upon the harder workers who

tear the bouquet to pieces to examine the stems. This was the chief narrowness of Wordsworth's mind; he could not understand that to break a rock with a hammer in search of crystal may sometimes be an act not disgraceful to human nature, and that to dissect a flower may sometimes be as proper as to dream over it; whereas all experience goes to teach us, that among men of average intellect the most useful members of society are the dissectors, not the dreamers. It is not that they love nature or beauty less, but that they love result, effect, and progress more; and when we glance broadly along the starry crowd of benefactors to the human race, and guides of human thought, we shall find that this dreaming love of natural beauty—or at least its expression—has been more or less checked by them all, and subordinated either to hard work or watching of *human* nature.—*M. P.*, III. IV. 17, § 7.

47. PAINTING CONSIDERED AS A LANGUAGE. —Painting, or art generally, as such, with all its technicalities, difficulties, and particular ends, is nothing but a noble and expressive language, invaluable as the vehicle of thought, but by itself nothing. He who has learned what is commonly considered the whole art of painting, that is, the art of representing any natural object faithfully, has as yet only learned the language by

which his thoughts are to be expressed. He has done just as much towards being that which we ought to respect as a great painter, as a man who has learnt how to express himself grammatically and melodiously has towards being a great poet. The language is, indeed, more difficult of acquirement in the one case than in the other, and possesses more power of delighting the sense, while it speaks to the intellect; but it is, nevertheless, nothing more than language, and all those excellences which are peculiar to the painter as such, are merely what rhythm, melody, precision, and force are in the words of the orator and the poet, necessary to their greatness, but not the tests of their greatness. It is not by the mode of representing and saying, but by what is represented and said, that the respective greatness either of the painter or the writer is to be finally determined.

Speaking with strict propriety, therefore, we should call a man a great painter only as he excelled in precision and force in the language of lines, and a great versifier, as he excelled in precision and force in the language of words. A great poet would then be a term strictly, and in precisely the same sense, applicable to both, if warranted by the character of the images or thoughts which each in their respective languages conveyed.

Take, for instance, one of the most perfect

poems or pictures (I use the word as synony-
mous) which modern times have seen:—the
"Old Shepherd's Chief-mourner." Here the
exquisite execution of the glossy and crisp hair
of the dog, the bright sharp touching of the
green bough beside it, the clear painting of the
wood of the coffin and the folds of the blanket,
are language—language clear and expressive in
the highest degree. But the close pressure of
the dog's breast against the wood, the convulsive
clinging of the paws, which has dragged the
blanket off the trestle, the total powerlessness
of the head laid, close and motionless, upon
its folds, the fixed and tearful fall of the eye in
its utter hopelessness, the rigidity of repose
which marks that there has been no motion nor
change in the trance of agony since the last blow
was struck on the coffin-lid, the quietness and
gloom of the chamber, the spectacles marking
the place where the Bible was last closed, indicating how lonely has been the life, how
unwatched the departure, of him who is now
laid solitary in his sleep;—these are all thoughts
—thoughts by which the picture is separated at
once from hundreds of equal merit, as far as
mere painting goes, by which it ranks as a work
of high art, and stamps its author, not as the
neat imitator of the texture of a skin, or the
fold of a drapery, but as the Man of Mind.—
M. P., I. I. i. 2, § 1–4.

48. A DEFINITION OF POETRY.—Poetry is "the suggestion, by the imagination, of noble grounds for the noble emotions." I mean, by the noble emotions, those four principal sacred passions—Love, Veneration, Admiration, and Joy (this latter especially, if unselfish); and their opposites—Hatred, Indignation (or Scorn), Horror, and Grief,—this last, when unselfish, becoming Compassion. These passions in their various combinations constitute what is called "poetical feeling," when they are felt on noble grounds, that is, on great and true grounds. Indignation, for instance, is a poetical feeling, if excited by serious injury; but it is not a poetical feeling if entertained on being cheated out of a small sum of money. It is very possible the manner of the cheat may have been such as to justify considerable indignation; but the feeling is nevertheless not poetical unless the grounds of it be large as well as just. In like manner, energetic admiration may be excited in certain minds by a display of fireworks, or a street of handsome shops; but the feeling is not poetical, because the grounds of it are false, and therefore ignoble. There is in reality nothing to deserve admiration either in the firing of packets of gunpowder, or in the display of the stocks of warehouses. But admiration excited by the budding of a flower is a poetical feeling, because it is impossible that this manifestation of spiritual power and vital beauty can ever be enough admired.

Farther, it is necessary to the existence of poetry that the grounds of these feelings should be *furnished by the imagination*. Poetical feeling, that is to say, mere noble emotion, is not poetry. It is happily inherent in all human nature deserving the name, and is found often to be purest in the least sophisticated. But the power of assembling, by *the help of the imagination*, such images as will excite these feelings, is the power of the poet or literally of the "Maker."—*M. P.*, III. IV. I, § 13, 14.

49. THE IMAGINATION IN POETRY.—When Milton's Satan first "rears from off the pool his mighty stature," the image of leviathan before suggested not being yet abandoned, the effect on the fire-wave is described as of the upheaved monster on the ocean stream:

> "On each hand the flames
> Driven backward, slope their pointed spires, and, rolled
> In billows, leave i' the midst a horrid vale."

And then follows a fiercely restless piece of volcanic imagery:

> "As when the force
> Of subterranean wind transports a hill
> Torn from Pelorus, or the shattered side
> Of thundering Ætna, whose combustible
> And fuelled entrails thence conceiving fire,

Sublimed with mineral fury, aid the winds,
And leave a singëd bottom all involved
With stench and smoke : such resting found the sole
Of unblest feet."

Yet I think all this is too far detailed, and deals too much with externals : we feel rather the form of the fire-waves than their fury ; we walk upon them too securely; and the fuel, sublimation, smoke, and singeing seem to me images only of partial combustion ; they vary and extend the conception, but they lower the thermometer. Look back, if you will, and add to the description the glimmering of the livid flames ; the sulphurous hail and red lightning ; yet all together, however they overwhelm us with horror, fail of making us thoroughly, unendurably *hot*. The essence of intense flame has not been given. Now hear Dante :

> " Feriami 'l Sole in su l' omero destro,
>   Che già raggiando tutto l' Occidente
>   *Mutava in bianco aspetto di cilestro.*
> Ed io facea *con l'ombra più rovente*
>   *Parer la fiamma.*"

That is a slight touch ; he has not gone to Ætna or Pelorus for fuel ; but we shall not soon recover from it, he has taken our breath away, and leaves us gasping. No smoke nor cinders there. Pure white, hurtling, formless flame ; very fire-crystal, we cannot make spires nor waves of it, nor divide it, nor walk on it ; there is no question

about singeing soles of feet.   It is lambent annihilation.

Such is always the mode in which the highest
imaginative faculty seizes its materials.   It never
stops at crusts or ashes, or outward images of
any kind ; it ploughs them all aside, and plunges
into the very central fiery heart ; nothing else
will content its spirituality ; whatever semblances
and various outward shows and phases its subject
may possess go for nothing ; it gets within all
fence, cuts down to the root, and drinks the very
vital sap of that it deals with : once therein, it
is at liberty to throw up what new shoots it will,
so always that the true juice and sap be in them,
and to prune and twist them at its pleasure, and
bring them to fairer fruit than grew on the old
tree ; but all this pruning and twisting is work
that it likes not, and often does ill ; its function
and gift are the getting at the root, its nature
and dignity depend on its holding things always
by the heart.   Take its hand from off the beating
of that, and it will prophesy no longer ; it looks
not in the eyes, it judges not by the voice, it
describes not by outward features ; all that it
affirms, judges, or describes, it affirms, from
within.

It may seem to the reader that I am incorrect in
calling this penetrating possession-taking faculty
Imagination.   Be it so ; the name is of little consequence ; the faculty itself, called by what name

we will, I insist upon as the highest intellectual power of man. There is no reasoning in it; it works not by algebra, nor by integral calculus; it is a piercing pholas-like mind's tongue, that works and tastes into the very rock heart; no matter what be the subject submitted to it, substance or spirit; all is alike divided asunder, joint and marrow, whatever utmost truth, life, principle it has, laid bare, and that which has no truth, life, nor principle, dissipated into its original smoke at a touch. The whispers at men's ears it lifts into visible angels. Vials that have lain sealed in the deep sea a thousand years it unseals, and brings out of them Genii.

Every great conception of poet or painter is held and treated by this faculty. Every character that is so much as touched by men like Æschylus, Homer, Dante, or Shakespere, is by them held by the heart; and every circumstance or sentence of their being, speaking, or seeming, is seized by process from within, and is referred to that inner secret spring of which the hold is never lost for an instant; so that every sentence, as it has been thought out from the heart, opens for us a way down to the heart, leads us to the centre, and then leaves us to gather what more we may. It is the Open Sesame of a huge, obscure, endless cave, with inexhaustible treasure of pure gold scattered in it; the wandering about and gathering the pieces may be left to any of us, all can accomplish that; but the first opening of that invisible door in the rock is of the imagination only.

Hence there is in every word set down by the imaginative mind an awful under-current of meaning, and evidence and shadow upon it of the deep places out of which it has come. It is often obscure, often half-told; for he who wrote it, in his clear seeing of the things beneath, may have been impatient of detailed interpretation: but, if we choose to dwell upon it and trace it, it will lead us always securely back to that metropolis of the soul's dominion from which we may follow out all the ways and tracks to its farthest coasts.

I think the "Quel giorno più non vi leggemmo avante" of Francesca di Rimini, and the "He has no children" of Macduff, are as fine instances as can be given; but the sign and mark of it are visible on every line of the four great men above instanced.

The unimaginative writer, on the other hand, as he has never pierced to the heart, so he can never touch it. If he has to paint a passion, he remembers the external signs of it, he collects expressions of it from other writers, he searches for similes, he composes, exaggerates, heaps term on term, figure on figure, till we groan beneath the cold disjointed heap: but it is all faggot and no fire; the life breath is not in it; his passion has the form of the leviathan, but it never makes the deep boil; he fastens us all at anchor in the scaly rind of it; our sympathies remain as idle as a painted ship upon a painted ocean.

And that virtue of originality that men so strain after is not *newness*, as they vainly think (there is nothing new), it is only *genuineness ;* it all depends on this single glorious faculty of getting to the spring of things and working out from that; it is the coolness, and clearness, and deliciousness of the water fresh from the fountain head, opposed to the thick, hot, unrefreshing drainage from other men's meadows.—*M. P.*, II. III. ii. 3, § 2–6.

50. MILTON AND DANTE.—Milton's effort, in all that he tells us of his Inferno, is to make it indefinite; Dante's, to make it *definite*. Both, indeed, describe it as entered through gates; but, within the gate, all is wild and fenceless with Milton, having indeed its four rivers,—the last vestige of the mediæval tradition,—but rivers which flow through a waste of mountain and moorland, and by "many a frozen, many a fiery Alp." But Dante's Inferno is accurately separated into circles drawn with well-pointed compasses ; mapped and properly surveyed in every direction, trenched in a thoroughly good style of engineering from depth to depth, and divided in the "*accurate* middle" (dritto mezzo) of its deepest abyss, into a concentric series of ten

moats and embankments, like those about a
castle, with bridges from each embankment to
the next; precisely in the manner of those
bridges over Hiddekel and Euphrates, which
Mr. Macaulay thinks so innocently designed,
apparently not aware that he is also laughing
at Dante. These larger fosses are of rock, and
the bridges also; but as he goes farther into
detail, Dante tells us of various minor fosses
and embankments, in which he anxiously points
out to us not only the formality, but the neatness
and perfectness, of the stonework. For instance,
in describing the river Phlegethon, he tells us
that it was "paved with stone at the bottom,
and at the sides, and *over the edges of the sides,*"
just as the water is at the baths of Bulicame;
and for fear we should think this embankment
at all *larger* than it really was, Dante adds,
carefully, that it was made just like the embankments of Ghent or Bruges against the sea, or
those in Lombardy which bank the Brenta, only
"not so high, nor so wide," as any of these.
And besides the trenches, we have two well-
built castles; one, like Ecbatana, with seven
circuits of wall (and surrounded by a fair
stream), wherein the great poets and sages of
antiquity live; and another, a great fortified
city with walls of iron, red-hot, and a deep fosse
round it, and full of "grave citizens,"—the
city of Dis.

Now, whether this be in what we moderns call "good taste," or not, I do not mean just now to inquire—Dante having nothing to do with taste, but with the facts of what he had seen; only, so far as the imaginative faculty of the two poets is concerned, note that Milton's vagueness is not the sign of imagination, but of its absence, so far as it is significative in the matter. For it does not follow, because Milton did not map out his Inferno as Dante did, that he *could* not have done so if he had chosen; only, it was the easier and less imaginative process to leave it vague than to define it. Imagination is always the seeing and asserting faculty; that which obscures or conceals may be judgment, or feeling, but not invention. The invention, whether good or bad, is in the accurate engineering, not in the fog and uncertainty.—*M. P.*, III. IV. 14, § 29, 30.

51. DANTE'S LANDSCAPE.—As Homer gave us an ideal landscape, which even a god might have been pleased to behold, so Dante gives us, fortunately, an ideal landscape, which is specially intended for the terrestrial paradise. And it will doubtless be with some surprise, after our reflections above on the general tone of Dante's feelings, that we find ourselves here first entering a *forest*, and that even a *thick* forest. But there is a peculiar meaning in this. With any other poet than Dante, it might have been regarded

as a wanton inconsistency. Not so with him:
by glancing back to the two lines which explain
the nature of Paradise, we shall see what he
means by it. Virgil tells him, as he enters it,
"Henceforward, take thine own pleasure for
guide; thou art beyond the steep ways, and
beyond all Art;"—meaning, that the perfectly
purified and noble human creature, having no
pleasure but in right, is past all effort, and past
all *rule*. Art has no existence for such a being.
Hence, the first aim of Dante, in his landscape
imagery, is to show evidence of this perfect
liberty, and of the purity and sinlessness of the
new nature, converting pathless ways into happy
ones. So that all those fences and formalisms
which had been needed for him in imperfection,
are removed in this paradise; and even the pathlessness of the wood, the most dreadful thing
possible to him in his days of sin and short-
coming, is now a joy to him in his days of
purity. And as the fencelessness and thicket of
sin led to the fettered and fearful order of eternal
punishment, so the fencelessness and thicket of
the free virtue lead to the loving and constellated
order of eternal happiness.

This forest, then, is very like that of Colonos
in several respects—in its peace and sweetness,
and number of birds; it differs from it only in
letting a light breeze through it, being therefore
somewhat thinner than the Greek wood; the

tender lines which tell of the voices of the birds mingling with the wind, and of the leaves all turning one way before it, have been more or less copied by every poet since Dante's time. They are, so far as I know, the sweetest passage of wood description which exists in literature.

Before, however, Dante has gone far in this wood,—that is to say, only so far as to have lost sight of the place where he entered it, or rather, I suppose, of the light under the boughs of the outside trees, and it must have been a very thin wood indeed if he did not do this in some quarter of a mile's walk,—he comes to a little river, three paces over, which bends the blades of grass to the left, with a meadow on the other side of it; and in this meadow

> "A lady, graced with solitude, who went
>   Singing, and setting flower by flower apart,
> By which the path she walked on was besprent."

This lady, observe, stands on the opposite side of the little stream, which, presently, she explains to Dante is Lethe, having power to cause forget-fulness of all evil, and she stands just among the bent blades of grass at its edge. She is first seen gathering flower from flower, then "passing continually the multitudinous flowers through her hands," smiling at the same time so brightly, that her first address to Dante is to prevent him from wondering at her, saying, "if he will remember

the verse of the ninety-second Psalm, beginning
'Delectasti,' he will know why she is so happy."

And turning to the verse of this Psalm we
find it written, "Thou, Lord, hast made me glad
through Thy works.   I will triumph *in the works
of Thy hands;*" or in the very words in which
Dante would read it,—

> " Quia delectasti me Domine, in factura Tua,
> Et in operibus manuum Tuarum exultabo."

. . Now, therefore, we see that Dante, as the
great prophetic exponent of the heart of the Middle
Ages, has, by the lips of the spirit of Matilda,
declared the mediæval faith,—that all perfect
active life was "the expression of man's delight
in God's work;" and that all their political and
warlike energy, as fully shown in the mortal life
of Matilda, was yet inferior and impure,—the
energy of the dream,—compared with that which
on the opposite bank of Lethe stood "choosing
flower from flower."   And what joy and peace
there were in this work is marked by Matilda's
being the person who draws Dante through the
stream of Lethe, so as to make him forget all
sin, and all sorrow : throwing her arms around
him, she plunges his head under the waves of
it ; then draws him through, crying to him,
"*hold me, hold me*" (tiemmi, tiemmi), and so
presents him, thus bathed, free from all painful
memory, at the feet of the spirit of the more

heavenly contemplation.—*M. P.*, III. IV. 14,
§ 34–36, 39.

52. SHAKESPERE.—He seems to have been
sent essentially to take universal and equal grasp
of the *human* nature ; and to have been removed,
therefore, from all influences which could in the
least warp or bias his thoughts.   It was necessary that he should lean *no* way ; that he should
contemplate, with absolute equality of judgment,
the life of the court, cloister, and tavern, and be
able to sympathise so completely with all creatures as to deprive himself, together with his
personal identity, even of his conscience, as he
casts himself into their hearts.   He must be able
to enter into the soul of Falstaff or Shylock
with no more sense of contempt or horror than
Falstaff or Shylock themselves feel for or in
themselves ; otherwise his own conscience and
indignation would make him unjust to them ;
he would turn aside from something, miss some
good, or overlook some essential palliation.   He
must be utterly without anger, utterly without
purpose ; for if a man has any serious purpose
in life, that which runs counter to it, or is foreign
to it, will be looked at frowningly or carelessly
by him.   Shakespere was forbidden of Heaven
to have any *plans*.   To *do* any good or *get* any
good, in the common sense of good, was not
to be within his permitted range of work.   Not,

for him, the founding of institutions, the preaching of doctrines, or the repression of abuses.
Neither he, nor the sun, did on any morning
that they rose together, receive charge from
their Maker concerning such things. They were
both of them to shine on the evil and good;
both to behold unoffendedly all that was upon
the earth, to burn unappalled upon the spears
of kings, and undisdaining, upon the reeds of
the river.

Therefore, so far as nature had influence over
the early training of this man, it was essential to
his perfectness that the nature should be quiet.
No mountain passions were to be allowed in him.
Inflict upon him but one pang of the monastic
conscience ; cast upon him but one cloud of
the mountain gloom ; and his serenity had been
gone for ever—his equity—his infinity. You
would have made another Dante of him ; and
all that he would have ever uttered about poor,
soiled, and frail humanity would have been the
quarrel between Sinon and Adam of Brescia,
—speedily retired from, as not worthy a man's
hearing, nay, not to be heard without heavy
fault. All your Falstaffs, Slenders, Quicklys,
Sir Tobys, Lances, Touchstones, and Quinces,
would have been lost in that. Shakespere could
be allowed no mountains ; nay, not even any
supreme natural beauty. He had to be left
with his kingcups and clover ;—pansies — the

passing clouds—the Avon's flow—and the undu-
lating hills and woods of Warwick ; nay, he was
not to love even these in any exceeding measure,
lest it might make him in the least overrate their
power upon the strong, full-fledged minds of men.
He makes the quarrelling fairies concerned about
them : poor lost Ophelia finds some comfort in
them ; fearful, fair, wise-hearted Perdita trust the
speaking of her good will and good hostess-ship
to them ; and one of the brothers of Imogen con-
fide his sorrow to them,—rebuked instantly by
his brother for "wench-like words;" but any
thought of them in his mighty men I do not find :
it is not usually in the nature of such men ; and
if he had loved the flowers the *least* better himself, he would assuredly have been offended at
this, and given a botanical turn of mind to Cæsar,
or Othello.

And it is even among the most curious proofs
of the necessity to all high imagination that it
should paint straight from the life, that he has
not given such a turn of mind to some of his
great men ;—Henry the Fifth, for instance.
Doubtless some of my readers, having been
accustomed to hear it repeated thoughtlessly
from mouth to mouth that Shakespere conceived
the spirit of all ages, were as much offended as
surprised at my saying that he only painted
human nature as he saw it in his own time.
They will find, if they look into his work closely,

as much antiquarianism as they do geography,
and no more. The commonly received notions
about the things that had been, Shakespere took
as he found them, animating them with pure
human nature, of any time and all time; but
inquiries into the minor detail of temporary feeling, he despised as utterly as he did maps; and
wheresoever the temporary feeling was in anywise contrary to that of his own day, he errs
frankly, and paints from his own time.—*M. P.*,
IV. v. 20, § 28–30.

53. OF THE PATHETIC FALLACY.—It is a
fallacy caused by an excited state of the feelings,
making us, for the time, more or less irrational.
. . . Thus, for instance, in Alton Locke,—

> " They rowed her in across the rolling foam—
>   The cruel, crawling foam."

The foam is not cruel, neither does it crawl.
The state of mind which attributes to it these
characters of a living creature is one in which
the reason is unhinged by grief. All violent
feelings have the same effect. They produce in
us a falseness in all our impressions of external
things, which I would generally characterise as
the "pathetic fallacy."

Now we are in the habit of considering this
fallacy as eminently a character of poetical description, and the temper of mind in which we

allow it, as one eminently poetical, because passionate. But I believe, if we look well into the matter, that we shall find the greatest poets do not often admit this kind of falseness,—that it is only the second order of poets who much delight in it.

Thus, when Dante describes the spirits falling from the bank of Acheron "as dead leaves flutter from a bough," he gives the most perfect image possible of their utter lightness, feebleness, passiveness, and scattering agony of despair, without, however, for an instant losing his own clear perception that *these* are souls, and *those* are leaves; he makes no confusion of one with the other. But when Coleridge speaks of

> " The one red leaf, the last of its clan,
>   That dances as often as dance it can,"

he has a morbid, that is to say, a so far false, idea about the leaf; he fancies a life in it, and will, which there are not; confuses its powerlessness with choice, its fading death with merriment, and the wind that shakes it with music. . . .

The temperament which admits the pathetic fallacy, is, as I said above, that of a mind and body in some sort too weak to deal fully with what is before them or upon them; borne away, or overclouded, or over-dazzled by emotion; and it is a more or less noble state, according to the force of the emotion which has induced it. For it is no credit to a man that he is not morbid or inaccurate in his perceptions, when he has no strength of feeling to warp them; and it is in general a sign of higher capacity and stand in the ranks of being, that the emotions should be strong enough to vanquish, partly, the intellect, and make it believe what they choose. But it is still a grander condition when the intellect also rises, till it is strong enough to assert its rule against, or together with, the utmost efforts of the passions; and the whole man stands in an iron glow, white hot, perhaps, but still strong, and in no wise evaporating; even if he melts, losing none of his weight.

So, then, we have the three ranks: the man who perceives rightly, because he does not feel, and to whom the primrose is very accurately the primrose, because he does not love it. Then, secondly, the man who perceives wrongly, because he feels, and to whom the primrose is anything else than a primrose: a star, or a sun, or a fairy's shield, or a forsaken maiden. And then, lastly, there is the man who perceives rightly in spite of his feelings, and to whom the primrose is for ever nothing else than itself—a little flower apprehended in the very plain and leafy fact of it, whatever and how many soever the associations and passions may be that crowd around it. And, in general, these three classes may be rated in comparative order, as the men who are not poets at all, and the poets of the second order, and the poets of the first; only however great a man may be, there are always some subjects which *ought* to throw him off his balance; some, by which his poor human capacity of thought should be conquered, and brought into the inaccurate and vague state of perception, so that the language of the highest inspiration becomes broken, obscure, and wild in metaphor, resembling that of the weaker man, overborne by weaker things.

And thus, in full, there are four classes: the men who feel nothing, and therefore see truly; the men who feel strongly, think weakly, and see untruly (second order of poets); the men who feel strongly, think strongly, and see truly (first order of poets); and the men who, strong as human creatures can be, are yet submitted to influences stronger than they, and see in a sort untruly, because what they see is inconceivably above them. This last is the usual condition of prophetic inspiration.—*M. P.*, III. IV. 12, § 5–9.

54. SCOTT.—Scott's habit of looking at nature neither as dead, or merely material, in the way that Homer regards it, nor as altered by his own feelings, in the way that Keats and Tennyson regard it, but as having an animation and pathos of *its own*, wholly irrespective of human presence or passion,—an animation which Scott loves and

sympathises with, as he would with a fellow-
creature, forgetting himself altogether, and subduing his own humanity before what seems to
him the power of the landscape.

> " And from the grassy slope he sees
>   The Greta flow to meet the Tees ;
>   Where issuing from her darksome bed,
>   She caught the morning's eastern red,
>   And through the softening vale below
>   Roll'd her bright waves in rosy glow,
>   All blushing to her bridal bed,
>   Like some shy maid, in convent bred ;
>   While linnet, lark, and blackbird gay
>   Sing forth her nuptial roundelay."

Is Scott, or are the persons of his story, gay at
this moment ? Far from it. Neither Scott nor
Risingham is happy, but the Greta is; and all
Scott's sympathy is ready for the Greta, on the
instant

Observe, therefore, this is not *pathetic* fallacy;
for there is no passion in *Scott* which alters
nature. It is not the lover's passion, making
him think the larkspurs are listening for his
lady's foot; it is not the miser's passion, making
him think that dead leaves are falling coins; but
it is an inherent and continual habit of thought,
which Scott shares with the moderns in general,
being, in fact, nothing else than the instinctive
sense which men must have of the Divine
presence, not formed into distinct belief. In
the Greek it created, as we saw, the faithfully

believed gods of the elements; in Dante and the mediævals, it formed the faithfully believed angelic presence: in the modern, it creates no perfect form, does not apprehend distinctly any Divine being or operation; but only a dim, slightly credited animation in the natural object, accompanied with great interest and affection for it. This feeling is quite universal with us, only varying in depth according to the greatness of the heart that holds it; and in Scott, being more than usually intense, and accompanied with infinite affection and quickness of sympathy, it enables him to conquer all tendencies to the pathetic fallacy, and, instead of making Nature anywise subordinate to himself, he makes himself subordinate to *her*—follows her lead simply —does not venture to bring his own cares and thoughts into her pure and quiet presence— paints her in her simple and universal truth, adding no result of momentary passion or fancy, and appears, therefore, at first shallower than other poets, being in reality wider and healthier. "What am I?" he says continually, "that I should trouble this sincere nature with my thoughts. I happen to be feverish and depressed, and I could see a great many sad and strange things in those waves and flowers; but I have no business to see such things. Gay Greta! sweet harebells! *you* are not sad nor strange to most people; you are but bright water and blue blossoms; you shall not be anything else to me, except that I cannot help thinking you are a little alive,—no one can help thinking that." And thus, as Nature is bright, serene, or gloomy, Scott takes her temper, and paints her as she is; nothing of himself being ever intruded, except that far-away Æolian tone, of which he is unconscious; and sometimes a stray syllable or two, like that about Blackford Hill, distinctly stating personal feeling, but all the more modestly for that distinctness, and for the clear consciousness that it is not the chiming brook, nor the cornfields, that are sad, but only the boy that rests by them; so returning on the instant to reflect, in all honesty, the image of Nature, as she is meant by all men to be received; nor that in fine words, but in the first that come; nor with comment of far-fetched thoughts, but with easy thoughts, such as all sensible men ought to have in such places, only spoken sweetly; and evidently also with an undercurrent of more profound reflection, which here and there murmurs for a moment, and which, I think, if we choose, we may continually pierce down to, and drink deeply from, but which Scott leaves us to seek, or shun, at our pleasure.—*M. P.*, III. IV. 16, § 36, 37.

55. THE AIMS OF LANDSCAPE PAINTING.—
The landscape painter must always have two

great and distinct ends: the first, to induce in
the spectator's mind the faithful conception of
any natural objects whatsoever; the second, to
guide the spectator's mind to those objects most
worthy of its contemplation, and to inform him
of the thoughts and feelings with which these
were regarded by the artist himself.

In attaining the first end the painter only places
the spectator where he stands himself; he sets
him before the landscape and leaves him. The
spectator is alone. He may follow out his own
thoughts as he would in the natural solitude;
or he may remain untouched, unreflecting and
regardless, as his disposition may incline him;
but he has nothing of thought given to him;
no new ideas, no unknown feelings, forced on
his attention or his heart. The artist is his
conveyance, not his companion,—his horse, not
his friend. But in attaining the second end,
the artist not only *places* the spectator, but
talks to him; makes him a sharer in his own
strong feelings and quick thoughts; hurries him
away in his own enthusiasm; guides him to
all that is beautiful; snatches him from all
that is base; and leaves him more than delighted,—ennobled and instructed, under the
sense of having not only beheld a new scene,
but of having held communion with a new
mind, and having been endowed for a time with
the keen perception and the impetuous emotions

I.　　　　　　　　　　　　K

of a nobler and more penetrating intelligence.
—*M. P.*, I. II. I, i., § I.

56. ON GREATNESS OF STYLE.—We have at
all times some instinctive sense that the function
of one painter is greater than that of another,
even supposing each equally successful in his
own way; and we feel that, if it were possible
to conquer prejudice, and do away with the
iniquities of personal feeling, and the insufficien-
cies of limited knowledge, we should all agree in
this estimate, and be able to place each painter
in his right rank, measuring them by a true scale
of nobleness. We feel that the men in the higher
classes of the scale would be, in the full sense of
the word, Great,—men whom one would give
much to see the faces of but for an instant; and
that those in the lower classes of the scale
(though none were admitted but who had true
merit of some kind) would be very small men,
not greatly exciting either reverence or curiosity.
And with this fixed instinct in our minds, we
permit our teachers daily to exhort their pupils
to the cultivation of "great art,"—neither they nor
we having any very clear notion as to what the
greatness consists in: but sometimes inclining to
think it must depend on the space of the canvas,
and that art on a scale of six feet by ten is something spiritually separated from that on a scale
of three feet by five;—sometimes holding it to

consist in painting the nude body, rather than the body decently clothed ;—sometimes being convinced that it is connected with the study of past history, and that the art is only great which represents what the painter never saw, and about which he knows nothing ;—and sometimes being firmly persuaded that it consists in generally finding fault with, and endeavouring to mend, whatsoever the Divine Wisdom has made. All which various errors, having yet some motes and atoms of truth in the make of each of them, deserve some attentive analysis, for they come under that general law,—that "the corruption of the best is the worst." There are not *worse* errors going than these four; and yet the truth they contain, and the instinct which urges many to preach them, are at the root of all healthy growth in art. We ruin one young painter after another by telling him to follow great art, without knowing ourselves what greatness is; and yet the feeling that it verily *is* something, and that there are depths and breadths, shallows and narrows, in the matter, is all that we have to look to, if we would ever make our art serviceable to ourselves or others. To follow art for the sake of being a great man, and therefore to cast about continually for some means of achieving position or attracting admiration, is the surest way of ending in total extinction. And yet it is only by honest reverence for art itself, and by great

self-respect in the practice of it, that it can be
rescued from dilettanteism, raised to approved
honourableness, and brought to the proper work
it has to accomplish in the service of man.—
M. P., III. IV. 3, § 3.

57. TOKENS OF GREATNESS. I. CHOICE OF
NOBLE SUBJECT. —Greatness of style consists,
then : first, in the habitual choice of subjects of
thought which involve wide interests and profound passions, as opposed to those which involve
narrow interests and slight passions. The style
is greater or less in exact proportion to the
nobleness of the interests and passions involved
in the subject. The habitual choice of sacred
subjects, such as the Nativity, Transfiguration,
Crucifixion (if the choice be sincere), implies that
the painter has a natural disposition to dwell on
the highest thoughts of which humanity is capable ; it constitutes him so far forth a painter
of the highest order, as, for instance, Leonardo,
in his painting of the Last Supper : he who
delights in representing the acts or meditations
of great men, as, for instance, Raphael painting
the School of Athens, is, so far forth, a painter
of the second order : he who represents the
passions and events of ordinary life, of the third.
And in this ordinary life, he who represents deep
thoughts and sorrows, as, for instance, Hunt, in
his Claudio and Isabella, and such other works,

is of the highest rank in his sphere; and he who
represents the slight malignities and passions of
the drawing-room, as, for instance, Leslie, of the
second rank; he who represents the sports of
boys, or simplicities of clowns, as Webster or
Teniers, of the third rank; and he who represents
brutalities and vices (for delight in them, and not
for rebuke of them), of no rank at all, or rather
of a negative rank, holding a certain order in the
abyss.

The reader will, I hope, understand how much
importance is to be attached to the sentence in
the first parenthesis, "if the choice be sincere;"
for choice of subject is, of course, only available
as a criterion of the rank of the painter, when
it is made from the heart. Indeed, in the lower
orders of painting, the choice is always made
from such heart as the painter has; for his
selection of the brawls of peasants or sports of
children can, of course, proceed only from the
fact that he has more sympathy with such brawls
or pastimes than with nobler subjects. But the
choice of the higher kind of subjects is often
insincere; and may, therefore, afford no real
criterion of the painter's rank. The greater
number of men who have lately painted religious
or heroic subjects have done so in mere ambition,
because they had been taught that it was a good
thing to be a "high art" painter; and the fact
is that, in nine cases out of ten, the so-called

historical or "high art" painter is a person
infinitely inferior to the painter of flowers or still
life. He is, in modern times, nearly always a
man who has great vanity without pictorial
capacity, and differs from the landscape or fruit
painter merely in misunderstanding and over-
estimating his own powers. He mistakes his
vanity for inspiration, his ambition for greatness
of soul, and takes pleasure in what he calls
"the ideal," merely because he has neither
humility nor capacity enough to comprehend
the real. . . .

It will follow, of course, from the above considerations, that the choice which characterises
the school of high art is seen as much in the
treatment of a subject as in its selection, and
that the expression of the thoughts of the persons
represented will always be the first thing considered by the painter who worthily enters that
highest school. For the artist who sincerely
chooses the noblest subject will also choose
chiefly to represent what makes that subject
noble, namely, the various heroism or other noble
emotions of the persons represented. If, instead
of this, the artist seeks only to make his picture
agreeable by the composition of its masses and
colours, or by any other merely pictorial merit,
as fine drawing of limbs, it is evident, not only
that any other subject would have answered his
purpose as well, but that he is unfit to approach

the subject he has chosen, because he cannot
enter into its deepest meaning, and therefore
cannot in reality have chosen it for that meaning.
Nevertheless, while the expression is always to
be the first thing considered, all other merits
must be added to the utmost of the painter's
power; for until he can both colour and draw
beautifully he has no business to consider himself
a painter at all, far less to attempt the noblest
subjects of painting; and, when he has once
possessed himself of these powers, he will naturally and fitly employ them to deepen and perfect
the impression made by the sentiment of his
subject.—*M. P.*, III. IV. 3, § 5, 6, 9.

58. TOKENS OF GREATNESS. II. LOVE OF
BEAUTY.—The second characteristic of the great
school of art is, that it introduces in the conception of its subject as much beauty as is possible,
consistently with truth.

For instance, in any subject consisting of a
number of figures, it will make as many of those
figures beautiful as the faithful representation of
humanity will admit. It will not deny the facts
of ugliness or decrepitude, or relative inferiority
and superiority of feature as necessarily manifested in a crowd, but it will, so far as it is in its
power, seek for and dwell upon the fairest forms,
and in all things insist on the beauty that is in
them, not on the ugliness. In this respect,

schools of art become higher in exact proportion
to the degree in which they apprehend and love
the beautiful. Thus, Angelico, intensely loving
all spiritual beauty, will be of the highest rank ;
and Paul Veronese and Correggio, intensely
loving physical and corporeal beauty, of the
second rank ; and Albert Dürer, Rubens, and in
general the Northern artists, apparently insensible to beauty, and caring only for truth,
whether shapely or not, of the third rank ; and
Teniers and Salvator, Caravaggio, and other
such worshippers of the depraved, of no rank,
or as we said before, of a certain order in the
abyss.

The corruption of the schools of high art,
so far as this particular quality is concerned,
consists in the sacrifice of truth to beauty.
Great art dwells on all that is beautiful ; but
false art omits or changes all that is ugly. Great
art accepts Nature as she is, but directs the eyes
and thoughts to what is most perfect in her ; false
art saves itself the trouble of direction by removing or altering whatever it thinks objection-
able. The evil results of which proceeding are
twofold.

First. That beauty deprived of its proper foils
and adjuncts ceases to be enjoyed as beauty, just
as light deprived of all shadow ceases to be
enjoyed as light. A white canvas cannot produce an effect of sunshine ; the painter must

darken it in some places before he can make it look luminous in others; nor can an uninterrupted succession of beauty produce the true effect of beauty; it must be foiled by inferiority before its own power can be developed. Nature has for the most part mingled her inferior and nobler elements as she mingles sunshine with shade, giving due use and influence to both, and the painter who chooses to remove the shadow, perishes in the burning desert he has created. The truly high and beautiful art of Angelico is continually refreshed and strengthened by his frank portraiture of the most ordinary features of his brother monks and of the recorded peculiarities of ungainly sanctity; but the modern German and Raphaelesque schools lose all honour and nobleness in barber-like admiration of handsome faces, and have, in fact, no real faith except in straight noses, and curled hair. Paul Veronese opposes the dwarf to the soldier, and the negress to the queen; Shakespere places Caliban beside Miranda, and Autolycus beside Perdita; but the vulgar idealist withdraws his beauty to the safety of the saloon, and his innocence to the seclusion of the cloister; he pretends that he does this in delicacy of choice and purity of sentiment, while in truth he has neither courage to front the monster, nor wit enough to furnish the knave.

It is only by the habit of representing faithfully all things, that we can truly learn what is beautiful, and what is not. The ugliest objects contain some element of beauty; and in all it is an element peculiar to themselves, which cannot be separated from their ugliness, but must either be enjoyed together with it or not at all. The more a painter accepts nature as he finds it, the more unexpected beauty he discovers in what he at first despised; but once let him arrogate the right of rejection, and he will gradually contract his circle of enjoyment, until what he supposed to be nobleness of selection ends in narrowness of perception. Dwelling perpetually upon one class of ideas, his art becomes at once monstrous and morbid; until at last he cannot faithfully represent even what he chooses to retain; his discrimination contracts into darkness, and his fastidiousness fades into fatuity.

High art, therefore, consists neither in altering, nor in improving nature; but in seeking throughout nature for "whatsoever things are lovely, and whatsoever things are pure;" in loving these, in displaying to the utmost of the painter's power such loveliness as is in them, and directing the thoughts of others to them by winning art or gentle emphasis.—*M. P.*, III. IV. 3, § 12–15.

59. TOKENS OF GREATNESS. III. SINCERITY. —The next* characteristic of great art is that it

* I name them in order of *in*creasing, not decreasing importance.

includes the largest possible quantity of Truth in the most perfect possible harmony. If it were possible for art to give all the truths of nature, it ought to do it. But this is not possible. Choice must always be made of some facts which *can* be represented, from among others which must be passed by in silence, or even, in some respects, misrepresented. The inferior artist chooses unimportant and scattered truths ; the great artist chooses the most necessary first, and afterwards the most consistent with these, so as to obtain the greatest possible and most harmonious *sum*. For instance, Rembrandt always chooses to represent the exact force with which the light on the most illumined part of an object is opposed to its obscurer portions. In order to obtain this, in most cases, not very important truth, he sacrifices the light and colour of five sixths of his picture ; and the expression of every character of objects which depends on tenderness of shape or tint. But he obtains his single truth, and what picturesque and forcible expression is dependent upon it, with magnificent skill and subtlety. Veronese, on the contrary, chooses to represent the great relations of visible things to each other, to the heaven above, and to the earth beneath them. He holds it more important to show how a figure stands relieved from delicate air, or marble wall; how as a red, or purple, or white figure, it separates itself, in clear discernibility,

from things not red, nor purple, nor white; how
infinite daylight shines round it; how innumerable veils of faint shadow invest it; how its
blackness and darkness are, in the excess of their
nature, just as limited and local as its intensity
of light: all this, I say, he feels to be more important than showing merely the exact *measure*
of the spark of sunshine that gleams on a dagger-
hilt, or glows on a jewel.   All this, moreover, he
feels to be harmonious,—capable of being joined
in one great system of spacious truth.   And with
inevitable watchfulness, inestimable subtlety, he
unites all this in tenderest balance, noting in each
hair's-breadth of colour, not merely what its rightness or wrongness is in itself, but what its relation is to every other on his canvas; restraining,
for truth's sake, his exhaustless energy, reining
back, for truth's sake, his fiery strength; veiling,
before truth, the vanity of brightness; penetrating,
for truth, the discouragement of gloom; ruling
his restless invention with a rod of iron;
pardoning no error, no thoughtlessness, no forgetfulness; and subduing all his powers, impulses,
and imaginations, to the arbitrament of a merciless justice, and the obedience of an incorruptible
verity.

I give this instance with respect to colour and
shade: but, in the whole field of art, the difference
between the great and inferior artists is of the
same kind, and may be determined at once by

the question, which of them conveys the largest sum of truth? . . .

As its greatness depends on the sum of truth, and this sum of truth can always be increased by delicacy of handling, it follows that all great art must have this delicacy to the utmost possible degree. This rule is infallible and inflexible. All coarse work is the sign of low art. Only, it is to be remembered, that coarseness must be estimated by the distance from the eye; it being necessary to consult this distance, when great, by laying on touches which appear coarse when seen near; but which, so far from being coarse, are, in reality, more delicate in a master's work than the finest close handling, for they involve a calculation of result, and are laid on with a subtlety of sense precisely correspondent to that with which a good archer draws his bow; the spectator seeing in the action nothing but the strain of the strong arm, while there is in reality, in the finger and eye, an ineffably delicate esti- mate of distance, and touch on the arrow plume. And, indeed, this delicacy is generally quite per- ceptible to those who know what the truth is, for strokes by Tintoret or Paul Veronese, which were done in an instant, and look to an ignorant spectator merely like a violent dash of loaded colour (and are, as such, imitated by blundering artists), are, in fact, modulated by the brush and finger to that degree of delicacy that no single grain of the colour could be taken from the touch without injury; and little golden particles of it, not the size of a gnat's head, have important share and function in the balances of light in a picture perhaps fifty feet long. Nearly *every* other rule applicable to art has some exception but this. This has absolutely none. All great art is delicate art, and all coarse art is bad art. —*M. P.*, III. IV. 3, § 16, 20.

60. TOKENS OF GREATNESS. IV. INVENTION.—The last characteristic of great art is that it must be inventive, that is, be produced by the imagination. In this respect, it must precisely fulfil the definition already given of poetry; and not only present grounds for noble emotion, but furnish these grounds by *imaginative power*. Hence there is at once a great bar fixed between the two schools of Lower and Higher Art. The lower merely copies what is set before it, whether in portrait, landscape, or still-life; the higher either entirely imagines its subject, or arranges the materials presented to it, so as to manifest the imaginative power. . . .

And now, finally, since this poetical power includes the historical, if we glance back to the other qualities required in great art, and put all together, we find that the sum of them is simply the sum of all the powers of man. For as (1) the choice of the high subject involves all conditions of right moral choice, and as (2) the love of beauty involves all conditions of right admiration, and as (3) the grasp of truth involves all strength of sense, evenness of judgment, and honesty of purpose, and as (4) the poetical power involves all swiftness of invention, and accuracy of historical memory, the sum of all these powers is the sum of the human soul. Hence we see why the word "Great" is used of this art. It is literally great. It compasses and calls forth the entire human spirit, whereas any other kind of art, being more or less small or narrow, compasses and calls forth only *part* of the human spirit. Hence the idea of its magnitude is a literal and just one, the art being simply less or greater in proportion to the number of faculties it exercises and addresses. And this is the ultimate meaning of the definition I gave of it long ago, as containing the "greatest number of the greatest ideas."

Therefore it is, that every system of teaching is false which holds forth "great art" as in any wise to be taught to students, or even to be aimed at by them. Great art is precisely that which never was, nor will be taught, it is pre-eminently and finally the expression of the spirits of great men; so that the only wholesome teaching is that which simply endeavours to fix those characters of nobleness in the pupil's mind, of which it seems easily susceptible; and without holding out to him, as a possible or even probable result, that he should ever paint like Titian, or carve like Michael Angelo, enforces upon him the manifest possibility, and assured duty, of endeavouring to draw in a manner at least honest and intelligible; and cultivates in him those general charities of heart, sincerities of thought, and graces of habit which are likely to lead him, throughout life, to prefer openness to affectation, realities to shadows, and beauty to corruption. —*M. P.*, III. IV. 3, § 21, 24, 28.

61. TRUTH IN PORTRAITURE.—We constantly recognise things by their least important attributes, and by help of very few of those: and if these attributes exist not in the imitation, though there may be thousands of others far higher and more valuable, yet if those be wanting, or imperfectly rendered, by which we are accustomed to recognise the object, we deny the likeness; while if these be given, though all the great and valuable and important attributes may be wanting, we affirm the likeness. Recognition is no proof of real and intrinsic resemblance. We recognise our books by their bindings, though the true and essential characteristics lie inside. A man is known to his dog by the smell, to his tailor by the coat, to his friend by the smile: each of these knows him, but how little, or how much, depends on the dignity of

the intelligence. That which is truly and indeed characteristic of the man, is known only to God. One portrait of a man may possess exact accuracy of feature, and no atom of expression; it may be, to use the ordinary terms of admiration bestowed on such portraits by those whom they please, "as like as it can stare." Everybody, down to his cat, would know this. Another portrait may have neglected or misrepresented the features, but may have given the flash of the eye, and the peculiar radiance of the lip, seen on him only in his hours of highest mental excitement. None but his friends would know this. Another may have given none of his ordinary expressions, but one which he wore in the most excited instant of his life, when all his secret passions and all his highest powers were brought into play at once. None but those who had then seen him might recognise *this* as like. But which would be the most truthful portrait of the *man*? The first gives the accidents of body—the sport of climate, and food, and time,—which corruption inhabits, and the worm waits for. The second gives the stamp of the soul upon the flesh; but it is the soul seen in the emotions which it shares with many, which may not be characteristic of its essence— the results of habit, and education, and accident, —a gloze, whether purposely worn or unconsciously assumed, perhaps totally contrary to all

I.

L

that is rooted and real in the mind which it
conceals. The third has caught the trace of all
that was most hidden and most mighty, when
all hypocrisy and all habit, and all petty and
passing emotion—the ice, and the bank, and the
foam of the immortal river—were shivered, and
broken, and swallowed up in the awakening of
its inward strength; when the call and claim of
some divine motive had brought into visible
being those latent forces and feelings which the
spirit's own volition could not summon, nor its
consciousness comprehend, which God only knew,
and God only could awaken—the depth and the
mystery of its peculiar and separating attributes.
And so it is with external Nature: she has a
body and a soul like man; but her soul is the
Deity. It is possible to represent the body
without the spirit; and this shall be like, to
those whose senses are only cognisant of body.
It is possible to represent the spirit in its
ordinary and inferior manifestations; and this
shall be like, to those who have not watched
for its moments of power. It is possible to
represent the spirit in its secret and high opera-
tions; and this shall be like, only to those to
whose watching they have been revealed. All
these are truth; but according to the dignity of
the truths he can represent or feel, is the power
of the painter—the justice of the judge.—*M. P.*,
I. II. i. 2, § 8.

62. TRUTH IN LANDSCAPE.—If we are now to go out to the fields, and to draw anything like a complete landscape, direct imitation becomes more or less impossible. It is always to be aimed at so far as it *is* possible; and when you have time and opportunity, some portions of a landscape may, as you gain greater skill, be rendered with an approximation almost to mirrored portraiture. Still, whatever skill you may reach, there will always be need of judgment to choose, and of speed to seize, certain things that are principal or fugitive; and you must give more and more effort daily to the observance of characteristic points, and the attainment of concise methods.

I have directed your attention early to foliage for two reasons. First, that it is always accessible as a study; and secondly, that its modes of growth present simple examples of the importance of leading or governing lines. It is by seizing these leading lines, when we cannot seize all, that likeness and expression are given to a portrait, and grace and a kind of vital truth to the rendering of every natural form. I call it vital truth, because these chief lines are always expressive of the past history and present action of the thing. They show in a mountain, first, how it was built or heaped up; and secondly, how it is now being worn away, and from what quarter the wildest storms strike it. In a tree, they show what kind of fortune it has had to endure from its childhood: how troublesome trees have come in its way, and pushed it aside, and tried to strangle or starve it; where and when kind trees have sheltered it, and grown up lovingly together with it, bending as it bent; what winds torment it most; what boughs of it behave best, and bear most fruit; and so on. In a wave or cloud, these leading lines show the run of the tide and of the wind, and the sort of change which the water or vapour is at any moment enduring in its form, as it meets shore, or counter-wave, or melting sunshine. Now remember, nothing distinguishes great men from inferior men more than their always, whether in life or in art, *knowing the way things are going.* Your dunce thinks they are standing still, and draws them all fixed; your wise man sees the change or changing in them, and draws them so, —the animal in its motion, the tree in its growth, the cloud in its course, the mountain in its wearing away. Try always, whenever you look at a form, to see the lines in it which have had power over its past fate and will have power over its futurity.—*E. D.*, II., § 102–104.

63. DECEPTIVE IMITATION.—But there is one source of pleasure in works of art totally different from all these, which I conceive to be properly and accurately expressed by the word "imitation;"

one which, though constantly confused in reasoning, because it is always associated in fact, with other means of pleasure, is totally separated from them in its nature, and is the real basis of whatever complicated or various meaning may be afterwards attached to the word in the minds of men.

I wish to point out this distinct source of pleasure clearly at once, and only to use the word " imitation " in reference to it.

Whenever anything looks like what it is not, the resemblance being so great as *nearly* to deceive, we feel a kind of pleasurable surprise, an agreeable excitement of mind, exactly the same in its nature as that which we receive from juggling. Whenever we perceive this in something produced by art, that is to say, whenever the work is seen to resemble something which we know it is not, we receive what I call an idea of imitation. *Why* such ideas are pleasing, it would be out of our present purpose to inquire; we only know that there is no man who does not feel pleasure in his animal nature from gentle surprise, and that such surprise can be excited in no more distinct manner than by the evidence that a thing is not what it appears to be. Now two things are requisite to our complete and most pleasurable perception of this: first, that the resemblance be so perfect as to amount to a deception; secondly, that there be some means

of proving at the same moment that it *is* a
deception.   The most perfect ideas and pleasures
of imitation are, therefore, when one sense is
contradicted by another, both bearing as positive
evidence on the subject as each is capable of
alone ; as when the eye says a thing is round,
and the finger says it is flat : they are, therefore,
never felt in so high a degree as in painting,
where appearance of projection, roughness, hair,
velvet, etc., are given with a smooth surface, or
in waxwork, where the first evidence of the
senses is perpetually contradicted by their experience.   But the moment we come to marble,
our definition checks us, for a marble figure does
not look like what it is not : it looks like marble,
and like the form of a man, but then it *is* marble,
and it *is* the form of a man.   It does not look
like a man, which it is not, but like the form of
a man, which it is.   Form is form, *bonâ fide* and
actual, whether in marble or in flesh—not an
imitation or resemblance of form, but real form.
The chalk outline of the bough of a tree on paper
is not an imitation ; it looks like chalk and paper
—not like wood, and that which it suggests to
the mind is not properly said to be *like* the form
of a bough, it *is* the form of a bough.   Now,
then, we see the limits of an idea of imitation ;
it extends only to the sensation of trickery and
deception occasioned by a thing's intentionally
seeming different from what it is ; and the degree

of the pleasure depends on the degree of difference and the perfection of the resemblance, not on the nature of the thing resembled. The simple pleasure in the imitation would be precisely of the same degree (if the accuracy could be equal), whether the subject of it were the hero or his horse. There are other collateral sources of pleasure which are necessarily associated with this, but that part of the pleasure which depends on the imitation is the same in both.

Ideas of imitation, then, act by producing the simple pleasure of surprise, and that not of surprise in its higher sense and function, but of the mean and paltry surprise which is felt in jugglery. These ideas and pleasures are the most contemptible which can be received from art.— *M. P.*, I. i. i. 4, § 1-4.

64. POWER IN ART.—The sensation of power is in proportion to the apparent inadequacy of the means to the end ; so that the impression is much greater from a partial success attained with slight effort, than from perfect success attained with greater proportional effort. Now, in all art, every touch or effort does individually less in proportion as the work approaches perfection. The first five chalk touches bring a head into existence out of nothing. No five touches in the whole course of the work will ever do so much as these, and the difference made by each touch is

more and more imperceptible as the work approaches completion. Consequently, the ratio between the means employed and the effect produced is constantly decreasing, and therefore the least sensation of power is received from the most perfect work.

It is thus evident that there are sensations of power about imperfect art, so that it be right art as far as it goes, which must always be wanting in its perfection; and that there are sources of pleasure in the hasty sketch and the rough-hewn block, which are partially wanting in the tinted canvas and the polished marble. But it is nevertheless wrong to prefer the sensation of power to the intellectual perception of it. There is in reality greater power in the completion than in the commencement; and though it be not so manifest to the senses, it ought to have higher influence on the mind; and therefore in praising pictures for the ideas of power they convey, we must not look to the keenest sensation, but to the highest estimate, accompanied with as much of the sensation as is compatible with it; and thus we shall consider those pictures as conveying the highest ideas of power which attain the most *perfect* end with the slightest possible means; not, observe, those in which, though much has been done with little, all has not been done, but from the picture, in which *all* has been done, and yet not a touch thrown away. The quantity of work in the sketch is necessarily less in proportion to the effect obtained than in the picture; but yet the picture involves the greater power, if, out of all the additional labour bestowed on it, not a touch has been lost.—*M. P.*, I. i. ii. 1, § 6, 7.

65. EXECUTION.—Let us, for instance, compare the execution of the bull's head in the left hand lowest corner of the Adoration of the Magi, in the Museum at Antwerp, with that in Berghem's landscape, No. 132, in the Dulwich Gallery. Rubens first scratches horizontally over his canvas a thin greyish brown, transparent and even, very much the colour of light wainscot; the horizontal strokes of the bristles being left so evident that the whole might be taken for an imitation of wood, were it not for its transparency. On this ground the eye, nostril, and outline of the cheek are given with two or three rude brown touches (about three or four minutes' work in all), though the head is colossal. The background is then laid in with thick solid, warm white, actually projecting all round the head, leaving it in dark intaglio. Finally, five thin and scratchy strokes of very cold bluish white are struck for the high light on the forehead and nose, and the head is complete. Seen within a yard of the canvas, it looks actually transparent—a flimsy, meaningless, distant shadow; while the background looks solid,

projecting, and near. From the right distance (ten or twelve yards off, whence alone the whole of the picture can be seen), it is a complete, rich, substantial, and living realisation of the projecting head of the animal; while the background falls far behind. Now there is no slight nor mean pleasure in perceiving such a result attained by means so strange. By Berghem, on the other hand, a dark background is first laid in with exquisite delicacy and transparency, and on this the cow's head is actually modelled in luminous white, the separate locks of hair projecting from the canvas. No surprise, nor much pleasure of any kind, would be attendant on this execution, even were the result equally successful; and what little pleasure we have in it vanishes, when on retiring from the picture, we find the head shining like a distant lantern, instead of seeming substantial or near. Yet strangeness is not to be considered as a legitimate source of pleasure. That means which is most conducive to the end, should always be the most pleasurable; and that which is most conducive to the end, can be strange only to the ignorance of the spectator. This kind of pleasure is illegitimate, therefore, because it implies and requires, in those who feel it, ignorance of art.

The legitimate sources of pleasure in execution are therefore truth, simplicity, mystery, inadequacy, decision, and velocity. But of these, be it observed, some are so far inconsistent with others, that they cannot be united in high degrees. Mystery with inadequacy, for instance; since to see that the means are inadequate, we must see what they are. Now the first three are the great qualities of execution, and the last three are the attractive ones, because on them are chiefly attendant the ideas of power. By the first three the attention is withdrawn from the means and fixed on the result: by the last three, withdrawn from the result, and fixed on the means. To see that execution is swift or that it is decided, we must look away from its creation to observe it in the act of creating; we must think more of the pallet than of the picture; but simplicity and mystery compel the mind to leave the means and fix itself on the conception. Hence the danger of too great fondness for those sensations of power which are associated with the last three qualities of execution; for, although it is most desirable that these should be present as far as they are consistent with the others, and though their visible absence is always painful and wrong, yet the moment the higher qualities are sacrificed to them in the least degree, we have a brilliant vice. —*M. P.*, I. I. ii. 2, § 7–9.

66. MYSTERY OF DETAIL.—Take the commonest, closest, most familiar thing, and strive to draw it verily as you see it. Be sure of this last fact, for otherwise you will find yourself

continually drawing, not what you *see*, but what you *know*. The best practice to begin with is, sitting about three yards from a bookcase (not your own, so that you may *know* none of the titles of the books), to try to draw the books accurately, with the titles on the backs, and patterns on the bindings, as you see them. You are not to stir from your place to look what they are, but to draw them simply as they appear, giving the perfect look of neat lettering; which, nevertheless, must be (as you will find it on most of the books) absolutely illegible. Next try to draw a piece of patterned muslin or lace (of which you do not know the pattern), a little way off, and rather in the shade; and be sure you get all the grace and *look* of the pattern without going a step nearer to see what it is. Then try to draw a bank of grass, with all its blades; or a bush, with all its leaves; and you will soon begin to understand under what a universal law of obscurity we live, and perceive that all *distinct* drawing must be *bad* drawing, and that nothing can be right, till it is unintelligible. . . .

" Well, but how of Veronese and all the firm, fearless draughtsmen of days gone by ? "

They are indeed firm and fearless, but they are all mysterious. Not one great man of them, but he will puzzle you, if you look close, to know what he means. Distinct enough, as to his general intent, indeed, just as Nature is distinct in her general intent, but examine his touches, and you will find in Veronese, in Titian, in Tintoret, in Correggio, and in all the great *painters*, properly so called, a peculiar melting and mystery about the pencilling, sometimes called softness, sometimes freedom, sometimes breadth; but in reality a most subtle confusion of colours and forms, obtained either by the apparently careless stroke of the brush, or by careful retouching with tenderest labour; but always obtained in one way or another: so that though, when compared with work that has no meaning, all great work is *distinct*,—compared with work that has narrow and stubborn meaning, all great work is *in*distinct; and if we find, on examining any picture closely, that it is all clearly to be made out, it cannot be, as painting, first-rate. There is no exception to this rule. EXCELLENCE OF THE HIGHEST KIND, WITHOUT OBSCURITY, CANNOT EXIST.—*M. P.*, IV. v. 4, § 7, 9.

67. THREE STAGES OF REALISATION.—There is a singular sense in which the child may peculiarly be said to be father of the man. In many arts and attainments, the first and last stages of progress, the infancy and the consummation, have many features in common; while the intermediate stages are wholly unlike either, and are farthest from the right. Thus it is in

the progress of a painter's handling. We see the perfect child, the absolute beginner, using of necessity a broken, imperfect, inadequate line, which, as he advances, becomes gradually firm, severe, and decided. Yet before he becomes a perfect artist, this severity and decision will again be exchanged for a light and careless stroke, which in many points will far more resemble that of his childhood than of his middle age, differing from it only by the consummate effect wrought out by the apparently inadequate means. So it is in many matters of opinion. Our first and last coincide, though on different grounds; it is the middle stage which is farthest from the truth. Childhood often holds a truth with its feeble fingers, which the grasp of manhood cannot retain, which it is the pride of utmost age to recover.

Perhaps this is in no instance more remarkable than in the opinion we form upon the subject of detail in works of art. Infants in judgment, we look for specific character, and complete finish; we delight in the faithful plumage of the well known bird, in the finely drawn leafage of the discriminated flower. As we advance in judgment, we scorn such detail altogether; we look for impetuosity of execution, and breadth of effect. But, perfected in judgment, we return in a great measure to our early feelings, and thank Raffaelle for the shells upon his sacred beach, and for the delicate stamens of the herbage beside his inspired St. Catharine.

Of those who take interest in art, nay, even of artists themselves, there are a hundred in the middle stage of judgment, for one who is in the last; and this, not because they are destitute of the power to discover, or the sensibility to enjoy, the truth, but because the truth bears so much semblance of error, the last stage of the journey to the first, that every feeling which guides to it is checked in its origin. The rapid and powerful artist necessarily looks with such contempt on those who seek minutiæ of detail *rather* than grandeur of impression, that it is almost impossible for him to conceive of the great last step in art by which both become compatible. He has so often to dash the delicacy out of the pupil's work, and to blot the details from his encumbered canvas; so frequently to lament the loss of breadth and unity, and so seldom to reprehend the imperfection of minutiæ, that he necessarily looks upon complete *parts* as the very sign of error, weakness, and ignorance. Thus, frequently to the latest period of his life, he separates, like Sir Joshua, as chief enemies, the details and the whole, which an artist cannot be great unless he reconciles; and because details alone, and unreferred to a final purpose, are the sign of a tyro's work, he loses sight of the remoter truth, that details perfect in unity, and contributing to a final purpose, are the sign of the production of a consummate master.—*M. P.*, I. Pref. 2nd Ed., § 24, 25.

68. FINISH.—Absolute finish is always right; finish, inconsistent with prudence and passion, wrong. The imperative demand for finish is ruinous, because it refuses better things than finish. The stopping short of the finish, which is honourably possible to human energy, is destructive on the other side, and not in less degree. Err, of the two, on the side of completion.— *M. P.*, V. IX. 7, *note*.

69. THE TWO-FOLD NATURE OF ART.—Good art always consists of two things: First, the observation of fact; secondly, the manifesting of human design and authority in the way that fact is told. Great and good art must unite the two; it cannot exist for a moment but in their unity; it consists of the two as essentially as water consists of oxygen and hydrogen, or marble of lime and carbonic acid. . . .

Wheresoever the search after truth begins, there life begins; wheresoever that search ceases, there life ceases. As long as a school of art holds any chain of natural facts, trying to discover more of them and express them better daily, it may play hither and thither as it likes on this side of the chain or that; it may design grotesques and conventionalisms, build the simplest buildings, serve the most practical utilities; yet all it does will be gloriously designed and gloriously done; but let it once quit hold of the chain of natural fact, cease to pursue that as the clue to its work; let it propose to itself any other end than preaching this living word, and think first of showing its own skill or its own fancy, and from that hour its fall is precipitate—its destruction sure; nothing that it does or designs will ever have life or loveliness in it more; its hour has come, and there is no work, nor device, nor knowledge, nor wisdom, in the grave whither it goeth. . . .

Thus, then, you will find—and the more profound and accurate your knowledge of the history of art the more assuredly you will find—that the living power in all the real schools, be they great or small, is love of nature. But do not mistake me by supposing that I mean this law to be all that is necessary to form a school. There needs to be much superadded to it, though there never must be anything superseding it. The main thing which needs to be superadded is the gift of design.

It is always dangerous, and liable to diminish the clearness of impression, to go over much ground in the course of one lecture. But I dare not present you with a maimed view of this important subject. I dare not put off to another

I. M

time, when the same persons would not be again
assembled, the statement of the great collateral
necessity which, as well as the necessity of truth,
governs all noble art.

That collateral necessity is *the visible operation
of human intellect in the presentation of truth*, the
evidence of what is properly called design or plan
in the work, no less than of veracity.   A looking-
glass does not design—it receives and communicates indiscriminately all that passes before it ; a
painter designs when he chooses some things,
refuses others, and arranges all.

This selection and arrangement must have
influence over everything that the art is concerned with, great or small—over lines, over
colours, and over ideas.   Given a certain group
of colours, by adding another colour at the side
of them, you will either improve the group and
render it more delightful, or injure it, and render
it discordant and unintelligible.   " Design " is the
choosing and placing the colour so as to help and
enhance all the other colours it is set beside.
So of thoughts: in a good composition, every
idea is presented in just that order, and with just
that force, which will perfectly connect it with
all the other thoughts in the work, and will
illustrate the others as well as receive illustration
from them ; so that the entire chain of thoughts
offered to the beholder's mind shall be received
by him with as much delight and with as little

effort as is possible. And thus you see design, properly so called, is human invention, consulting human capacity. Out of the infinite heap of things around us in the world, it chooses a certain number which it can thoroughly grasp, and presents this group to the spectator in the form best calculated to enable him to grasp it also, and to grasp it with delight.

And accordingly, the capacities of both gatherer and receiver being limited, the object is to make *everything that you offer helpful and precious.* If you give one grain of weight too much, so as to increase fatigue without profit, or bulk without value—that added grain is hurtful: if you put one spot or one syllable out of its proper place, that spot or syllable will be destructive—how far destructive it is almost impossible to tell: a misplaced touch may sometimes annihilate the labour of hours. Nor are any of us prepared to understand the work of any great master, till we feel this, and feel it as distinctly as we do the value of arrangement in the notes of music. Take any noble musical air, and you find, on examining it, that not one even of the faintest or shortest notes can be removed without destruction to the whole passage in which it occurs; and that every note in the passage is twenty times more beautiful so introduced, than it would have been if played singly on the instrument. Precisely this degree of arrangement and relation must exist between every touch * and line in a great picture. You may consider the whole as a prolonged musical composition: its parts, as separate airs connected in the story; its little bits and fragments of colour and line, as separate passages or bars in melodies; and down to the minutest note of the whole— down to the minutest *touch*,—if there is one that can be spared—that one is doing mischief.

Remember therefore always, you have two characters in which all greatness of art consists :— First, the earnest and intense seizing of natural facts: then the ordering those facts by strength of human intellect, so as to make them, for all who look upon them, to the utmost serviceable, memorable and beautiful.—*T. P.*, I. § 19, 23, 41–45.

70. COMPOSITION AND INVENTION.—When an unimaginative painter is about to draw a tree, (and we will suppose him, for better illustration of the point in question, to have good feeling and correct knowledge of the nature of trees,) he probably lays on his paper such a general form as he knows to be characteristic of the tree to be drawn, and such as he believes will fall in agreeably with the other masses of his picture, which we will suppose partly prepared. When this form is set down, he assuredly finds it has done

---

* Literally. I know how exaggerated this statement sounds; but I mean it,—every syllable of it.

something he did not intend it to do. It has mimicked some prominent line, or overpowered some necessary mass. He begins pruning and changing, and, after several experiments, succeeds in obtaining a form which does no material mischief to any other. To this form he proceeds to attach a trunk, and, working probably on a received notion or rule (for the unimaginative painter never works without a principle) that tree trunks ought to lean first one way and then the other as they go up, and ought not to stand under the middle of the tree, he sketches a serpentine form of requisite propriety; when it has gone up far enough, that is, till it looks disagreeably long, he will begin to ramify it; and if there be another tree in the picture with two large branches, he knows that this, by all laws of composition, ought to have three or four, or some different number; and because he knows that if three or four branches start from the same point they will look formal, therefore he makes them start from points one above another; and because equal distances are improper, therefore they shall start at unequal distances. When they are fairly started, he knows they must undulate or go backwards and forwards, which accordingly he makes them do at random; and because he knows that all forms ought to be contrasted, he makes one bend down while the other three go up. The three that go up he knows must not go up without

interfering with each other, and so he makes two
of them cross. He thinks it also proper that
there should be variety of character in them; so
he makes the one that bends down graceful and
flexible, and, of the two that cross, he splinters
one and makes a stump of it. He repeats the process among the more complicated minor boughs,
until coming to the smallest, he thinks farther
care unnecessary, but draws them freely, and by
chance. Having to put on the foliage, he will
make it flow properly in the direction of the tree's
growth; he will make all the extremities graceful;
but will be tormented by finding them come all
alike, and at last will be obliged to spoil a number
of them altogether, in order to obtain opposition.
They will not, however, be united in this their
spoliation, but will remain uncomfortably separate
and individually ill-tempered. He consoles himself by the reflection that it is unnatural for all of
them to be equally perfect.

Now, I suppose that through the whole of this
process, he has been able to refer to his definite
memory or conception of nature for every one of
the fragments he has successively added; that
the details, colour, fractures, insertions, etc., of
his boughs, are all either actual recollections or
based on secure knowledge of the tree (and
herein I allow far more than is commonly the
case with unimaginative painters). But, as far
as the process of combination is concerned, it is

evident that, from beginning to end, his laws have been his safety, and his plague has been his liberty. He has been compelled to work at random or under the guidance of feeling only, whenever there was anything left to his own decision. He has never been decided in anything except in what he *must* or *must not* do. He has walked as a drunken man on a broad road; his guides are the hedges; and, between these limits, the broader the way, the more difficult his progress.

The advance of the imaginative artist is precisely the reverse of this. He owns no laws. He defies all restraint, and cuts down all hedges. There is nothing within the limits of natural possibility that he dares not do, or that he allows the necessity of doing. The laws of nature he knows; these are to him no restraint. They are his own nature. All other laws or limits he sets at utter defiance; his journey is over an untrodden and pathless plain. But he sees his end over the waste from the first, and goes straight at it; never losing sight of it, nor throwing away a step. Nothing can stop him, nothing turn him aside; falcons and lynxes are of slow and uncertain sight compared with his. He saw his tree, trunk, boughs, foliage and all, from the first moment; not only the tree, but the sky behind it; not only that tree or sky, but all the other great features of his picture: by what intense power of instantaneous selection and amalgamation cannot be explained, but by this it may be proved and tested; that, if we examine the tree of the unimaginative painter, we shall find that on removing any part or parts of it, though the rest will indeed suffer, as being deprived of the proper development of a tree, and as involving a blank space that wants occupation, yet the portions left are not made discordant or disagreeable. They are absolutely and in themselves as valuable as they can be; every stem is a perfect stem, and every twig a graceful twig, or at least as perfect and as graceful as they were before the removal of the rest. But if we try the same experiment on the imaginative painter's work, and break off the merest stem or twig of it, it all goes to pieces like a Prince Rupert's drop. There is not so much as a seed of it but it lies on the tree's life, like the grain upon the tongue of Chaucer's sainted child. Take it away, and the boughs will sing to us no longer. All is dead and cold.—*M. P.*, II. III. ii. 2, § 11–13.

71. "PAINT YOUR IMPRESSIONS."—And now, once for all, let it be clearly understood, that an "impression on the mind" does not mean a piece of manufacture. The way in which most artists proceed to "invent," as they call it, a picture, is this: they choose their subject, for the most part well, with a sufficient quantity of towers,

mountains, ruined cottages, and other materials, to be generally interesting; then they fix on some object for a principal light; behind this they put a dark cloud, or, in front of it, a dark piece of foreground; then they repeat this light somewhere else in a less degree, and connect the two lights together by some intermediate ones. If they find any part of the foreground uninteresting, they put a group of figures into it; if any part of the distance, they put something there from some other sketch; and proceed to inferior detail in the same manner, taking care always to put white stones near black ones, and purple colours near yellow ones, and angular forms near round ones;—all this being, as simply a matter of recipe and practice as cookery; like that, not by any means a thing easily done well, but still having no reference whatever to "impressions on the mind."

But the artist who has real invention sets to work in a totally different way. First, he receives a true impression from the place itself, and takes care to keep hold of that as his chief good; indeed, he needs no care in the matter, for the distinction of his mind from that of others consists in his instantly receiving such sensations strongly, and being unable to lose them; and then he sets himself as far as possible to reproduce that impression on the mind of the spectator of his picture.—*M. P.*, IV. V. 2, § 8, 9.

72. FORM AND COLOUR.—All men, completely organised and justly tempered, enjoy colour; it is meant for the perpetual comfort and delight of the human heart; it is richly bestowed on the highest works of creation, and the eminent sign and seal of perfection in them; being associated with *life* in the human body, with *light* in the sky, with *purity* and hardness in the earth,— death, night, and pollution of all kinds being colourless. And although if form and colour be brought into complete opposition, so that it should be put to us as a matter of stern choice whether we should have a work of art all of form, without colour (as an Albert Dürer's engraving), or all of colour, without form (as an imitation of mother-of-pearl), form is beyond all comparison the more precious of the two; and in explaining the essence of objects, form is essential, and colour more or less accidental; yet if colour be introduced at all, it is necessary that, whatever else may be wrong *that* should be right: just as, though the music of a song may not be so essential to its influence as the meaning of the words, yet if the music be given at all, *it* must be right, or its discord will spoil the words; and it would be better, of the two, that the words should be indistinct, than the notes false.

Hence, as I have said elsewhere, the business of a painter is to paint. If he can colour, he is a painter, though he can do nothing else; if he cannot colour, he is no painter, though he may do everything else. But it is, in fact, impossible, if he can colour, but that he should be able to do more; for a faithful study of colour will always give power over form, though the most intense study of form will give no power over colour. The man who can see all the greys, and reds, and purples in a peach, will paint the peach rightly round, and rightly altogether; but the man who has only studied its roundness, may not see its purples and greys, and if he does not, will never get it to look like a peach; so that great power over colour is always a sign of large general art-intellect. Expression of the most subtle kind can be often reached by the slight studies of caricaturists; sometimes elaborated by the toil of the dull, and sometimes by the sentiment of the feeble; but to colour well requires real talent and earnest study, and to colour perfectly is the rarest and most precious power an artist can possess. Every other gift may be erroneously cultivated, but this will guide to all healthy, natural, and forcible truth; the student may be led into folly by philosophers, and into falsehood by purists; but he is always safe, if he holds the hand of a colourist.—*M. P.*, IV. v. 3, § 24.

73. TEMPERANCE IN COLOUR AND CURVATURE.—The safeguard of highest beauty, in all

visible work, is exactly that which is also the
safeguard of conduct in the soul,—Temperance,
in the broadest sense; the Temperance which
we have seen sitting on an equal throne with
Justice amidst the Four Cardinal virtues, and,
wanting which, there is not any other virtue
which may not lead us into desperate error.
Now observe: Temperance, in the nobler sense,
does not mean a subdued and imperfect energy;
it does not mean a stopping short in any good
thing, as in Love or in Faith; but it means the
power which governs the most intense energy,
and prevents its acting in any way but as it
ought. And with respect to things in which
there may be excess, it does not mean imperfect
enjoyment of them; but the regulation of their
quantity, so that the enjoyment of them shall be
greatest. For instance, in the matter we have
at present in hand, temperance in colour does
not mean imperfect or dull enjoyment of colour;
but it means that government of colour which
shall bring the utmost possible enjoyment out
of all hues. A bad colourist does not *love*
beautiful colour better than the best colourist
does, not half so much. But he indulges in it
to excess; he uses it in large masses, and un-
subdued; and then it is a law of nature, a law
as universal as that of gravitation, that he shall
not be able to enjoy it so much as if he had used
it in less quantity. His eye is jaded and satiated,

and the blue and red have life in them no more.
He tries to paint them bluer and redder, in vain:
all the blue has become grey, and gets greyer
the more he adds to it; all his crimson has
become brown, and gets more sere and autumnal
the more he deepens it. But the great painter
is sternly temperate in his work; he loves the
vivid colour with all his heart; but for a long
time he does not allow himself anything like it,
nothing but sober browns and dull greys, and
colours that have no conceivable beauty in them;
but these by his government become lovely: and
after bringing out of them all the life and power
they possess, and enjoying them to the uttermost,
—cautiously, and as the crown of the work, and
the consummation of its music, he permits the
momentary crimson and azure, and the whole
canvas is in a flame.

Again, in curvature, which is the cause of loveliness in all form, the bad designer does not
enjoy it more than the great designer, but he
indulges in it till his eye is satiated, and he
cannot obtain enough of it to touch his jaded
feeling for grace. But the great and temperate
designer does not allow himself any violent
curves; he works much with lines in which the
curvature, though always existing, is long before
it is perceived. He dwells on all these subdued
curvatures to the uttermost, and opposes them
with still severer lines to bring them out in fuller

sweetness; and, at last, he allows himself a momentary curve of energy, and all the work is, in an instant, full of life and grace.—*S. V.*, III. I., § 7, 8.

74. THE SANCTITY OF COLOUR.—God has employed colour in His creation as the unvarying accompaniment of all that is purest, most innocent, and most precious; while for things precious only in material uses, or dangerous, common colours are reserved. Consider for a little while what sort of a world it would be if all flowers were grey, all leaves black, and the sky *brown*. Imagine that, as completely as may be, and consider whether you would think the world any whit more sacred for being thus transfigured into the hues of the shadows in Raphael's Transfiguration. Then observe how constantly innocent things are bright in colour; look at a dove's neck, and compare it with the grey back of a viper; I have often heard talk of brilliantly coloured serpents; and I suppose there are such,—as there are gay poisons, like the foxglove and kalmia—types of deceit: but all the venomous serpents I have really *seen* are grey, brick-red, or brown, variously mottled; and the most awful serpent I have seen, the Egyptian asp, is precisely of the colour of gravel, or only a little greyer. So, again, the crocodile and alligator are grey, but the innocent lizard green and

beautiful. I do not mean that the rule is invariable, otherwise it would be more convincing than the lessons of the natural universe are intended ever to be; there are beautiful colours on the leopard and tiger, and in the berries of the nightshade; and there is nothing very notable in brilliancy of colour either in sheep or cattle (though, by the way, the velvet of a brown bull's hide in the sun, or the tawny white of the Italian oxen, is, to my mind, lovelier than any leopard's or tiger's skin): but take a wider view of nature, and compare generally rainbows, sunrises, roses, violets, butterflies, birds, gold-fish, rubies, opals, and corals, with alligators, hippopotami, lions, wolves, bears, swine, sharks, slugs, bones, fungi, fogs, and corrupting, stinging, destroying things in general, and you will feel then how the question stands between the colourists and chiaroscurists,—which of them have nature and life on their side, and which have sin and death.—*M. P.*, IV. v. 3, § 23.

75. THE SIGNIFICANCE OF THE GIFT OF COLOURING.—Of all God's gifts to the sight of man, colour is the holiest, the most divine, the most solemn. We speak rashly of gay colour and sad colour, for colour cannot at once be good and gay. All good colour is in some degree pensive; the loveliest is melancholy, and the

purest and most thoughtful minds are those which love colour the most.

I know that this will sound strange in many ears, and will be especially startling to those who have considered the subject chiefly with reference to painting; for the great Venetian schools of colour are not usually understood to be either pure or pensive, and the idea of its pre-eminence is associated in nearly every mind with the coarseness of Rubens, and the sensualities of Correggio and Titian. But a more comprehensive view of art will soon correct this impression. It will be discovered, in the first place, that the more faithful and earnest the religion of the painter, the more pure and prevalent is the system of his colour. It will be found, in the second place, that where colour becomes a primal intention with a painter otherwise mean or sensual, it instantly elevates him, and becomes the one sacred and saving element in his work. The very depth of the stoop to which the Venetian painters and Rubens sometimes condescend, is a consequence of their feeling confidence in the power of their colour to keep them from falling. They hold on by it, as by a chain let down from heaven, with one hand, though they may sometimes seem to gather dust and ashes with the other. And, in the last place, it will be found that so surely as a painter is irreligious, thoughtless, or obscene in disposition, so surely is his colouring cold, gloomy, and valueless. The opposite poles of art in this respect are Frà Angelico and Salvator Rosa; of whom the one was a man who smiled seldom, wept often, prayed constantly, and never harboured an impure thought. His pictures are simply so many pieces of jewellery, the colours of the draperies being perfectly pure, as various as those of a painted window, chastened only by paleness, and relieved upon a gold ground. Salvator was a dissipated jester and satirist, a man who spent his life in masquing and revelry. But his pictures are full of horror, and their colour is for the most part gloomy grey. Truly it would seem as if art had so much of eternity in it, that it must take its dye from the close rather than the course of life: "In such laughter the heart of man is sorrowful, and the end of that mirth is heaviness."—*S. V.*, II. v., § 30, 31.

76. CHIAROSCURO.—Chiaroscuro is a very noble subject of study; but it is not so noble a study as human nature: nor is it the subject which should mainly occupy our thoughts when we have human nature before us. Generally, we ought to see more in man or woman than that their foreheads come dark against the sky, or their petticoats and pantaloons white against it. If we see nothing but this, and think of nothing else in the company of our

fellow-creatures but the depth of their shadows,
we are assuredly in such insensitive state of mind
as must render all true painting impossible to us.
It may be the most important thing about a
pollard willow that it comes greyly against a
cloud, or gloomily out of a pool. But respecting
a man, his greyness or opacity are not the principal facts which it is desirable to state of him.
If you cannot see his human beauty, and have
no sympathy with his mind, don't paint him.
Go and paint logs, or stones, or weeds;—you
will not, indeed, paint even these at all supremely,
for *their* best beauty is also in a sort human:
nevertheless, you will not insult them, as you
do living creatures, by perceiving in them only
opacity. Immense harm has been done in this
matter by the popular misunderstanding of
Rembrandt — for Rembrandt's strength is in
rendering of human character—not in chiaroscuro. Rembrandt's chiaroscuro is always forced
—generally false, and wholly vulgar: it is in
all possible ways inferior, *as* chiaroscuro, to
Correggio's, Titian's, Tintoret's, Veronese's, or
Velasquez's. But in rendering human character,
such as he saw about him, Rembrandt is nearly
equal to any of these men, and the real power
of him is in his stern and steady touch on lip
and brow—seen best in his lightest etchings—
or in the lightest parts of the handling of his
portraits, the head of the Jew in our own Gallery

being about as good and thorough work as it is possible to see of his. And when this is so, and the great qualities of character and of form are first secured—after them, and in due subordination to them—chiaroscuro and everything else will come rightly and gloriously; and they always do come in such order; no chiaroscuro ever was good, as such, which was not subordinate to character and to form; and all search after it as a first object ends in the loss of the thing itself so sought.—*Notes on the Academy,* No. V. p. 51.

77. THE FALSE IDEAL.—Every one can easily appreciate the merit of regular features and well-formed limbs, but it requires some attention, sympathy, and sense, to detect the charm of passing expression, or life-disciplined character. The beauty of the Apollo Belvidere, or Venus de' Medici, is perfectly palpable to any shallow fine lady or fine gentleman, though they would have perceived none in the face of an old weather-beaten St. Peter, or a grey-haired "Grandmother Lois." The knowledge that long study is necessary to produce these regular types of the human form renders the facile admiration matter of eager self-complacency; the shallow spectator, delighted that he can really, and without hypocrisy, admire what required much thought to produce, supposes himself endowed with the highest critical faculties,

and easily lets himself be carried into rhapsodies
about the "ideal," which, when all is said, if they
be accurately examined, will be found literally to
mean nothing more than that the figure has got
handsome calves to its legs, and a straight
nose. . . .

But even this vulgar pursuit of physical beauty
(vulgar in the profoundest sense, for there is no
vulgarity like the vulgarity of education) would
be less contemptible if it really succeeded in its
object; but, like all pursuits carried to inordinate
length, it defeats itself. Physical beauty *is* a
noble thing when it is seen in perfectness; but the
manner in which the moderns pursue their ideal
prevents their ever really seeing what they are
always seeking; for, requiring that all forms
should be regular and faultless, they permit, or
even compel, their painters and sculptors to work
chiefly by rule, altering their models to fit their
preconceived notions of what is right. When
such artists look at a face, they do not give it
the attention necessary to discern what beauty is
already in its peculiar features; but only to see
how best it may be altered into something for
which they have themselves laid down the laws.
Nature never unveils her beauty to such a gaze.
She keeps whatever she has done best, close sealed
until it is regarded with reverence. To the
painter who honours her she will open a revelation in the face of a street mendicant; but in the

work of the painter who alters her she will make Portia become ignoble, and Perdita graceless.

Nor is the effect less for evil on the mind of the general observer. The lover of ideal beauty, with all his conceptions narrowed by rule, never looks carefully enough upon the features which do not come under his law (or any others) to discern the inner beauty in them. The strange intricacies about the lines of the lips, and marvellous shadows and watch-fires of the eye, and wavering traceries of the eyelash, and infinite modulations of the brow, wherein high humanity is embodied, are all invisible to him. He finds himself driven back at last, with all his idealism, to the lionne of the ball-room, whom youth and passion can as easily distinguish as his utmost critical science; whereas, the observer who has accustomed himself to take human faces as God made them, will often find as much beauty on a village green as in the proudest room of state, and as much in the free seats of a church aisle, as in all the sacred paintings of the Vatican or the Pitti.—*M. P.*, III. IV. 5, § 8–11.

78. SYMBOLISM IN ART.—We hear it not unfrequently asserted that symbolism or personification should not be introduced in painting at all. Such assertions are in their grounds unintelligible, and in their substance absurd. Whatever is in words described as visible, may

with all logical fitness * be rendered so by
colours; and not only is this a legitimate branch
of ideal art, but I believe there is hardly any
other so widely useful and instructive; and I
heartily wish that every great allegory which
the poets ever invented were powerfully put on
canvas, and easily accessible by all men, and
that our artists were perpetually exciting themselves to invent more. And as far as authority
bears on the question, the simple fact is that
allegorical painting has been the delight of the
greatest men and of the wisest multitudes, from
the beginning of art, and will be till art expires.
Orcagna's Triumph of Death; Simon Memmi's
frescoes in the Spanish Chapel; Giotto's principal works at Assisi, and partly at the Arena;
Michael Angelo's two best statues, the Night
and Day; Albert Dürer's noble Melancholy, and
hundreds more of his best works; a full third,
I should think, of the works of Tintoret and
Veronese, and nearly as large a portion of those
of Raphael and Rubens, are entirely symbolical
or personifiant; and, except in the case of the
last-named painter, are always among the most
interesting works the painters executed. The
greater and more thoughtful the artists, the more
they delight in symbolism, and the more fearlessly
they employ it. Dead symbolism, second-hand

* Though, perhaps, only in a subordinate degree.

symbolism, pointless symbolism, are indeed objec-
tionable enough ; but so are most other things
that are dead, second-hand, and pointless. It
is also true that both symbolism and personification are somewhat more apt than most things
to have their edges taken off by too much
handling; and what with our modern Fames,
Justices, and various metaphorical ideals, largely
used for signs and other such purposes, there
is some excuse for our not well knowing what
the real power of personification is. But that
power is gigantic and inexhaustible, and ever
to be grasped with peculiar joy by the painter,
because it permits him to introduce picturesque
elements and flights of fancy into his work, which
otherwise would be utterly inadmissible ;—to
bring the wild beasts of the desert into the room
of state, fill the air with inhabitants as well as
the earth, and render the least (visibly) interesting incidents themes for the most thrilling drama.
Even Tintoret might sometimes have been hard put
to it, when he had to fill a large panel in the Ducal
Palace with the portrait of a nowise interesting
Doge, unless he had been able to lay a winged
lion beside him, ten feet long from the nose to the
tail, asleep upon the Turkey carpet ; and Rubens
could certainly have made his flatteries of Mary
of Medicis palatable to no one but herself, without
the help of rosy-cheeked goddesses of abundance,
and seven-headed hydras of rebellion.

For observe, not only does the introduction of these imaginary beings permit greater fantasticism of *incident*, but also infinite fantasticism of *treatment;* and, I believe, so far from the pursuit of the false ideal having in any wise exhausted the realms of fantastic imagination, those realms have hardly yet been entered, and that a universe of noble dream-land lies before us, yet to be conquered. For, hitherto, when fantastic creatures have been introduced, either the masters have been so realistic in temper that they made the spirits as substantial as their figures of flesh and blood,—as Rubens, and, for the most part, Tintoret; or else they have been weak and unpractised in realisation, and have painted transparent or cloudy spirits because they had no power of painting grand ones. But if a really great painter, thoroughly capable of giving substantial truth, and master of the elements of pictorial effect which have been developed by modern art, would solemnly, and yet fearlessly, cast his fancy free in the spiritual world, and faithfully follow out such masters of that world as Dante and Spenser, there seems no limit to the splendour of thought which painting might express.—*M. P.,* III. IV. 8, § 6, 7.

79. THE ARTIST AND THE MAN OF SCIENCE. —Science and art are commonly distinguished by the nature of their actions; the one as knowing,

the other as changing, producing, or creating. But there is a still more important distinction in the nature of the things they deal with. Science deals exclusively with things as they are in themselves; and art exclusively with things as they affect the human sense and human soul. Her work is to portray the appearances of things, and to deepen the natural impressions which they produce upon living creatures. The work of science is to substitute facts for appearances, and demonstrations for impressions. Both, observe, are equally concerned with truth; the one with truth of aspect, the other with truth of essence. Art does not represent things falsely, but truly as they appear to mankind. Science studies the relations of things to each other: but art studies only their relations to man: and it requires of everything which is submitted to it imperatively this, and only this,—what that thing is to the human eyes and human heart, what it has to say to men, and what it can become to them: a field of question just as much vaster than that of science, as the soul is larger than the material creation.

This, then, being the kind of truth with which art is exclusively concerned, how is such truth as this to be ascertained and accumulated? Evidently, and only, by perception and feeling. Never either by reasoning or report. Nothing must come between Nature and the artist's sight; nothing between God and the artist's soul. Neither calculation nor hearsay,—be it the most subtle of calculations, or the wisest of sayings,—may be allowed to come between the universe, and the witness which art bears to its visible nature. The whole value of that witness depends on its being *eye*-witness; the whole genuineness, acceptableness, and dominion of it depend on the personal assurance of the man who utters it. All its victory depends on the veracity of the one preceding word, "Vidi."

The whole function of the artist in the world is to be a seeing and feeling creature; to be an instrument of such tenderness and sensitiveness, that no shadow, no hue, no line, no instantaneous and evanescent expression of the visible things around him, nor any of the emotions which they are capable of conveying to the spirit which has been given him, shall either be left unrecorded, or fade from the book of record. It is not his business either to think, to judge, to argue, or to know. His place is neither in the closet, nor on the bench, nor at the bar, nor in the library. They are for other men, and other work. He may think, in a by-way; reason, now and then, when he has nothing better to do; know, such fragments of knowledge as he can gather without stooping, or reach without pains; but none of these things are to be his care. The work of his life is to be two-fold only; to see, to feel.

Nay, but, the reader perhaps pleads with me, one of the great uses of knowledge is to open the eyes; to make things perceivable which never would have been seen, unless first they had been known.

Not so. This could only be said or believed by those who do not know what the perceptive faculty of a great artist is, in comparison with that of other men. There is no great painter, no great workman in any art, but he sees more with the glance of a moment than he can learn by the labour of a thousand hours.

God has made every man fit for his work; He has given to the man whom He means for a student, the reflective, logical, sequential faculties; and to the man whom He means for an artist, the perceptive, sensitive, retentive faculties. And neither of these men, so far from being able to do the other's work, can even comprehend the way in which it is done. The student has no understanding of the vision, nor the painter of the process; but chiefly, the student has no idea of the colossal grasp of the true painter's vision and sensibility.

The labour of the whole Geological Society, for the last fifty years, has but now arrived at the ascertainment of those truths respecting mountain form which Turner saw and expressed with a few strokes of a camel's hair pencil fifty years ago, when he was a boy. The knowledge of all

the laws of the planetary system, and of all the
curves of the motion of projectiles, would never
enable the man of science to draw a waterfall or
a wave; and all the members of Surgeons' Hall
helping each other could not at this moment see,
or represent, the natural movement of a human
body in vigorous action, as a poor dyer's son did
two hundred years ago.*

But surely, it is still insisted, granting this
peculiar faculty to the painter, he will see more,
as he knows more, and the more knowledge he
obtains, therefore, the better. No; not even so.
It is indeed true that, here and there, a piece of
knowledge will enable the eye to detect a truth
which might otherwise have escaped it; as, for
instance, in watching a sunrise, the knowledge
of the true nature of the orb may lead the painter
to feel more profoundly, and express more fully,
the distance between the bars of cloud that cross
it, and the sphere of flame that lifts itself slowly
beyond them into the infinite heaven. But, for
one visible truth to which knowledge thus opens
the eyes, it seals them to a thousand: that is to
say, if the knowledge occur to the mind so as
to occupy its powers of contemplation at the
moment when the sight-work is to be done, the
mind retires inward, fixes itself upon the known
fact, and forgets the passing visible ones; and
a *moment* of such forgetfulness loses more to the

* Tintoret.

painter than a day's thought can gain. This is
no new or strange assertion. Every person
accustomed to careful reflection of any kind
knows that its natural operation is to close his
eyes to the external world. While he is thinking
deeply, he neither sees nor feels, even though
naturally he may possess strong powers of sight
and emotion. He who, having journeyed all day
beside the Leman Lake, asked of his companions,
at evening, where it was,* probably was not
wanting in sensibility; but he was generally
a thinker, not a perceiver. And this instance is
only an extreme one of the effect which, in all
cases, knowledge, becoming a subject of reflection,
produces upon the sensitive faculties. It must
be but poor and lifeless knowledge, if it has no
tendency to force itself forward, and become
ground for reflection, in despite of the succession
of external objects. It will not obey their succession. The first that comes gives it food
enough for its day's work; it is its habit, its
duty, to cast the rest aside, and fasten upon that.
The first thing that a thinking and knowing man
sees in the course of the day, he will not easily
quit. It is not his way to quit anything without
getting to the bottom of it, if possible. But the
artist is bound to receive all things on the broad,
white, lucid field of his soul, not to grasp at one.
For instance, as the knowing and thinking man

* St. Bernard.

watches the sunrise, he sees something in the colour of a ray, or the change of a cloud, that is new to him; and this he follows out forthwith into a labyrinth of optical and pneumatical laws, perceiving no more clouds nor rays all the morning. But the painter must catch all the rays, all the colours that come, and see them all truly, all in their real relations and succession; therefore, everything that occupies room in his mind he must cast aside for the time as completely as may be. The thoughtful man is gone far away to seek; but the perceiving man must sit still, and open his heart to receive. The thoughtful man is knitting and sharpening himself into a two-edged sword, wherewith to pierce. The perceiving man is stretching himself into a four-cornered sheet, wherewith to catch. And all the breadth to which he can expand himself, and all the white emptiness into which he can blanch himself, will not be enough to receive what God has to give him.

What then, it will be indignantly asked, is an utterly ignorant and unthinking man likely to make the best artist? No, not so neither. Knowledge is good for him so long as he can keep it utterly, servilely, subordinate to his own divine work, and trample it under his feet, and out of his way, the moment it is likely to entangle him.

And in this respect, observe, there is an enormous difference between knowledge and education. An artist need not be a *learned* man; in all probability it will be a disadvantage to him to become so; but he ought, if possible, always to be an *educated* man; that is, one who has understanding of his own uses and duties in the world, and therefore of the general nature of the things done and existing in the world; and who has so trained himself, or been trained, as to turn to the best and most courteous account whatever faculties or knowledge he has. The mind of an educated man is greater than the knowledge it possesses; it is like the vault of heaven, encompassing the earth which lives and flourishes beneath it : but the mind of an un-educated and learned man is like a caoutchouc band, with an everlasting spirit of contraction in it, fastening together papers which it cannot open, and keeps others from opening.

Half our artists are ruined for want of educa-tion, and by the possession of knowledge; the best that I have known have been educated and illiterate. The ideal of an artist, however, is not that he should be illiterate, but well read in the best books, and thoroughly high bred, both in heart and in bearing. In a word, he should be fit for the best society, *and should keep out of it*. —*S. V.*, III. II., § 8–13.

80. LAST WORDS TO THE LANDSCAPE STU-DENT.—The noisy life of modern days is wholly

incompatible with any true perception of natural
beauty. If you go down into Cumberland by
the railroad, live in some frequented hotel, and
explore the hills with merry companions, however much you may enjoy your tour or their
conversation, depend upon it you will never
choose so much as one pictorial subject rightly;
you will not see into the depth of any. But
take knapsack and stick, walk towards the hills
by short day's journeys,—ten or twelve miles a
day—taking a week from some starting-place
sixty or seventy miles away: sleep at the pretty
little wayside inns, or the rough village ones;
then take the hills as they tempt you, following
glen or shore as your eye glances or your heart
guides, wholly scornful of local fame or fashion,
and of everything which it is the ordinary
traveller's duty to see, or pride to do. Never
force yourself to admire anything when you are
not in the humour; but never force yourself
away from what you feel to be lovely, in search
of anything better; and gradually the deeper
scenes of the natural world will unfold themselves to you in still increasing fulness of passionate power; and your difficulty will be no
more to seek or to compose subjects, but only
to choose one from among the multitude of
melodious thoughts with which you will be
haunted, thoughts which will of course be noble
or original in proportion to your own depth of

character and general power of mind; for it is not so much by the consideration you give to any single drawing, as by the previous discipline of your powers of thought, that the character of your composition will be determined. Simplicity of life will make you sensitive to the refinement and modesty of scenery, just as inordinate excitement and pomp of daily life will make you enjoy coarse colours and affected forms. Habits of patient comparison and accurate judgment will make your art precious, as they will make your actions wise; and every increase of noble enthusiasm in your living spirit will be measured by the reflection of its light upon the works of your hands.—*E. D.*, III., § 246.

81. THE USE OF AMATEUR STUDY.—Keep clear of the notion of following Art as dilettantism: it ought to delight you, as your reading delights you—but you never think of your reading as dilettantism. It ought to delight you as your studies of physical science delight you—but you don't call physical science dilettantism. If you are determined only to think of Art as a play or a pleasure, give it up at once: you will do no good to yourselves, and you will degrade the pursuit in the sight of others. Better, infinitely better, that you should never enter a picture gallery, than that you should enter only to saunter and to smile: better, infinitely better,

I.

that you should never handle a pencil at all, than handle it only for the sake of complacency in your small dexterity: better, infinitely better, that you should be wholly uninterested in pictures, and uninformed respecting them, than that you should just know enough to detect blemishes in great works,—to give a colour of reasonableness to presumption, and an appearance of acuteness to misunderstanding.

Men employed in any kind of manual labour, by which they must live, are not likely to take up the notion that they can learn any other art for amusement only; but amateurs are: and it is of the highest importance, nay, it is just the one thing of all importance, to show them what drawing really means; and not so much to teach them to produce a good work themselves, as to know it when they see it done by others. Good work, in the stern sense of the word, as I before said, no mere amateur can do; and good work, in any sense, that is to say, profitable work for himself or for any one else, he can only do by being made in the beginning to see what is possible for him, and what not;—what is accessible, and what not; and by having the majesty and sternness of the everlasting laws of fact set before him in their infinitude. It is no matter for appalling him: the man is great already who is made well capable of being appalled; nor do we ever wisely hope, nor truly understand, till we

are humiliated by our hope, and awestruck by our understanding. Nay, I will go farther than this, and say boldly, that what you have mainly to teach the young men here is, not so much what they can do, as what they cannot;—to make them see how much there is in nature which cannot be imitated, and how much in man which cannot be emulated. He only can be truly said to be educated in Art to whom all his work is only a feeble sign of glories which he cannot convey, and a feeble means of measuring, with ever-enlarging admiration, the great and untraversable gulf which God has set between the great and the common intelligences of mankind : and all the triumphs of Art which man can commonly achieve are only truly crowned by pure delight in natural scenes themselves, and by the sacred and self-forgetful veneration which can be nobly abashed, and tremblingly exalted, in the presence of a human spirit greater than his own.
—*Inaugural Address, Cambridge School of Art.*

82. THE "PUBLIC." Whom does it include ? People continually forget that there is a *separate* public for every picture, and for every book. Appealed to with reference to any particular work, the public is that class of persons who possess the knowledge which it presupposes, and the faculties to which it is addressed. With reference to a new edition of Newton's Principia,

the "public" means little more than the Royal Society. With reference to one of Wordsworth's poems, it means all who have hearts. With reference to one of Moore's, all who have passions. With reference to the works of Hogarth, it means those who have worldly knowledge,—to the works of Giotto, those who have religious faith. Each work must be tested exclusively by the fiat of the *particular* public to whom it is addressed. We will listen to no comments on Newton from people who have no mathematical knowledge; to none on Wordsworth from those who have no hearts; to none on Giotto from those who have no religion. Therefore, when we have to form a judgment of any new work, the question, "What do the public say to it?" is indeed of vital importance; but we must always inquire, first, who are *its* public?—*Letter to " The Artist and Amateur's Magazine," Jan.* 1844 (*A. C.,* I. pp. 21, 22).

83. SOUND CRITICISM of art is impossible to young men; for it consists principally, and in a far more exclusive sense than has yet been felt, in the recognition of the facts represented by the art. A great artist represents many and abstruse facts; it is necessary, in order to judge of his works, that all those facts should be experimentally (not by hearsay) known to the observer; whose recognition of them constitutes

his approving judgment. A young man *cannot* know them.

Criticism of art by young men must, therefore, consist either in the more or less apt retailing and application of received opinions, or in a more or less immediate and dexterous use of the knowledge they already possess, so as to be able to assert of given works of art that they are true up to a certain point: the probability being then that they are true farther than the young man sees.

The first kind of criticism is, in general useless, if not harmful; the second is that which the youths will employ who are capable of becoming critics in after years.

Secondly. All criticism of art, at whatever period of life, must be partial; warped more or less by the feelings of the person endeavouring to judge. Certain merits of art (as energy, for instance) are pleasant only to certain temperaments; and certain tendencies of art (as, for instance, to religious sentiment) can only be sympathised with by one order of minds. . . .

Thirdly. The history of art, or the study, in your accurate words, "*about* the subject," is in no wise directly connected with the studies which promote or detect art-capacity or art-judgment. It is quite possible to acquire the most extensive and useful knowledge of the forms of art existing in different ages, and among different nations, without thereby acquiring any power whatsoever of determining respecting any of them (much less respecting a modern work of art) whether it is good or bad.—*Letter to the Rev. F. Temple (Bishop of London)*, 1857 (*A. C.*, I. pp. 40, 41).

84. CHEAP ART AND LITERATURE.—Art ought not to be made cheap beyond a certain point; for the amount of pleasure that you can receive from any great work depends wholly on the quantity of attention and energy of mind you can bring to bear upon it. Now, that attention and energy depend much more on the freshness of the thing than you would at all suppose, unless you very carefully studied the movements of your own minds. If you see things of the same kind and of equal value very frequently, your reverence for them is infallibly diminished, your powers of attention get gradually wearied, and your interest and enthusiasm worn out; and you cannot in that state bring to any given work the energy necessary to enjoy it. . . . Hence, it is wisely appointed for us that few of the things we desire can be had without considerable labour, and at considerable intervals of time. We cannot generally get our dinner without working for it, and that gives us appetite for it; we cannot get our holiday without waiting for it, and that gives us zest for it; and we ought not to get our picture without paying for it, and that gives us a mind to look at it.

Nay, I will even go so far as to say we ought not to get books too cheaply. No book, I believe, is ever worth half so much to its reader as one that has been coveted for a year at a bookstall, and bought out of saved halfpence, and perhaps a day or two's fasting. That's the way to get at the cream of a book.—*Political Economy of Art*, II. (*J. E.*, § 63–65).

85. THE APPEAL OF GREAT ART.—All great art is the work of the whole living creature, body and soul, and chiefly of the soul. But it is not only *the work* of the whole creature, it likewise *addresses* the whole creature. That in which the perfect being speaks must also have the perfect being to listen. I am not to spend my utmost spirit, and give all my strength and life to my work, while you, spectator or hearer, will give me only the attention of half your soul. You must be all mine, as I am all yours; it is the only condition on which we can meet each other. All your faculties, all that is in you of greatest and best, must be awake in you, or I have no reward. The painter is not to cast the entire treasure of his human nature into his labour merely to please a part of the beholder: not merely to delight his senses, not merely to amuse his fancy, not merely to beguile him into emotion, not merely to lead him into thought; but to do *all* this. Senses, fancy, feeling, reason, the whole

of the beholding spirit, must be stilled in attention or stirred with delight; else the labouring spirit has not done its work well. For observe, it is not merely its *right* to be thus met, face to face, heart to heart; but it is its *duty* to evoke this answering of the other soul: its trumpet call must be so clear, that though the challenge may by dulness or indolence be unanswered, there shall be no error as to the meaning of the appeal; there must be a summons in the work, which it shall be our own fault if we do not obey. We require this of it, we beseech this of it. Most men do not know what is in them till they receive this summons from their fellows: their hearts die within them, sleep settles upon them, the lethargy of the world's miasmata; there is nothing for which they are so thankful as that cry, " Awake, thou that sleepest."—*S. V.*, III. IV., § 21.

IV.

PAINTERS AND PICTURES.

86. THE PROGRESS OF REALISM.—As soon as art obtained the power of realisation, it obtained also that of *assertion*. As fast as the painter advanced in skill he gained also in credibility, and that which he perfectly represented was perfectly believed, or could be disbelieved only by an actual effort of the beholder to escape from the fascinating deception. What had been faintly declared, might be painlessly denied; but it was difficult to discredit things forcibly alleged; and representations, which had been innocent in discrepancy, became guilty in consistency. . . .

The continual presentment to the mind of this beautiful and fully realised imagery more and more chilled its power of apprehending the real truth; and when pictures of this description met the eye in every corner of every chapel, it was physically impossible to dwell distinctly upon facts the direct reverse of those represented. The word "Virgin" or "Madonna," instead of calling up the vision of a simple Jewish girl, bearing the calamities of poverty, and the dishonours of inferior station, summoned instantly the idea of a graceful princess, crowned with gems, and surrounded by obsequious ministry of kings and saints. The fallacy which was presented to the imagination was indeed discredited, but also the fact which was *not* presented to the imagination was forgotten; all true grounds of faith were gradually undermined, and the beholder was either enticed into mere luxury of fanciful enjoyment, believing nothing; or left, in his confusion of mind, the prey of vain tales and traditions; while in his best feelings he was unconsciously subject to the power of the fallacious picture, and, with no sense of the real cause of his error, bowed himself, in prayer or adoration, to the lovely lady on her golden throne, when he would never have dreamed of doing so to the Jewish girl in her outcast poverty, or, in her simple household, to the carpenter's wife.

But a shadow of increasing darkness fell upon the human mind as art proceeded to still more perfect realisation. These fantasies of the earlier painters, though they darkened faith, never hardened *feeling;* on the contrary, the frankness of their unlikelihood proceeded mainly from the endeavour on the part of the painter to express, not the actual fact, but the enthusiastic state of his own feelings about the fact; he covers the Virgin's dress with gold, not with any idea of representing the Virgin as she ever was, or ever will be seen, but with a burning desire to show what his love and reverence would think fittest for her. He erects for the stable a Lombardic portico, not because he supposes the Lombardi to have built stables in Palestine in the days of Tiberius, but to show that the manger in which Christ was laid is, in his eyes, nobler than the greatest architecture in the world. He fills his landscape with church spires and silver streams, not because he supposes that either were in sight at Bethlehem, but to remind the beholder of the peaceful course and succeeding power of Christianity. And, regarded with due sympathy and clear understanding of these thoughts of the artist, such pictures remain most impressive and touching, even to this day. I shall refer to them in future, in general terms, as the pictures of the "Angelican Ideal"—Angelico being the central master of the school.

It was far otherwise in the next step of the Realistic progress. The greater his powers became, the more the mind of the painter was absorbed in their attainment, and complacent in their display. The early arts of laying on bright colours smoothly, of burnishing golden ornaments, or tracing, leaf by leaf, the outlines of flowers, were not so difficult as that they should materially occupy the thoughts of the artist, or furnish foundation for his conceit; he learned

these rudiments of his work without pain, and
employed them without pride, his spirit being
left free to express, so far as it was capable of
them, the reaches of higher thought. But when
accurate shade, and subtle colour, and perfect
anatomy, and complicated perspective, became
necessary to the work, the artist's whole energy
was employed in learning the laws of these, and
his whole pleasure consisted in exhibiting them.
His life was devoted, not to the objects of art,
but to the cunning of it; and the sciences of
composition and light and shade were pursued
as if there were abstract good in them ;—as if,
like astronomy or mathematics, they were ends
in themselves, irrespective of anything to be
effected by them. And without perception, on
the part of any one, of the abyss to which all
were hastening, a fatal change of aim took place
throughout the whole world of art. In early
times *art was employed for the display of religious facts ;* now, *religious facts were employed
for the display of art.* The transition, though
imperceptible, was consummate ; it involved the
entire destiny of painting. It was passing from
the paths of life to the paths of death.

And this change was all the more fatal, because at first veiled by an appearance of greater
dignity and sincerity than were possessed by
the older art. One of the earliest results of the
new knowledge was the putting away the greater

part of the *unlikelihoods* and fineries of the
ancient pictures, and an apparently closer following of nature and probability. All the fantasy
which I have just been blaming as disturbant
of the simplicity of faith, was first subdued,—
then despised and cast aside. The appearances
of nature were more closely followed in everything ; and the crowned Queen-Virgin of Perugino
sank into a simple Italian mother in Raphael's
Madonna of the Chair.

Was not this, then, a healthy change ? No.
It *would* have been healthy if it had been effected
with a pure motive, and the new truths would
have been precious if they had been sought for
truth's sake. But they were not sought for truth's
sake, but for pride's ; and truth which is sought
for display may be just as harmful as truth which
is spoken in malice. The glittering childishness
of the old art was rejected, not because it was
false, but because it was easy ; and, still more,
because the painter had no longer any religious
passion to express. He could think of the
Madonna now very calmly, with no desire to
pour out the treasures of earth at her feet, or
crown her brows with the golden shafts of heaven.
He could think of her as an available subject for
the display of transparent shadows, skilful tints,
and scientific fore-shortenings,—as a fair woman,
forming, if well painted, a pleasant piece of
furniture for the corner of a boudoir, and best

imagined by combination of the beauties of the prettiest contadinas.   He could think of her, in her last maternal agony, with academical discrimination ; sketch in first her skeleton, invest her, in serene science, with the muscles of misery and the fibres of sorrow ; then cast the grace of antique drapery over the nakedness of her desolation, and fulfil, with studious lustre of tears and delicately painted pallor, the perfect type of the " Mater Dolorosa."—*M. P.*, III. IV. 4, § 8–13.

87. WOUVERMANS AND ANGELICO.—The technical disposition of Wouvermans, in his search after delicate form and minute grace, much resembles that of Angelico.   But the thoughts of Wouvermans are wholly of this world.   For him there is no heroism, awe, or mercy, hope, or faith.   Eating and drinking, and slaying; rage and lust; the pleasures and distresses of the debased body—from these, his thoughts, if so we may call them, never for an instant rise or range.

The soul of Angelico is in all ways the precise reverse of this ; habitually as incognisant of any earthly pleasure as Wouvermans of any heavenly one.   Both are exclusive with absolute exclusiveness ;—neither desiring nor conceiving anything beyond their respective spheres.   Wouvermans lives under gray clouds, his lights come out as spots.   Angelico lives in an unclouded light : his shadows themselves are colour ; his lights are not the spots, but his darks.   Wouvermans lives in perpetual tumult—tramp of horse—clash of cup—ring of pistol-shot.   Angelico in perpetual peace.   Not seclusion from the world.   No shutting out of the world is needful for him.   There is nothing to shut out.   Envy, lust, contention, discourtesy, are to him as though they were not ; and the cloister walk of Fiesole no penitential solitude, barred from the stir and joy of life, but a possessed land of tender blessing, guarded from the entrance of all but holiest sorrow.   The little cell was as one of the houses of heaven prepared for him by his Master.   "What need had it to be elsewhere ?   Was not the Val d'Arno, with its olive woods in white blossom, paradise enough for a poor monk ? or could Christ be indeed in heaven more than here ? Was He not always with him ?   Could he breathe or see, but that Christ breathed beside him, and looked into his eyes ?   Under every cypress avenue the angels walked ; he had seen their white robes, whiter than the dawn, at his bedside, as he awoke in early summer.   They had sung with him, one on each side, when his voice failed for joy at sweet vesper and matin time ; his eyes were blinded by their wings in the sunset, when it sank behind the hills of Luni."

There may be weakness in this, but there is

no baseness; and while I rejoice in all recovery from monasticism which leads to practical and healthy action in the world, I must, in closing this work, severely guard my pupils from the thought that sacred rest may be honourably exchanged for selfish and mindless activity.—*M. P.*, V. IX. 8, § 12, 13.

88. THE VENETIANS.—All the nobleness, as well as the faults, of the Greek art were dependent on its making the most of this present life. It might do so in the Anacreontic temper —*Τί Πλειάδεσσι, κἀμοί;* "What have I to do with the Pleiads?" or in the defiant or the trustful endurance of fate;—but its dominion was in this world.

Florentine art was essentially Christian, ascetic, expectant of a better world, and antagonistic, therefore, to the Greek temper. So that the Greek element, once forced upon it, destroyed it. There was absolute incompatibility between them. Florentine art, also, could not produce landscape. It despised the rock, the tree, the vital air itself, aspiring to breathe empyreal air.

Venetian art began with the same aim and under the same restrictions. Both are healthy in the youth of art. Heavenly aim and severe law for boyhood; earthly work and fair freedom for manhood.

The Venetians began, I repeat, with asceticism;

always, however, delighting in more massive and deep colour than other religious painters. They are especially fond of saints who have been cardinals, because of their red hats, and they sun-burn all their hermits into splendid russet brown.

They differed from the Pisans in having no Maremma between them and the sea; from the Romans, in continually quarrelling with the Pope; and from the Florentines in having no gardens.

They had another kind of garden, deep fur-rowed, with blossom in white wreaths — fruit-less. Perpetual May therein, and singing of wild, nestless birds. And they had no Maremma to separate them from this garden of theirs. The destiny of Pisa was changed, in all probability, by the ten miles of marsh-land and poisonous air between it and the beach. The Genoese energy was feverish; too much heat reflected from their torrid Apennine. But the Venetian had his free horizon, his salt breeze, and sandy Lido shore; sloped far and flat,—ridged some-times under the Tramontane winds with half a mile's breadth of rollers ;—sea and sand shrivelled up together in one yellow careering field of fall and roar.

They were, also, we said, always quarrelling with the Pope. Their religious liberty came, like their bodily health, from that wave training; for it is one notable effect of a life passed on shipboard to destroy weak beliefs in appointed

I   P

forms of religion. A sailor may be grossly superstitious, but his superstitions will be connected with amulets and omens, not cast in systems. He must accustom himself, if he prays at all, to pray anywhere and anyhow. Candlesticks and incense not being portable into the maintop, he perceives those decorations to be, on the whole, inessential to a maintop mass. Sails must be set and cables bent, be it never so strict a saint's day, and it is found that no harm comes of it. Absolution on a lee-shore must be had of the breakers, it appears, if at all, and they give it plenary and brief, without listening to confession.

Whereupon our religious opinions become vague, but our religious confidences strong; and the end of it all is that we perceive the Pope to be on the other side of the Apennines, and able, indeed, to sell indulgences, but not winds, for any money. Whereas, God and the sea are with us, and we must even trust them both, and take what they shall send.

Then, farther. This ocean-work is wholly adverse to any morbid conditions of sentiment. Reverie, above all things, is forbidden by Scylla and Charybdis. By the dogs and the depths, no dreaming! The first thing required of us is presence of mind. Neither love, nor poetry, nor piety, must ever so take up our thoughts as to make us slow or unready. In sweet Val d'Arno it is permissible enough to dream among the orange-blossoms, and forget the day in twilight of ilex. But along the avenues of the Adrian waves there can be no careless walking. Vigilance, night and day, required of us, besides learning of many practical lessons in severe and humble dexterities. It is enough for the Florentine to know how to use his sword and to ride. We Venetians, also, must be able to use our swords, and on ground which is none of the steadiest; but, besides, we must be able to do nearly everything that hands can turn to— rudders, and yards, and cables, all needing workmanly handling and workmanly knowledge, from captain as well as from men. To drive a nail, lash a spar, reef a sail—rude work this for noble hands; but to be done sometimes, and done well, on pain of death. All which not only takes mean pride out of us, and puts nobler pride of power in its stead ; but it tends partly to soothe, partly to chasten, partly to employ and direct, the hot Italian temper, and make us every way greater, calmer, and happier.

Moreover, it tends to induce in us great respect for the whole human body ; for its limbs, as much as for its tongue or its wit. Policy and eloquence are well ; and, indeed, we Venetians can be politic enough, and can speak melodiously when we choose ; but to put the helm up at the right moment is the beginning of all cunning—and

for that we need arm and eye;—not tongue.
And with this respect for the body as such, comes
also the sailor's preference of massive beauty in
bodily form.   The landsmen, among their roses
and orange-blossoms, and chequered shadows
of twisted vine, may well please themselves with
pale faces, and finely-drawn eyebrows, and fantastic braiding of hair.   But from the sweeping
glory of the sea we learn to love another kind
of beauty; broad-breasted; level-browed, like
the horizon;—thighed and shouldered like the
billows;—footed like their stealing foam;—bathed
in cloud of golden hair, like their sunsets.—*M. P.*,
V. IX. iii., § 1–5.

89. VENETIAN ART.—The Venetian possessed,
and cared for, neither fields nor pastures.   Being
delivered, to his loss, from all the wholesome
labours of tillage, he was also shut out from the
sweet wonders and charities of the earth, and
from the pleasant natural history of the year.
Birds and beasts, and times and seasons, all
unknown to him.   No swallow chattered at his
window, nor, nested under his golden roofs,
claimed the sacredness of his mercy ; no Pytha-
gorean fowl taught him the blessings of the poor,
nor did the grave spirit of poverty rise at his side
to set forth the delicate grace and honour of
lowly life.   No humble thoughts of grasshopper
sire had he, like the Athenian ; no gratitude for

gifts of olive ; no childish care for figs, any more
than thistles. The rich Venetian feast had no
need of the figtree spoon. Dramas about birds,
and wasps and frogs, would have passed un-
heeded by his proud fancy ; carol or murmur of
them had fallen unrecognised on ears accustomed
only to grave syllables of war-tried men, and
wash of songless wave.

No simple joy was possible to him. Only
stateliness and power ; high intercourse with
kingly and beautiful humanity, proud thoughts,
or splendid pleasures ; throned sensualities, and
ennobled appetites. But of innocent, childish,
helpful, holy pleasures, he had none. As in the
classical landscape, nearly all rural labour is
banished from the Titianesque : there is one bold
etching of a landscape, with grand ploughing in
the foreground, but this is only a caprice ; the
customary Venetian background is without sign
of laborious rural life. We find, indeed, often
a shepherd with his flock, sometimes a woman
spinning, but no division of fields, no growing
crops, nor nestling villages. In the numerous
drawings and woodcuts variously connected with
or representative of Venetian work, a watermill
is a frequent object, a river constant, generally
the sea. But the prevailing idea in all the great
pictures I have seen is that of mountainous land
with wild but graceful forest, and rolling or
horizontal clouds. The mountains are dark blue ;

the clouds glowing or soft gray, always massive;
the light, deep, clear, melancholy; the foliage,
neither intricate nor graceful, but compact and
sweeping (with undulated trunks), dividing much
into horizontal flakes, like the clouds; the ground
rocky and broken somewhat monotonously, but
richly green with wild herbage; here and there
a flower, by preference white or blue, rarely
yellow, still more rarely red.

It was stated that this heroic landscape of
theirs was peopled by spiritual beings of the
highest order. And in this rested the dominion
of the Venetians over all later schools. They
were the *last believing* school of Italy. Although,
as I said above, always quarrelling with the Pope,
there is all the more evidence of an earnest
faith in their religion. People who trusted the
Madonna less, flattered the Pope more. But
down to Tintoret's time, the Roman Catholic
religion was still real and sincere at Venice; and
though faith in it was compatible with much
which to us appears criminal or absurd, the
religion itself was entirely sincere.

Perhaps when you see one of Titian's splendidly
passionate subjects, or find Veronese making the
marriage in Cana one blaze of worldly pomp, you
imagine that Titian must have been a sensualist,
and Veronese an unbeliever.

Put the idea from you at once, and be assured
of this for ever; it will guide you through many

a labyrinth of life, as well as of painting,—that
of an evil tree, men never gather good fruit—
good of any sort or kind; even good sensualism.
—*M. P.*, V. IX. 3, § 10–13.

90. TITIAN.—No painter's name is oftener
in the mouth of the ordinary connoisseur, and
no painter was ever less understood.   His power
of colour is indeed perfect, but so is Bonifazio's.
Titian's *supremacy* above all the other Venetians,
except Tintoret and Veronese, consists in the
firm truth of his portraiture, and more or less
masterly understanding of the nature of stones,
trees, men, or whatever else he took in hand to
paint; so that, without some correlative understanding in the spectator, Titian's work, in its
highest qualities, must be utterly dead and un-
appealing to him.—*M. P.*, IV. V. 18, § 9.

There is only one way of *seeing* things rightly,
and that is, seeing the whole of them, without
any choice, or more intense perception of one
point than another, owing to our special idiosyn-
crasies.   Thus, when Titian or Tintoret look at
a human being, they see at a glance the whole
of its nature, outside and in; all that it has of
form, of colour, of passion, or of thought; saintli-
ness, and loveliness; fleshly body, and spiritual
power; grace, or strength, or softness, or whatsoever other quality, those men will see to the

full, and so paint, that, when narrower people
come to look at what they have done, every one
may, if he chooses, find his own special pleasure
in the work.   The sensualist will find sensuality
in Titian ; the thinker will find thought; the saint,
sanctity ;   the   colourist,   colour ;   the anatomist,
form ; and yet the picture will never be a popular
one in the full sense, for none of these narrower
people will find their special taste so alone consulted, as that the qualities which would ensure
their gratification shall be sifted or separated
from others ; they are checked by the presence
of the other qualities which ensure the gratification   of   other   men.   Thus,   Titian   is   not
soft enough for the sensualist,—Correggio suits
him better ; Titian is not defined enough for the
formalist,—Leonardo suits him better ; Titian is
not pure   enough for   the   religionist,—Raphael
suits him better ; Titian is not polite enough for
the man of the world,—Vandyke suits him better;
Titian is not forcible enough for the lover of the
picturesque,—Rembrandt suits him better.   So
Correggio is popular with a certain set, and
Vandyke with a certain set, and Rembrandt with
a certain set.   All are great men, but of inferior
stamp, and therefore Vandyke is popular, and
Rembrandt is popular, but nobody cares much
at heart about Titian ; only there is a strange
undercurrent of everlasting murmur about his
name, which means the deep consent of all great

men that he is greater than they—the consent of those who, having sat long enough at his feet, have found in that restrained harmony of his strength that there are indeed depths of each balanced power more wonderful than all those separate manifestations in inferior painters; that there is a softness more exquisite than Correggio's, a purity loftier than Leonardo's, a force mightier than Rembrandt's, a sanctity more solemn even than Raphael's.—*T. P.*, II., § 57.

91. VERONESE'S FAMILY, PAINTED BY HIM-SELF.—He wishes to represent them as happy and honoured. The best happiness and highest honour he can imagine for them is that they should be presented to the Madonna, to whom, therefore, they are being brought by the three virtues—Faith, Hope, and Charity.

The Virgin stands in a recess behind two marble shafts, such as may be seen in any house belonging to an old family in Venice. She places the boy Christ on the edge of a balustrade before her. At her side are St. John the Baptist, and St. Jerome. This group occupies the left side of the picture. The pillars, seen sideways, divide it from the group formed by the Virtues, with the wife and children of Veronese. He himself stands a little behind, his hands clasped in prayer.

His wife kneels full in front, a strong Venetian

woman, well advanced in years. She has brought up her children in fear of God, and is not afraid to meet the Virgin's eyes. She gazes steadfastly on them; her proud head and gentle, self-possessed face are relieved in one broad mass of shadow against a space of light, formed by the white robes of Faith, who stands beside her,—guardian, and companion. Perhaps a somewhat disappointing Faith at the first sight, for her face is not in any special way exalted or refined. Veronese knew that Faith had to companion simple and slow-hearted people, perhaps oftener than able or refined people—does not therefore insist on her being severely intellectual, or looking as if she were always in the best company. So she is only distinguished by her pure white (not bright white) dress, her delicate hand, her golden hair drifted in light ripples across her breast, from which the white robes fall nearly in the shape of a shield—the shield of Faith. A little behind her stands Hope; she also, at first, not to most people a recognisable Hope. We usually paint Hope as young, and joyous. Veronese knows better. That young hope is vain hope—passing away in rain of tears; but the Hope of Veronese is aged, assured, remaining when all else has been taken away. "For tribulation worketh patience, and patience experience, and experience hope;" and *that* hope maketh not ashamed.

She has a black veil on her head.

Then again, in the front, is Charity, red-robed; stout in the arms,—a servant of all work, she; but small-headed, not being specially given to thinking; soft-eyed, her hair braided brightly; her lips rich red, sweet-blossoming. She has got some work to do even now, for a nephew of Veronese's is doubtful about coming forward, and looks very humbly and penitently towards the Virgin — his life perhaps not having been quite so exemplary as might at present be wished. Faith reaches her small white hand lightly back to him, lays the tips of her fingers on his; but Charity takes firm hold of him by the wrist from behind, and will push him on presently, if he still hangs back.

In front of the mother kneel her two eldest children, a girl of about sixteen, and a boy a year or two younger. They are both rapt in adoration—the boy's being the deepest. Nearer us, at their left side, is a younger boy, about nine years old—a black-eyed fellow, full of life —and evidently his father's darling (for Veronese has put him full in light in the front; and given him a beautiful white silken jacket, barred with black, that nobody may ever miss seeing him to the end of time). He is a little shy about being presented to the Madonna, and for the present has got behind the pillar, blushing, but opening his black eyes wide; he is just

summoning courage to peep round, and see if
she looks kind. A still younger child, about six
years old, is really frightened, and has run back
to his mother, catching hold of her dress at the
waist. She throws her right arm round him and
over him, with exquisite instinctive action, not
moving her eyes from the Madonna's face. Last
of all, the youngest child, perhaps about three
years old, is neither frightened nor interested,
but finds the ceremony tedious, and is trying to
coax the dog to play with him; but the dog,
which is one of the little curly, short-nosed,
fringy-pawed things, which all Venetian ladies
petted, will not now be coaxed. For the dog
is the last link in the chain of lowering feeling,
and takes his doggish views of the matter. He
cannot understand, first, how the Madonna got
into the house; nor, secondly, why she is allowed
to stay, disturbing the family, and taking all their
attention from his dogship. And he is walking
away, much offended. . . .

Throughout the rest of Italy, piety had become
abstract, and opposed theoretically to worldly
life; hence the Florentine and Umbrian painters
generally separated their saints from living men.
They delighted in imagining scenes of spiritual
perfectness;—Paradises, and companies of the
redeemed at the judgment;—glorified meetings
of martyrs;—madonnas surrounded by circles of
angels. If, which was rare, definite portraitures

of living men were introduced, these real characters formed a kind of chorus or attendant company, taking no part in the action. At Venice
all this was reversed, and so boldly as at first to
shock, with its seeming irreverence, a spectator
accustomed to the formalities and abstractions of
the so-called sacred schools. The madonnas are
no more seated apart on their thrones, the saints
no more breathe celestial air. They are on our
own plain ground—nay, here in our houses with
us. All kind of worldly business going on in
their presence, fearlessly; our own friends and
respected acquaintances, with all their mortal
faults, and in their mortal flesh, looking at them
face to face unalarmed: nay, our dearest children
playing with their pet dogs at Christ's very feet.

I once myself thought this irreverent. How
foolishly! As if children whom He loved *could*
play anywhere else.—*M. P.*, V. IX. 3, § 18–21.

92. THE ANNUNCIATION, BY TINTORET.—
No subject has been more frequently or exquisitely treated by the religious painters than
that of the Annunciation; though, as usual, the
most perfect type of its pure ideal has been given
by Angelico, and by him with the most radiant
consummation (so far as I know) in a small reli-
quary in the sacristy of St^a. Maria Novella. The
background there, however, is altogether decorative; but, in the fresco of the corridor of St.

Mark's, the concomitant circumstances are of exceeding loveliness. The Virgin sits in an open loggia, resembling that of the Florentine Church of L'Annunziata. Before her is a meadow of rich herbage, covered with daisies. Behind her is seen, through the door at the end of the loggia, a chamber with a single grated window, through which a starlike beam of light falls into the silence. All is exquisite in feeling, but not inventive nor imaginative. Severe would be the shock and painful the contrast, if we could pass in an instant from that pure vision to the wild thought of Tintoret. For not in meek reception of the adoring messenger, but startled by the rush of his horizontal and rattling wings, the Virgin sits, not in the quiet loggia, not by the green pasture of the restored soul, but houseless, under the shelter of a palace vestibule ruined and abandoned, with the noise of the axe and the hammer in her ears, and the tumult of a city round about her desolation. The spectator turns away at first, revolted, from the central object of the picture forced painfully and coarsely forward, a mass of shattered brickwork, with the plaster mildewed away from it and the mortar mouldering from its seams; and if he look again, either at this or at the carpenter's tools beneath it, will perhaps see, in the one and the other, nothing more than such a study of scene as Tintoret could but too easily obtain

among the ruins of his own Venice, chosen to
give a coarse explanation of the calling and the
condition of the husband of Mary. But there
is more meant than this. When he looks at
the composition of the picture, he will find the
whole symmetry of it depending on a narrow
line of light, the edge of a carpenter's square,
which connects these unused tools with an object
at the top of the brickwork, a white stone, four
square, the corner-stone of the old edifice, the
base of its supporting column. This, I think,
sufficiently explains the typical character of the
whole. The ruined house is the Jewish dispen-
sation ; that obscurely arising in the dawning of
the sky is the Christian ; but the corner-stone of
the old building remains, though the builders'
tools lie idle beside it, and the stone which the
builders refused is become the Headstone of the
Corner.—*M. P.*, II. III. ii., 3, § 17.

93. THE MASSACRE OF THE INNOCENTS, BY
TINTORET.—All the ordinary representations of
this subject are, I think, false and cold : the artist
has not heard the shrieks, nor mingled with the
fugitives ; he has sat down in his study to con-
vulse features methodically, and philosophise over
insanity. Not so Tintoret. Knowing, or feeling,
that the expression of the human face was, in
such circumstances, not to be rendered, and that
the effort could only end in an ugly falsehood, he

denies himself all aid from the features, he feels
that if he is to place himself or us in the midst of
that maddened multitude, there can be no time
allowed for watching expression.   Still less does
he depend on details of murder or ghastliness of
death; there is no blood, no stabbing or cutting,
but there is an awful substitute for these in the
chiaroscuro.   The scene is the outer vestibule of
a palace, the slippery marble floor is fearfully
barred across by sanguine shadows, so that our
eyes seem to become bloodshot and strained with
strange horror and deadly vision; a lake of life
before them, like the burning seen of the doomed
Moabite on the water that came by the way of
Edom; a huge flight of stairs, without parapet,
descends on the left; down this rush a crowd of
women mixed with the murderers; the child in
the arms of one has been seized by the limbs,
*she hurls herself over the edge, and falls head
downmost, dragging the child out of the grasp by
her weight;*—she will be dashed dead in a
second;—close to us is the great struggle; a
heap of the mothers entangled in one mortal
writhe with each other and the swords, one of
the murderers dashed down and crushed beneath
them, the sword of another caught by the blade
and dragged at by a woman's naked hand; the
youngest and fairest of the women, her child just
torn away from a death grasp, and clasped to
her breast with the grip of a steel vice, falls

backwards, helplessly over the heap, right on the sword points; all knit together and hurled down in one hopeless, frenzied, furious abandonment of body and soul in the effort to save. Far back, at the bottom of the stairs, there is something in the shadow like a heap of clothes. It is a woman, sitting quiet,—quite quiet,—still as any stone; she looks down steadfastly on her dead child, laid along on the floor before her, and her hand is pressed softly upon her brow.

This, to my mind, is the only Imaginative, that is, the only true, real, heartfelt representation of the being and actuality of the subject, in existence.—*M. P.*, II. III. ii. 3, § 21, 22.

94. The Last Judgment, by Tintoret.— By Tintoret only has this unimaginable event been grappled with, in its Verity; not typically nor symbolically, but as they may see it who shall not sleep, but be changed. Only one traditional circumstance he has received with Dante and Michael Angelo, the Boat of the Condemned; but the impetuosity of his mind bursts out even in the adoption of this image; he has not stopped at the scowling ferryman of the one, nor at the sweeping blow and demon dragging of the other, but seized Hylas-like by the limbs, and tearing up the earth in his agony, the victim is dashed into his destruction: nor is it the sluggish Lethe, nor the fiery lake that bears the

I.   Q cursed vessel, but the oceans of the earth and the waters of the firmament gathered into one white, ghastly cataract; the river of the wrath of God, roaring down into the gulf where the world has melted with its fervent heat, choked with the ruin of nations, and the limbs of its corpses tossed out of its whirling, like water-wheels. Bat-like, out of the holes and caverns and shadows of the earth, the bones gather and the clay heaps heave, rattling and adhering into half-kneaded anatomies, that crawl, and startle, and struggle up among the putrid weeds, with the clay clinging to their clotted hair, and their heavy eyes sealed by the earth darkness yet, like his of old who went his way unseeing to the Siloam Pool; shaking off one by one the dreams of the prison-house, hardly hearing the clangour of the trumpets of the armies of God, blinded yet more, as they awake, by the white light of the new Heaven, until the great vortex of the four winds bears up their bodies to the judgment-seat: the Firmament is all full of them, a very dust of human souls, that drifts, and floats, and falls in the interminable, inevitable light; the bright clouds are darkened with them as with thick snow, currents of atom life in the arteries of heaven, now soaring up slowly, and higher and higher still, till the eye and the thought can follow no farther, borne up, wingless, by their inward faith and by the angel powers invisible, now hurled in countless drifts of horror before the breath of their condemnation.—*M. P.*, II. III. ii. 3, § 24.

95. St. Sebastian, by Tintoret.—I never saw a man die a violent death, and therefore cannot say whether this figure be true or not, but it gives the grandest and most intense impression of truth. The figure is dead, and well it may be, for there is one arrow through the forehead and another through the heart; but the eyes are open, though glazed, and the body is rigid in the position in which it last stood, the left arm raised and the left limb advanced, something in the attitude of a soldier sustaining an attack under his shield, while the dead eyes are still turned in the direction from which the arrows came: but the most characteristic feature is the way these arrows are fixed. In the common martyrdoms of St. Sebastian they are stuck into him here and there like pins, as if they had been shot from a great distance and had come faltering down, entering the flesh but a little way, and rather bleeding the saint to death than mortally wounding him; but Tintoret had no such ideas about archery. He must have seen bows drawn in battle, like that of Jehu when he smote Jehoram between the harness: all the arrows in the saint's body lie straight in the same direction, broad-feathered and strong-shafted, and sent apparently with the force of thunderbolts; every one of them

has gone through him like a lance, two through the limbs, one through the arm, one through the heart, and the last has crashed through the forehead, nailing the head to the tree behind, as if it had been dashed in by a sledge-hammer. The face, in spite of its ghastliness, is beautiful, and has been serene; and the light which enters first and glistens on the plumes of the arrows, dies softly away upon the curling hair, and mixes with the glory upon the forehead. There is not a more remarkable picture in Venice, and yet I do not suppose that one in a thousand of the travellers who pass through the Scuola so much as perceives there is a picture in the place which it occupies.—*S. V.*, III. *V. I.*

96. THE FALL OF VENETIAN ART.—In all its roots of power, and modes of work;—in its belief, its breadth, and its judgment, I find the Venetian mind perfect. How, then, did its art so swiftly pass away? How become, what it became unquestionably, one of the chief causes of the corruption of the mind of Italy, and of her subsequent decline in moral and political power?

By reason of one great, one fatal fault;—recklessness in aim. Wholly noble in its sources, it was wholly unworthy in its purposes.

Separate and strong, like Samson, chosen from its youth, and with the Spirit of God visibly resting on it,—like him, it warred in careless strength, and wantoned in untimely pleasure. No Venetian painter ever worked with any aim beyond that of delighting the eye, or expressing fancies agreeable to himself or flattering to his nation. They could not be either, unless they were religious. But he did not desire the religion. He desired the delight.

The Assumption is a noble picture, because Titian believed in the Madonna. But he did not paint it to make any one else believe in her. He painted it, because he enjoyed rich masses of red and blue, and faces flushed with sunlight.

Tintoret's Paradise is a noble picture, because he believed in Paradise. But he did not paint it to make any one think of heaven; but to form a beautiful termination for the hall of the greater council.

Other men used their effete faiths and mean faculties with a high moral purpose. The Venetian gave the most earnest faith, and the lordliest faculty, to gild the shadows of an antechamber, or heighten the splendours of a holiday.

Strange and lamentable as this carelessness may appear, I find it to be almost the law with the great workers. Weak and vain men have acute consciences, and labour under a profound sense of responsibility. The strong men, sternly disdainful of themselves, do what they can, too often merely as it pleases them at the moment, reckless what comes of it.

I know not how far in humility, or how far in bitter and hopeless levity, the great Venetians gave their art to be blasted by the sea-winds or wasted by the worm. I know not whether in sorrowful obedience, or in wanton compliance, they fostered the folly, and enriched the luxury of their age. This only I know, that in proportion to the greatness of their power was the shame of its desecration and the suddenness of its fall. The enchanter's spell, woven by centuries of toil, was broken in the weakness of a moment; and swiftly, and utterly, as a rainbow vanishes, the radiance and the strength faded from the wings of the Lion.—*M. P.*, V. IX. 3, § 31–33.

97. SALVATOR ROSA.—Born with a wild and coarse nature (how coarse I will show you soon), but nevertheless an honest one, he set himself in youth hotly to the war, and cast himself carelessly on the current, of life. No rectitude of ledger-lines stood in his way; no tender precision of household customs; no calm successions of rural labour. But past his half-starved lips rolled profusion of pitiless wealth; before him glared and swept the troops of shameless pleasure. Above him muttered Vesuvius; beneath his feet shook the Solfatara.

In heart disdainful, in temper adventurous; conscious of power, impatient of labour, and yet more of the pride of the patrons of his youth, he

fled to the Calabrian hills, seeking, not knowledge, but freedom.   If he was to be surrounded
by cruelty and deceit, let them at least be those
of brave men or savage beasts, not of the timorous
and the contemptible.   Better the wrath of the
robber, than enmity of the priest; and the cunning of the wolf than of the hypocrite. . . .

Yet even among such scenes as these, Salvator
might have been calmed and exalted, had he been,
indeed, capable of exaltation.   But he was not
of high temper enough to perceive beauty.   He
had not the sacred sense—the sense of colour;
all the loveliest hues of the Calabrian air were
invisible to him; the sorrowful desolation of the
Calabrian villages unfelt.   He saw only what was
gross and terrible,—the jagged peak, the splintered tree, the flowerless bank of grass, and
wandering weed, prickly and pale.   His temper
confirmed itself in evil, and became more and
more fierce and morose; though not, I believe,
cruel, ungenerous, or lascivious.   I should not
suspect Salvator of wantonly inflicting pain.   His
constantly painting it does not prove he delighted
in it; he felt the horror of it, and in that horror,
fascination.   Also, he desired fame, and saw that
here was an untried field rich enough in morbid
excitement to catch the humour of his indolent
patrons.   But the gloom gained upon him, and
grasped him.   He could jest, indeed, as men jest
in prison-yards (he became afterwards a renowned

mime in Florence); his satires are full of good mocking, but his own doom to sadness is never repealed.

Of all men whose work I have ever studied, he gives me most distinctly the idea of a lost spirit. Michelet calls him, "Ce damné Salvator," perhaps in a sense merely harsh and violent; the epithet to me seems true in a more literal, more merciful sense,—"That condemned Salvator." I see in him, notwithstanding all his baseness, the last traces of spiritual life in the art of Europe. He was the last man to whom the thought of a spiritual existence presented itself as a conceivable reality. All succeeding men, however powerful—Rembrandt, Rubens, Vandyck, Reynolds—would have mocked at the idea of a spirit. They were men of the world; they are never in earnest, and they are never appalled. But Salvator was capable of pensiveness, of faith, and of fear. The misery of the earth is a marvel to him; he cannot leave off gazing at it. The religion of the earth is a horror to him. He gnashes his teeth at it, rages at it, mocks and gibes at it. He would have acknowledged religion, had he seen any that was true. Anything rather than that baseness which he did see. "If there is no other religion than this of pope and cardinals, let us to the robber's ambush and the dragon's den." He was capable of fear also. The grey spectre, horse-headed, striding across the sky—(in the

Pitti Palace)—its bat wings spread, green bars of the twilight seen between its bones; it was no play to him—the painting of it. Helpless Salvator! A little early sympathy, a word of true guidance, perhaps, had saved him. What says he of himself? "Despiser of wealth and of death." Two grand scorns; but, oh, condemned Salvator! the question is not for man what he can scorn, but what he can love.—*M. P.*, V. IX. 4, § 11–14.

98. DÜRER.—In the sight of Dürer, things were for the most part as they ought to be. Men did their work in his city and in the fields round it. The clergy were sincere. Great social questions unagitated; great social evils either non-existent, or seemingly a part of the nature of things, and inevitable. His answer was that of patient hope; and twofold, consisting of one design in praise of Fortitude, and another in praise of Labour. The Fortitude, commonly known as the "Knight and Death," represents a knight riding through a dark valley overhung by leafless trees, and with a great castle on a hill beyond. Beside him, but a little in advance, rides Death on a pale horse. Death is grey-haired and crowned;—serpents wreathed about his crown; (the sting of death involved in the kingly power). He holds up the hour-glass, and looks earnestly into the knight's face. Behind

him follows Sin; but Sin powerless; he has
been conquered and passed by, but follows yet,
watching if any way of assault remains. On his
forehead are two horns—I think of sea-shell—
to indicate his insatiableness and instability. He
has also the twisted horns of the ram, for stubbornness, the ears of an ass, the snout of a swine,
the hoofs of a goat. Torn wings hang useless from his shoulders, and he carries a spear
with two hooks, for catching as well as wounding. The knight does not heed him, nor even
Death, though he is conscious of the presence
of the last.

He rides quietly, his bridle firm in his hand,
and his lips set close in a slight sorrowful smile,
for he hears what Death is saying; and hears it
as the word of a messenger who brings pleasant
tidings, thinking to bring evil ones. A little
branch of delicate heath is twisted round his
helmet. His horse trots proudly and straight;
its head high, and with a cluster of oak on the
brow where on the fiend's brow is the sea-shell
horn. But the horse of Death stoops its head;
and its rein catches the little bell which hangs
from the knight's horse-bridle, making it toll as
a passing-bell.

Dürer's second answer is the plate of " Melancholia," which is the history of the sorrowful toil
of the earth, as the " Knight and Death " is of its
sorrowful patience under temptation.

Salvator's answer, remember, is in both respects that of despair. Death as he reads, lord of temptation, is victor over the spirit of man; and lord of ruin, is victor over the work of man. Dürer declares the sad but unsullied conquest over Death the tempter; and the sad but enduring conquest over Death the destroyer.

Though the general intent of the Melancholia is clear, and to be felt at a glance, I am in some doubt respecting its special symbolism. I do not know how far Dürer intended to show that labour, in many of its most earnest forms, is closely connected with the morbid sadness or "dark anger," of the Northern nations. Truly some of the best work ever done for man, has been in that dark anger; but I have not yet been able to determine for myself how far this is necessary, or how far great work may also be done with cheerfulness. If I knew what the truth was, I should be able to interpret Dürer better; meantime the design seems to me his answer to the complaint, "Yet is his strength labour and sorrow."

"Yes," he replies, "but labour and sorrow are his strength."

The labour indicated is in the daily work of men. Not the inspired or gifted labour of the few (it is labour connected with the sciences, not with the arts), shown in its four chief functions: thoughtful, faithful, calculating and executing.

Thoughtful, first ; all true power coming of that resolved, resistless calm of melancholy thought. This is the first and last message of the whole design. Faithful, the right arm of the spirit resting on the book. Calculating (chiefly in the sense of self-command), the compasses in her right hand. Executive—roughest instruments of labour at her feet : a crucible, and geometrical solids, indicating her work in the sciences. Over her head the hour-glass and the bell, for their continual words, " Whatsoever thy hand findeth to do." Beside her, childish labour (lesson-learning ?) sitting on an old millstone, with a tablet on its knees. I do not know what instrument it has in its hand. At her knees a wolf-hound asleep. In the distance a comet (the disorder and threatening of the universe) setting, the rainbow dominant over it. Her strong body is close girded for work ; at her waist hang the keys of wealth ; but the coin is cast aside contemptuously under her feet. She has eagle's wings, and is crowned with fair leafage of spring.

Yes, Albert of Nuremberg, it was a noble answer, yet an imperfect one. This is indeed the labour which is crowned with laurel and has the wings of the eagle. It was reserved for another country to prove, for another hand to pourtray, the labour which is crowned with fire, and has the wings of the bat.—*M. P.*, V. IX. 4, § 16–19.

99. ITALIANS AND TEUTONS.—A man long trained to love the monk's visions of Fra Angelico, turns in proud and ineffable disgust from the first work of Rubens which he encounters on his return across the Alps. But is he right in his indignation? He has forgotten, that while Angelico prayed and wept in his *olive shade*, there was different work doing in the dank fields of Flanders;—wild seas to be banked out; endless canals to be dug, and boundless marshes to be drained; hard ploughing and harrowing of the frosty clay; careful breeding of stout horses and fat cattle; close setting of brick walls against cold winds and snow; much hardening of hands and gross stoutening of bodies in all this; gross jovialities of harvest homes and Christmas feasts, which were to be the reward of it; rough affections, and sluggish imaginations; fleshy, substantial, iron-shod humanities, but humanities still; humanities which God had his eye upon, and which won, perhaps, here and there, as much favour in his sight as the wasted aspects of the whispering monks of Florence (Heaven forbid it should not be so, since the most of us cannot be monks, but must be ploughmen and reapers still). And are we to suppose there is no nobility in Rubens' masculine and universal sympathy with all this, and with his large human rendering of it, gentleman though he was, by birth, and feeling, and education, and place; and, when

he chose, lordly in conception also ? He had his faults, perhaps great and lamentable faults, though more those of his time and his country than his own ; he has neither cloister breeding nor boudoir breeding, and is very unfit to paint either in missals or annuals ; but he has an open sky and wide-world breeding in him, that we may not be offended with, fit alike for king's court, knight's camp, or peasant's cottage. On the other hand, a man trained here in England, in our Sir Joshua school, will not and cannot allow that there is any art at all in the technical work of Angelico. But he is just as wrong as the other. Fra Angelico is as true a master of the art necessary to his purposes, as Rubens was of that necessary for his. We have been taught in England to think there can be no virtue but in a loaded brush and rapid hand; but if we can shake our common sense free of such teaching we shall understand that there is art also in the delicate point and in the hand which trembles as it moves ; not because it is more liable to err, but because there is more danger in its error, and more at stake upon its precision. The art of Angelico, both as a colourist and a draughtsman, is consummate ; so perfect and beautiful, that his work may be recognised at any distance by the rainbow-play and brilliancy of it. However closely it may be surrounded by other works of the same school, glowing with enamel and gold, Angelico's may be told from them at a glance, like so many huge pieces of opal lying among common marbles.—*S. V.*, I., App. 15.

100. THE FLEMISH MASTERS.—There is just this difference between the men of this modern period, and the Florentines or Venetians—that whereas the latter never exert themselves fully except on a sacred subject, the Flemish and Dutch masters are always languid unless they are profane. Leonardo is only to be seen in the Cena; Titian only in the Assumption; but Rubens only in the Battle of the Amazons, and Vandyck only at court.

Altar-pieces, when wanted, of course either of them will supply as readily as anything else. Virgins in blue, or St. Johns in red, as many as you please. Martyrdoms also, by all means: Rubens especially delights in these. St. Peter, head downwards, is interesting anatomically; writhings of impenitent thieves, and bishops having their tongues pulled out, display our powers to advantage, also. Theological instruction, if required: "Christ armed with thunder, to destroy the world, spares it at the intercession of St. Francis." Last Judgments even, quite Michael-Angelesque, rich in twistings of limbs, with spiteful biting, and scratching; and fine aerial effects in smoke of the pit.

In all this, however, there is not a vestige of religious feeling or reverence. We have even some visible difficulty in meeting our patron's pious wishes. Daniel in the lions' den is indeed an available subject, but duller than a lion hunt: and Mary of Nazareth must be painted if an order come for her; but (says polite Sir Peter), Mary of Medicis, or Catherine, her bodice being fuller, and better embroidered, would, if we might offer a suggestion, probably give greater satisfaction.

No phenomenon in human mind is more extraordinary than the junction of this cold and worldly temper with great rectitude of principle and tranquil kindness of heart. Rubens was an honourable and entirely well-intentioned man, earnestly industrious, simple and temperate in habits of life, high-bred, learned and discreet. His affection for his mother was great; his generosity to contemporary artists unfailing. He is a healthy, worthy, kind-hearted, courtly-phrased — Animal — without any clearly perceptible traces of a soul, except when he paints his children. . . . He is religious too, after his manner; hears mass every morning, and perpetually uses the phrase " by the grace of God," or some other such, in writing of any business he takes in hand; but the tone of his religion may be determined by one fact.

We saw how Veronese painted himself and his family, as worshipping the Madonna.

Rubens has also painted himself and his family in an equally elaborate piece. But they are not *worshipping* the Madonna. They are *performing* the Madonna, and her saintly entourage. His favourite wife "en Madonne;" his youngest boy "as Christ;" his father-in-law (or father, it matters not which) "as Simeon;" another elderly relation, with a beard, "as St. Jerome;" and he himself "as St. George."

Rembrandt has also painted (it is, on the whole, his greatest picture, so far as I have seen) himself and his wife in a state of ideal happiness. He sits at supper with his wife on his knee, flourishing a glass of champagne, with a roast peacock on the table.

The Rubens is in the Church of St. James at Antwerp; the Rembrandt at Dresden—marvellous pictures, both. No more precious works by either painter exist. Their hearts, such as they have, are entirely in them; and the two pictures, not inaptly, represent the Faith and Hope of the 17th century.—*M. P.*, V. IX. 6, § 5–10.

101. VANDYCK.—The following extract from my private diary refers to two portraits which happened to be placed opposite to each other in the arrangement of a gallery; one, modern, of a (foreign) general on horseback at a review; the other, by Vandyck, also an equestrian

I.
R

portrait, of an ancestor of his family, whom I
shall here simply call "the knight :"

"I have seldom seen so noble a Vandyck,
chiefly because it is painted with less flightiness
and flimsiness than usual, with a grand quietness
and reserve—almost like Titian. The other is,
on the contrary, as vulgar and base a picture
as I have ever seen, and it becomes a matter
of extreme interest to trace the cause of the
difference.

"In the first place, everything the general and
his horse wear is evidently just made. It has
not only been cleaned that morning, but has
been sent home from the tailor's in a hurry last
night. Horse bridle, saddle housings, blue coat,
stars and lace thereupon, cocked hat, and sword
hilt—all look as if they had just been taken from
a shopboard in Pall Mall; the irresistible sense
of the coat having been brushed to perfection
is the first sentiment which the picture summons.
The horse has also been rubbed down all the
morning, and shines from head to tail.

"The knight rides in a suit of rusty armour.
It has evidently been polished also carefully,
and gleams brightly here and there; but all the
polishing in the world will never take the battle-
dints and battle-darkness out of it. His horse
is grey, not lustrous, but a dark, lurid grey.
Its mane is deep and soft; part of it shaken in
front over its forehead—the rest, in enormous

masses of waving gold, six feet long, falls streaming on its neck, and rises in currents of softest light, rippled by the wind over the rider's armour. The saddle cloth is of a dim red, fading into leathern brown, gleaming with sparkles of obscure gold. When, after looking a little while at the soft mane of the Vandyck horse, we turn back to the general's, we are shocked by the evident coarseness of its hair, which hangs, indeed, in long locks over the bridle, but is stiff, crude, sharp pointed, coarsely coloured (a kind of buff); no fine drawing of nostril or neck can give any look of nobleness to the animal which carries such hair; it looks like a hobby horse with tow glued to it, which riotous children have half pulled or scratched out. The next point of difference is the isolation of Vandyck's figure, compared with the modern painter's endeavour to ennoble his by subduing others. The knight seems to be just going out of his castle gates; his horse rears as he passes their pillars; there is nothing behind, but the sky. But the general is reviewing a regiment; the ensign lowers his colours to him; he takes off his hat in return. All which reviewing and bowing is in its very nature ignoble, wholly unfit to be painted: a gentleman might as well be painted leaving his card on somebody. And, in the next place, the modern painter has thought to enhance his officer by putting the regiment some distance back and in the shade, so that the men look only about five feet high, being besides very ill painted to keep them in better subordination. One does not know whether most to despise the feebleness of the painter who must have recourse to such an artifice, or his vulgarity in being satisfied with it. I ought by the way, before leaving the point of dress, to have noted that the vulgarity of the painter is considerably assisted by the vulgarity of the costume itself. Not only is it base in being new, but base in that it cannot last to be old. If one wanted a lesson on the ugliness of modern costume, it could not be more sharply received than by turning from one to the other horseman. The knight wears steel plate armour, chased here and there with gold; the delicate, rich, pointed lace collar falling on the embossed breastplate; his dark hair flowing over his shoulders; a crimson silk scarf fastened round his waist, and floating behind him; buff boots, deep folded at the instep, set in silver stirrup. The general wears his hair cropped short; blue coat, padded and buttoned; blue trowsers and red stripe; black shiny boots; common saddler's stirrups; cocked hat in hand, suggestive of absurd completion, when assumed.

"Another thing noticeable as giving nobleness to the Vandyck is its feminineness: the rich, light silken scarf, the flowing hair, the delicate, sharp, though sunburnt features, and the lace collar, do not in the least diminish the manliness, but *add* feminineness. One sees that the knight is indeed a soldier, but not a soldier only; that he is accomplished in all ways, and tender in all thoughts: while the general is represented as nothing but a soldier—and it is very doubtful if he is even that—one is sure, at a glance, that if he can do anything but put his hat off and on, and give words of command, the anything must, at all events, have something to do with the barracks; that there is no grace, nor music, nor softness, nor learnedness, in the man's soul; that he is made up of forms and accoutrements.

"Lastly, the modern picture is as bad painting as it is wretched conceiving; and one is struck, in looking from it to Vandyck's, peculiarly by the fact that good work is always *enjoyed* work. There is not a touch of Vandyck's pencil but he seems to have revelled in—not grossly, but delicately—tasting the colour in every touch as an epicure would wine. While the other goes on daub, daub, daub, like a bricklayer spreading mortar—nay, with far less lightness of hand or lightness of spirit than a good bricklayer's— covering his canvas heavily and conceitedly at once, caring only but to catch the public eye with his coarse, presumptuous, ponderous, illiterate work."

Thus far my diary. In case it should be

discovered by any one where these pictures are, it should be noted that the vulgarity of the modern one is wholly the painter's fault. It implies none in the general (except bad taste in pictures). The same painter would have made an equally vulgar portrait of Bayard. And as for taste in pictures, the general's was not singular. I used to spend much time before the Vandyck; and among all the tourist visitors to the gallery, who were numerous, I never saw one look at it twice, but all paused in respectful admiration before the padded surtout.—*M. P.*, V. IX. 7, *note*.

102. ANIMAL PAINTING.—I stated, in speaking of Venetian religion, that the Venetians always introduced the dog as a contrast to the high aspects of humanity. They do this, not because they consider him the basest of animals, but the highest—the connecting link between men and animals; in whom the lower forms of really human feeling may be best exemplified, such as conceit, gluttony, indolence, petulance. But they saw the noble qualities of the dog, too;—all his patience, love, and faithfulness; therefore Veronese, hard as he is often on lap-dogs, has painted one great heroic poem on the dog.

Two mighty brindled mastiffs, and beyond them, darkness. You scarcely see them at first, against the gloomy green. No other sky for them—poor things. They are gray themselves, spotted with black all over; their multitudinous doggish vices may not be washed out of them,— are in grain of nature. Strong thewed and sinewed, however,—no blame on them as far as bodily strength may reach; their heads coal-black, with drooping ears and fierce eyes, blood-shot a little. Wildest of beasts perhaps they would have been, by nature. But between them stands the spirit of their human love, dove-winged and beautiful, the resistless Greek boy, golden-quivered; his glowing breast and limbs the only light upon the sky,—purple and pure. He has cast his chain about the dogs' necks, and holds it in his strong right hand, leaning proudly a little back from them. They will never break loose.

This is Veronese's highest, or spiritual view of the dog's nature. He can only give this when looking at the creature alone. When he sees it in company with men, he subdues it, like an inferior light in presence of the sky; and gene-rally then gives it a merely brutal nature, not insisting even on its affection. It is thus used in the Marriage in Cana to symbolise gluttony. That great picture I have not yet had time to examine in all its bearings of thought; but the chief purpose of it is, I believe, to express the pomp and pleasure of the world, pursued without thought of the presence of Christ; therefore the Fool with the bells is put in the centre, immediately underneath the Christ; and in front are the couple of dogs in leash, one gnawing a bone. A cat lying on her back scratches at one of the vases which hold the wine of the miracle.

In the picture of Susannah, her little pet dog is merely doing his duty, barking at the Elders. But in that of the Magdalen (at Turin) a noble piece of by-meaning is brought out by a dog's help. On one side is the principal figure, the Mary washing Christ's feet; on the other, a dog has just come out from beneath the table (the dog under the table eating of the crumbs), and in doing so, has touched the robe of one of the Pharisees, thus making it unclean. The Pharisee gathers up his robe in a passion, and shows the hem of it to a bystander, pointing to the dog at the same time.

In the Supper at Emmaus, the dog's affection is, however, fully dwelt upon. Veronese's own two little daughters are playing, on the hither side of the table, with a great wolf-hound, larger than either of them. One with her head down, nearly touching his nose, is talking to him—asking him questions it seems, nearly pushing him over at the same time:—the other, raising her eyes, half archly, half dreamily,—some far-away thought coming over her,—leans against him on the other side, propping him with her little hand, laid slightly on his neck. He, all passive, and glad at heart, yielding himself to the pushing or sustaining hand, looks earnestly into the face of the child close to his; would answer her with the gravity of a senator, if so it might be:—can only look at her, and love her.

To Velasquez and Titian dogs seem less interesting than to Veronese; they paint them simply as noble brown beasts, but without any special character; perhaps Velasquez' dogs are sterner and more threatening than the Venetian's, as are also his kings and admirals. This fierceness in the animal increases, as the spiritual power of the artist declines; and, with the fierceness, another character. One great and infallible sign of the absence of spiritual power is the presence of the slightest taint of obscenity. Dante marked this strongly in all his representations of demons, and as we pass from the Venetians and Florentines to the Dutch, the passing away of the soul-power is indicated by every animal becoming savage or foul. The dog is used by Teniers, and many other Hollanders, merely to obtain unclean jest; while by the more powerful men, Rubens, Snyders, Rembrandt, it is painted only in savage chase, or butchered agony. I know no pictures more shameful to humanity than the boar and lion hunts of Rubens and Snyders, signs of disgrace all the deeper, because the powers desecrated are so great. The painter of the village alehouse sign may, not dishonourably, paint the fox-hunt for the village squire;

but the occupation of magnificent art-power in giving semblance of perpetuity to those bodily pangs which Nature has mercifully ordained to be transient, and in forcing us, by the fascination of its stormy skill, to dwell on that from which eyes of merciful men should instinctively turn away, and eyes of high-minded men scornfully, is dishonourable, alike in the power which it degrades, and the joy to which it betrays.— *M. P.*, V. IX. 6, § 14–19.

103. CLAUDE.—He had a fine feeling for beauty of form and considerable tenderness of perception. His aërial effects are unequalled. Their character appears to me to arise rather from a delicacy of bodily constitution in Claude, than from any mental sensibility: such as they are, they give a kind of feminine charm to his work, which partly accounts for its wide influence. To whatever the character may be traced, it renders him incapable of enjoying or painting anything energetic or terrible. Hence the weakness of his conceptions of rough sea.

He had sincerity of purpose; but in common with other landscape painters of his day, neither earnestness, humility, nor love, such as would ever cause him to forget himself.

That is to say, so far as he felt the truth, he tried to be true; but he never felt it enough to sacrifice supposed propriety, or habitual method to it. Very few of his sketches, and none of his pictures, show evidence of interest in other natural phenomena than the quiet afternoon sunshine which would fall methodically into a composition. One would suppose he had never seen scarlet in a morning cloud, nor a storm burst on the Apennines. But he enjoys a quiet misty afternoon in a ruminant sort of way, yet truly; and strives for the likeness of it, therein differing from Salvator, who never attempts to be truthful, but only to be impressive.

His seas are the most beautiful in old art. For he studied tame waves, as he did tame skies, with great sincerity, and some affection; and modelled them with more care not only than any other landscape painter of his day, but even than any of the great men; for they, seeing the perfect painting of sea to be impossible, gave up the attempt, and treated it conventionally. But Claude took so much pains about this, feeling it was one of his *fortes*, that I suppose no one can model a small wave better than he.

He first set the pictorial sun in the pictorial heaven. We will give him the credit of this, with no drawbacks.

He had hardly any knowledge of physical science, and shows a peculiar incapacity of understanding the main point of a matter. Connected with which incapacity is his want of harmony in expression.

Such were the principal qualities of the leading
painter of classical landscape, his effeminate softness carrying him to dislike all evidences of toil,
or distress, or terror, and to delight in the calm
formalities which mark the school.

Although he often introduces romantic incidents
and mediæval as well as Greek or Roman person-
ages, his landscape is always in the true sense
classic—everything being "elegantly" (select-
ingly or tastefully), not passionately, treated.
The absence of indications of rural labour, of
hedges, ditches, haystacks, ploughed fields, and
the like; the frequent occurrence of ruins of
temples, or masses of unruined palaces; and the
graceful wildness of growth in his trees, are the
principal sources of the "elevated" character
which so many persons feel in his scenery. . . .

The admiration of his works was legitimate, so
far as it regarded their sunlight effects and their
graceful details. It was base, in so far as it
involved irreverence both for the deeper powers
of nature, and carelessness as to conception of
subject. Large admiration of Claude is wholly
impossible in any period of national vigour in art.
He may by such tenderness as he possesses,
and by the very fact of his banishing painful-
ness, exercise considerable influence over certain
classes of minds; but this influence is almost
exclusively hurtful to them.

Nevertheless, on account of such small sterling

qualities as they possess, and of their general pleasantness, as well as their importance in the history of art, genuine Claudes must always possess a considerable value, either as drawing-room ornaments or museum relics. They may be ranked with fine pieces of china manufacture, and other agreeable curiosities, of which the price depends on the rarity rather than the merit, yet always on a merit of a certain low kind.—*M. P.*, V. IX. 5, § 10–16.

104. N. POUSSIN.—The other characteristic master of classical landscape is Nicolo Poussin.

I named Claude first, because the forms of scenery he has represented are richer and more general than Poussin's; but Poussin has a far greater power, and his landscapes, though more limited in material, are incomparably nobler than Claude's. It would take considerable time to enter into accurate analysis of Poussin's strong but degraded mind; and bring us no reward, because whatever he has done, has been done better by Titian. His peculiarities are, without exception, weaknesses, induced in a highly intellectual and inventive mind by being fed on medals, books, and bassi-relievi instead of nature, and by the want of any deep sensibility. His best works are his Bacchanalian revels, always brightly wanton and wild, full of frisk and fire; but they are coarser than Titian's, and infinitely less beautiful. In all minglings of the human and brutal character he leans on the bestial, yet with a sternly Greek severity of treatment. This restraint, peculiarly classical, is much too manifest in him; for, owing to his habit of never letting himself be free, he does nothing as well as it ought to be done, rarely even as well as he can himself do it; and his best beauty is poor, incomplete, and characterless, though refined. The Nymph pressing the honey in the "Nursing of Jupiter," and the Muse leaning against the tree, in the "Inspiration of Poet" (both in the Dulwich Gallery), appear to me examples of about his highest reach in this sphere.

His want of sensibility permits him to paint frightful subjects, without feeling any true horror: his pictures of the Plague, the Death of Polydectes, etc., are thus ghastly in incident, sometimes disgusting, but never impressive. The prominence of the bleeding head in the Triumph of David marks the same temper. His battle pieces are cold and feeble; his religious subjects wholly nugatory, they do not excite him enough to develop even his ordinary powers of invention. Neither does he put much power into his landscape when it becomes principal; the best pieces of it occur in fragments behind his figures. Beautiful vegetation, more or less ornamental in character, occurs in nearly all his mythological subjects, but his pure landscape is notable only for its dignified reserve; the great squareness and horizontality of its masses, with lowness of tone, giving it a deeply meditative character.   His Deluge might be much depreciated, under this head of ideas of relation, but it is so uncharacteristic of him that I pass it by.   Whatever power this lowness of tone, light in the distance, etc., give to his landscape, or to Gaspar's,* is in both conventional and artificial.—*M. P.*, V. IX. 5, § 17, 18.

105. THE "HOLY FAMILY" AND THE "GRACES" OF REYNOLDS.—Great, as ever was work wrought by man.   In placid strength, and subtlest science, unsurpassed;—in sweet felicity, incomparable.   If you truly want to know what good work of painter's hand is, study those two pictures from side to side, and miss no inch of them (you will hardly, eventually, be inclined to miss one): in some respects there is no execution like it; none so open in the magic. For the work of other great men is hidden in its wonderfulness—you cannot see how it was done. But in Sir Joshua's there is no mystery; it is all amazement.   No question but that the touch was so laid; only that it *could* have been so laid, is a marvel for ever.   So also there is no painting so majestic in sweetness.   He is lily-sceptred:

* Compare § 21, "The Distant Gleam."

his power blossoms, but burdens not. All men
of equal dignity paint more slowly; all others
of equal force paint less lightly. Tintoret lays
his line like a king marking the boundaries of
conquered lands; but Sir Joshua leaves it as
a summer wind its trace on a lake; he could
have painted on a silken veil, where it fell free,
and not bent it.

Such at least is his touch when it is life that
he paints: for things lifeless he has a severer
hand. If you examine that picture of the *Graces*
you will find it reverses all the ordinary ideas
of expedient treatment. By other men flesh is
firmly painted, but accessories lightly. Sir
Joshua paints accessories firmly, flesh lightly;
—nay, flesh not at all, but spirit. The wreath
of flowers he feels to be material; and gleam by
gleam strikes fearlessly the silver and violet
leaves out of the darkness. But the three maidens
are less substantial than rose petals. No flushed
nor frosted tissue that ever faded in night-wind
is so tender as they; no hue may reach, no
line measure, what is in them so gracious and
so fair. Let the hand move softly—itself as a
spirit; for this is Life, of which it touches the
imagery.

"And yet——" Yes: you do well to pause.
There is a "yet" to be thought of. I did not
bring you to these pictures to see wonderful
work merely, or womanly beauty merely.   I

brought you chiefly to look at that Madonna, believing that you might remember other Madonnas, unlike her; and might think it desirable to consider wherein the difference lay:— other Madonnas not by Sir Joshua, who painted Madonnas but seldom. Who perhaps, if truth must be told, painted them *never:* for surely this dearest pet of an English girl, with the little curl of lovely hair under her ear, is *not* one.—*Cornhill Magazine*, March 1860 (*O. R.*, I., § 149–152).

106. REYNOLDS AND GAINSBOROUGH.—It was a faultful temper which, having so mighty a power of realisation at command, never became so much interested in any fact of human history as to spend one touch of heartfelt skill upon it; —which, yielding momentarily to indolent imagination, ended, at best, in a Puck, or a Thais; a Mercury as Thief, or a Cupid as Linkboy. How wide the interval between this gently trivial humour, guided by the wave of a feather, or arrested by the enchantment of a smile,—and the habitual dwelling of the thoughts of the great Greeks and Florentines among the beings and the interests of the eternal world!

In some degree it may indeed be true that the modesty and sense of the English painters are the causes of their simple practice. All that they did, they did well, and attempted nothing over which conquest was doubtful. . . . Meaner men, their contemporaries or successors, raved of high art with incoherent passion; arrogated to themselves an equality with the masters of elder time, and declaimed against the degenerate tastes of a public which acknowledged not the return of the Heraclidæ. But the two great—the two only painters of their age, happy in a reputation founded as deeply in the heart as in the judgment of mankind, demanded no higher function than that of soothing the domestic affections; and achieved for themselves at last an immortality not the less noble, because in their lifetime they had concerned themselves less to claim it, than to bestow.

Yet while we acknowledge the discretion and simple-heartedness of these men, honouring them for both: and the more when we compare their tranquil powers with the hot egotism and hollow ambition of their inferiors: we have to remember, on the other hand, that the measure they thus set to their aims was, if a just, yet a narrow one; that amiable discretion is not the highest virtue, nor to please the frivolous, the best success. There is probably some strange weakness in the painter, and some fatal error in the age, when, in thinking over the examples of their greatest work, for some type of culminating loveliness or veracity, we remember no expression either of religion or heroism, and instead of reverently naming a Madonna di San Sisto, can only whisper, modestly, " Mrs. Pelham feeding chickens."—*Cornhill Magazine*, March 1860 (*O. R.*, I., § 155–158).

107. SIR JOSHUA REYNOLDS.—I am inclined to think that, considering all the disadvantages of circumstances and education under which his genius was developed, there was perhaps hardly ever born a man with a more intense and innate gift of insight into nature than our own Sir Joshua Reynolds. Considered as a painter of individuality in the human form and mind, I think him, even as it is, the prince of portrait painters. Titian paints nobler pictures, and Vandyke had nobler subjects, but neither of them entered so subtly as Sir Joshua did into the minor varieties of human heart and temper; and when you consider that, with a frightful conventionality of social habitude all around him, he yet conceived the simplest types of all feminine and childish loveliness;—that in a northern climate, and with grey, and white, and black, as the principal colours around him, he yet became a colourist who can be crushed by none, even of the Venetians;—and that with Dutch painting and Dresden china for the prevailing types of art in the saloons of his day, he threw himself at once at the feet of the great masters of Italy, and arose from their feet to share their throne—I know not that in the whole

history of art you can produce another instance of so strong, so unaided, so unerring an instinct for all that was true, pure, and noble.—*The Two Paths*, Lect. 2, § 63.

108. STOTHARD'S IDEALISM.—The works of our own Stothard are examples of the operation of a mind, singular in gentleness and purity, upon mere worldly subject. It seems as if Stothard could not conceive wickedness, coarseness, or baseness; every one of his figures looks as if it had been copied from some creature who had never harboured an unkind thought, or permitted itself in an ignoble action. With this intense love of mental purity is joined, in Stothard, a love of mere physical smoothness and softness, so that he lived in a universe of soft grass and stainless fountains, tender trees, and stones at which no foot could stumble.

All this is very beautiful, and may sometimes urge us to an endeavour to make the world itself more like the conception of the painter. At least, in the midst of its malice, misery, and baseness, it is often a relief to glance at the graceful shadows, and take, for momentary companionship, creatures full only of love, gladness, and honour. But the perfect truth will at last vindicate itself against the partial truth ; the help which we can gain from the unsubstantial vision will be only like that which we may sometimes receive,

in weariness, from the scent of a flower or the
passing of a breeze. For all firm aid, and steady
use, we must look to harder realities; and, as far
as the painter himself is regarded, we can only
receive such work as the sign of an amiable imbecility. It is indeed ideal; but ideal as a fair
dream is in the dawn of morning, before the
faculties are astir. The apparent completeness of
grace can never be attained without much definite
falsification as well as omission; stones, over
which we cannot stumble, must be ill-drawn
stones; trees, which are all gentleness and softness, cannot be trees of wood; nor companies
without evil in them, companies of flesh and
blood. The habit of falsification (with whatever
aim) begins always in dulness and ends always
in incapacity: nothing can be more pitiable than
any endeavour by Stothard to express facts
beyond his own sphere of soft pathos or graceful mirth, and nothing more unwise than the
aim at a similar ideality by any painter who
has power to render a sincerer truth.—*M. P.*,
III. IV. 6, § 5.

109. TWO BOYHOODS, — GIORGIONE AND
TURNER.—Born half-way between the mountains
and the sea—that young George of Castelfranco
—of the Brave Castle :—Stout George they called
him, George of Georges, so goodly a boy he was
—Giorgione.

Have you ever thought what a world his eyes opened on—fair, searching eyes of youth? What a world of mighty life, from those mountain roots to the shore;—of loveliest life, when he went down, yet so young, to the marble city— and became himself as a fiery heart to it?

A city of marble, did I say? nay, rather a golden city, paved with emerald. For truly, every pinnacle and turret glanced or glowed, overlaid with gold, or bossed with jasper. Beneath, the unsullied sea drew, in deep breathing, to and fro, its eddies of green wave. Deephearted, majestic, terrible as the sea,—the men of Venice moved in sway of power and war; pure as her pillars of alabaster, stood her mothers and maidens; from foot to brow, all noble, walked her knights; the low bronzed gleaming of sea-rusted armour shot angrily under their blood-red mantle-folds. Fearless, faithful, patient, impenetrable, implacable,—every word a fate—sate her senate. In hope and honour, lulled by flowing of wave around their isles of sacred sand, each with his name written and the cross graved at his side, lay her dead. A wonderful piece of world. Rather, itself a world. It lay along the face of the waters, no larger, as its captains saw it from their masts at evening, than a bar of sunset that could not pass away; but for its power, it must have seemed to them as if they were sailing in the expanse of heaven, and this a great planet, whose orient edge widened through ether. A world from which all ignoble care and petty thoughts were banished, with all the common and poor elements of life. No foulness, nor tumult, in those tremulous streets, that filled, or fell, beneath the moon; but rippled music of majestic change, or thrilling silence. No weak walls could rise above them; no low-roofed cottage, nor straw-built shed. Only the strength as of rock, and the finished setting of stones most precious. And around them, far as the eye could reach, still the soft moving of stainless waters, proudly pure; as not the flower, so neither the thorn nor the thistle, could grow in the glancing fields. Ethereal strength of Alps, dreamlike, vanishing in high procession beyond the Torcellan shore; blue islands of Paduan hills, poised in the golden west. Above, free winds and fiery clouds ranging at their will;—brightness out of the north, and balm from the south, and the stars of the evening and morning clear in the limitless light of arched heaven and circling sea.

Such was Giorgione's school—such Titian's home.

Near the south-west corner of Covent Garden, a square brick pit or well is formed by a close-set block of houses, to the back windows of which it admits a few rays of light. Access to the bottom of it is obtained out of Maiden Lane,

through a low archway and an iron gate; and if
you stand long enough under the archway to
accustom your eyes to the darkness you may see
on the left hand a narrow door, which formerly
gave quiet access to a respectable barber's shop,
of which the front window, looking into Maiden
Lane, is still extant, filled, in this year (1860),
with a row of bottles, connected, in some defunct
manner, with a brewer's business. A more
fashionable neighbourhood, it is said, eighty
years ago than now—never certainly a cheerful
one—wherein a boy being born on St. George's
day, 1775, began soon after to take interest in
the world of Covent Garden, and put to service
such spectacles of life as it afforded.

No knights to be seen there, nor, I imagine,
many beautiful ladies; their costume at least
disadvantageous, depending much on incumbency
of hat and feather, and short waists; the majesty
of men founded similarly on shoebuckles and
wigs;—impressive enough when Reynolds will
do his best for it; but not suggestive of much
ideal delight to a boy.

"Bello ovile dov' io dormii agnello:" of things
beautiful, besides men and women, dusty sunbeams up or down the street on summer morn-
ings; deep furrowed cabbage-leaves at the
greengrocer's; magnificence of oranges in wheel-
barrows round the corner; and Thames' shore
within three minutes' race.

None of these things very glorious; the best, however, that England, it seems, was then able to provide for a boy of gift: who, such as they are, loves them—never, indeed, forgets them. The short waists modify to the last his visions of Greek ideal. His foregrounds had always a succulent cluster or two of greengrocery at the corners. Enchanted oranges gleam in Covent Gardens of the Hesperides; and great ships go to pieces in order to scatter chests of them on the waves. That mist of early sunbeams in the London dawn crosses, many and many a time, the clearness of Italian air; and by Thames' shore, with its stranded barges and glidings of red sail, dearer to us than Lucerne lake or Venetian lagoon—by Thames' shore we will die.

With such circumstance round him in youth, let us note what necessary effects followed upon the boy. I assume him to have had Giorgione's sensibility (and more than Giorgione's, if that be possible) to colour and form. I tell you farther, and this fact you may receive trustfully, that his sensibility to human affection and distress was no less keen than even his sense for natural beauty—heart-sight deep as eyesight.

Consequently, he attaches himself with the faithfullest child-love to everything that bears an image of the place he was born in. No matter how ugly it is—has it anything about

it like Maiden Lane, or like Thames shore?
If so, it shall be painted for their sake. Hence,
to the very close of life, Turner could endure
uglinesses which no one else, of the same sensibility, would have borne with for an instant.
Dead brick walls, blank square windows, old
clothes, market-womanly types of humanity—
anything fishy and muddy, like Billingsgate or
Hungerford Market, had great attraction for him ;
black barges, patched sails, and every possible
condition of fog.

You will find these tolerations and affections
guiding or sustaining him to the last hour of his
life ; the notablest of all such endurances being
that of dirt. No Venetian ever draws anything
foul ; but Turner devoted picture after picture
to the illustration of effects of dinginess, smoke,
soot, dust, and dusty texture ; old sides of boats,
weedy roadside vegetation, dung-hills, straw-
yards, and all the soilings and stains of every
common labour.

And more than this, he not only could endure,
but enjoyed and looked for *litter*, like Covent
Garden wreck after the market. His pictures are
often full of it, from side to side ; their foregrounds
differ from all others in the natural way that
things have of lying about in them. Even his
richest vegetation, in ideal work, is confused ;
and he delights in shingle, débris, and heaps of
fallen stones. The last words he ever spoke

to me about a picture were in gentle exultation about his St. Gothard; "that *litter* of stones which I endeavoured to represent."

The second great result of this Covent Garden training was, understanding of and regard for the poor, whom the Venetians, we saw, despised ; whom, contrarily, Turner loved, and more than loved—understood. He got no romantic sight of them, but an infallible one, as he prowled about the end of his lane, watching night effects in the wintry streets ; nor sight of the poor alone, but of the poor in direct relations with the rich. He knew, in good and evil, what both classes thought of, and how they dealt with, each other.

Reynolds and Gainsborough, bred in country villages, learned there the country boy's reverential theory of "the squire," and kept it. They painted the squire and the squire's lady as centres of the movements of the universe, to the end of their lives. But Turner perceived the younger squire in other aspects about his lane, occurring prominently in its night scenery, as a dark figure, or one of two, against the moonlight. He saw also the working of city commerce, from endless warehouse, towering over Thames, to the back shop in the lane, with its stale herrings—highly interesting these last ; one of his father's best friends, whom he often afterwards visited affectionately at Bristol, being a fishmonger and glue-boiler ; which gives us a friendly turn of mind

towards herring-fishing, whaling, Calais pois-
sardes, and many other of our choicest subjects
in after-life; all this being connected with that
mysterious forest below London Bridge on one
side; and, on the other, with these masses of
human power and national wealth which weigh
upon us, at Covent Garden here, with strange
compression, and crush us into narrow Hand
Court.

"That mysterious forest below London Bridge"
—better for the boy than wood of pine, or grove
of myrtle. How he must have tormented the
watermen, beseeching them to let him crouch
anywhere in the bows, quiet as a log, so only
that he might get floated down there among the
ships, and round and round the ships, and with
the ships, and by the ships, and under the ships,
staring, and clambering;—these the only quite
beautiful things he can see in all the world,
except the sky; but these, when the sun is on
their sails, filling or falling, endlessly disordered
by sway of tide and stress of anchorage, beautiful
unspeakably; which ships also are inhabited by
glorious creatures—red-faced sailors, with pipes,
appearing over the gunwales, true knights, over
their castle parapets—the most angelic beings in
the whole compass of London world. And
Trafalgar happening long before we can draw
ships, we, nevertheless coax all current stories
out of the wounded sailors, do our best at

present to show Nelson's funeral streaming up the Thames; and vow that Trafalgar shall have its tribute of memory some day. Which, accordingly, is accomplished—once, with all our might, for its death; twice, with all our might, for its victory; thrice, in pensive farewell to the old Téméraire, and, with it, to that order of things.

Now this fond companying with sailors must have divided his time, it appears to me, pretty equally between Covent Garden and Wapping (allowing for incidental excursions to Chelsea on one side, and Greenwich on the other), which time he would spend pleasantly, but not magnificently, being limited in pocket-money, and leading a kind of " Poor-Jack " life on the river.

In some respects, no life could be better for a lad. But it was not calculated to make his ear fine to the niceties of language, nor form his moralities on an entirely regular standard. Picking up his first scraps of vigorous English chiefly at Deptford and in the markets, and his first ideas of female tenderness and beauty among nymphs of the barge and the barrow,—another boy might, perhaps, have become what people usually term "vulgar." But the original make and frame of Turner's mind being not vulgar, but as nearly as possible a combination of the minds of Keats and Dante, joining capricious waywardness, and intense openness to every fine pleasure of sense, and hot defiance of formal precedent, with a quite infinite tenderness, generosity, and desire of justice and truth—this kind of mind did not become vulgar, but very tolerant of vulgarity, even fond of it in some forms; and on the outside, visibly infected by it, deeply enough; the curious result, in its combination of elements, being to most people wholly incomprehensible. It was as if a cable had been woven of blood-crimson silk, and then tarred on the outside. People handled it, and the tar came off on their hands; red gleams were seen through the black, underneath, at the places where it had been strained. Was it ochre?—said the world—or red lead?

Schooled thus in manners, literature, and general moral principles at Chelsea and Wapping, we have finally to inquire concerning the most important point of all. We have seen the principal differences between this boy and Giorgione, as respects sight of the beautiful, understanding of poverty, of commerce, and of order of battle; then follows another cause of difference in our training—not slight,—the aspect of religion, namely, in the neighbourhood of Covent Garden. I say the aspect; for that was all the lad could judge by. Disposed, for the most part, to learn chiefly by his eyes, in this special matter he finds there is really no other way of learning. His father taught him "to lay one penny upon another." Of mother's teaching, we hear of none; of parish pastoral teaching, the reader may guess how much.— *M. P.*, V. IX. 9, § 1–10.

110. TURNER'S YOUTH.—Under these influences pass away the first reflective hours of life, with such conclusion as they can reach. In consequence of a fit of illness, he was taken—I cannot ascertain in what year—to live with an aunt, at Brentford; and here, I believe, received some schooling, which he seems to have snatched vigorously; getting knowledge, at least by translation, of the more picturesque classical authors, which he turned presently to use, as we shall see. Hence also, walks about Putney and Twickenham in the summer time acquainted him with the look of English meadow-ground in its restricted states of paddock and park; and with some round-headed appearances of trees, and stately entrances to houses of mark: the avenue at Bushey, and the iron gates and carved pillars of Hampton, impressing him apparently with great awe and admiration; so that in after-life his little country house is,—of all places in the world,—at Twickenham! Of swans and reedy shores he now learns the soft motion and the green mystery, in a way not to be forgotten.

And at last fortune wills that the lad's true life shall begin; and one summer's evening, after various wonderful stage-coach experiences on the north road, which gave him a love of stage-coaches ever after, he finds himself sitting alone among the Yorkshire hills.* For the first time, the silence of Nature round him, her freedom sealed to him, her glory opened to him. Peace at last; no roll of cart-wheel, nor mutter of sullen voices in the back shop; but curlew-cry in space of heaven, and welling of bell-toned streamlet by its shadowy rock. Freedom at last. Dead-wall, dark railing, fenced field, gated garden, all passed away like the dream of a prisoner; and behold, far as foot or eye can race or range, the moor, and cloud. Loveliness at last. It is here then, among these deserted vales! Not among men. Those pale, poverty-struck, or cruel faces;—that multitudinous, marred humanity—are not the only things that God has made. Here is something He has made which no one has marred. Pride of purple rocks, and river pools of blue, and tender wilderness of glittering trees, and misty lights of evening on immeasurable hills.

Beauty, and freedom, and peace; and yet another teacher, graver than these. Sound preaching at last here, in Kirkstall crypt, concerning fate and life. Here, where the dark pool reflects the chancel pillars, and the cattle lie

---

* I do not mean that this is his first acquaintance with the country, but the first impressive and touching one, after his mind was formed. The earliest sketches I found in the National collection are at Clifton and Bristol; the next, at Oxford.

in unhindered rest, the soft sunshine on their dappled bodies, instead of priests' vestments; their white furry hair ruffled a little, fitfully, by the evening wind deep-scented from the meadow thyme.

Consider deeply the import to him of this, his first sight of ruin, and compare it with the effect of the architecture that was around Giorgione. There were indeed aged buildings, at Venice, in his time, but none in decay. All ruin was removed, and its place filled as quickly as in our London; but filled always by architecture loftier and more wonderful than that whose place it took, the boy himself happy to work upon the walls of it; so that the idea of the passing away of the strength of men and beauty of their works never could occur to him sternly. Brighter and brighter the cities of Italy had been rising and broadening on hill and plain, for three hundred years. He saw only strength and immortality, could not but paint both; conceived the form of man as deathless, calm with power, and fiery with life.

Turner saw the exact reverse of this. In the present work of men, meanness, aimlessness, unsightliness: thin-walled, lath-divided, narrow-garreted houses of clay; booths of a darksome Vanity Fair, busily base.

But on Whitby Hill, and by Bolton Brook, remained traces of other handiwork. Men who

I.

T

could build had been there; and who also had
wrought, not merely for their own days. But
to what purpose? Strong faith, and steady
hands, and patient souls—can this, then, be all
you have left! this the sum of your doing on
the earth;—a nest whence the night-owl may
whimper to the brook, and a ribbed skeleton of
consumed arches, looming above the bleak banks
of mist, from its cliff to the sea?

As the strength of men to Giorgione, to Turner.
their weakness and vileness, were alone visible.
They themselves, unworthy or ephemeral; their
work, despicable, or decayed. In the Venetian's
eyes, all beauty depended on man's presence and
pride; in Turner's, on the solitude he had left,
and the humiliation he had suffered.

And thus the fate and issue of all his work
were determined at once. He must be a painter
of the strength of nature, there was no beauty
elsewhere than in that; he must paint also the
labour and sorrow and passing away of men:
this was the great human truth visible to him.

Their labour, their sorrow, and their death.
Mark the three. Labour; by sea and land, in
field and city, at forge and furnace, helm and
plough. No pastoral indolence nor classic pride
shall stand between him and the troubling of
the world; still less between him and the toil
of his country,—blind, tormented, unwearied,
marvellous England.

Also their Sorrow; Ruin of all their glorious
work, passing away of their thoughts and their
honour, mirage of pleasure, FALLACY OF HOPE;
gathering of weed on temple step; gaining of
wave on deserted strand; weeping of the mother
for the children, desolate by her breathless first-
born in the streets of the city, desolate by her
last sons slain, among the beasts of the field.

And their Death. That old Greek question
again;—yet unanswered. · The unconquerable
spectre still flitting among the forest trees at
twilight; rising ribbed out of the sea-sand;—
white, a strange Aphrodite,—out of the sea-
foam; stretching its gray, cloven wings among
the clouds; turning the light of their sunsets
into blood. This has to be looked upon, and
in a more terrible shape than ever Salvator or
Dürer saw it. The wreck of one guilty country
does not infer the ruin of all countries, and
need not cause general terror respecting the
laws of the universe. Neither did the orderly
and narrow succession of domestic joy and
sorrow in a small German community bring
the question in its breadth, or in any unresolv-
able shape, before the mind of Dürer. But
the English death—the European death of the
nineteenth century—was of another range and
power; more terrible a thousand-fold in its
merely physical grasp and grief; more terrible,
incalculably, in its mystery and shame. What

were the robber's casual pang, or the range
of the flying skirmish, compared to the work of
the axe, and the sword, and the famine, which
was done during this man's youth on all the
hills and plains of the Christian earth, from
Moscow to Gibraltar? He was eighteen years
old when Napoleon came down on Arcola. Look
on the map of Europe, and count the blood-stains
on it, between Arcola and Waterloo.

Not alone those blood-stains on the Alpine
snow, and the blue of the Lombard plain. The
English death was before his eyes also. No
decent, calculable, consoled dying; no passing
to rest like that of the aged burghers of Nuremberg town. No gentle processions to church-
yards among the fields, the bronze crests bossed
deep on the memorial tablets, and the skylark
singing above them from among the corn. But
the life trampled out in the slime of the street,
crushed to dust amidst the roaring of the wheel,
tossed countlessly away into howling winter wind
along five hundred leagues of rock-fanged shore.
Or, worst of all, rotted down to forgotten graves
through years of ignorant patience, and vain
seeking for help from man, for hope in God—
infirm, imperfect yearning, as of motherless
infants starving at the dawn; oppressed royalties
of captive thought, vague ague-fits of bleak,
amazed despair.

This was the sight which opened on the young

eyes, this the watchword sounding within the heart of Turner in his youth.

So taught, and prepared for his life's labour, sate the boy at last alone among his fair English hills; and began to paint, with cautious toil, the rocks, and fields, and trickling brooks, and soft white clouds of heaven.—*M. P.*, V. IX. 9, § 15–24.

111. TURNER'S MERIT.—There seems to be an impression on the minds of many students that Turner's merit consists in a peculiar style or manner, which, by reverent copying, may be caught from him; and that when they have once mastered this "dodge," and got into the way of the thing, they will all become Turners directly. Now they cannot possibly be under a graver or more consummate mistake. Turner's merit consists neither in style, nor in want of style, nor in any other copiable or communicable quality. It consists in this,—that, from the time he was ten years old till he was seventy, he never passed a day, and seldom an hour, without obtaining the accurate knowledge of some great natural fact; and, never forgetting anything he once knew, he keeps expressing this enormous and accumulated knowledge more and more redundantly till his death; so that you cannot understand one line of his work until you know the fact it represents, nor any part of the merit or wonderfulness of his

work till you have obtained a commensurate part of the knowledge which it contains. . . . And this being so, it is not only hopeless to attain any of his power by mere imitation of his drawings, but it is even harmful to copy them unintelligently, because they contain thousands of characters which are mere shorthand writing for things not otherwise representable in the given space or time; and which, until long looking at Nature has enabled you to read the cipher, will be in your imitations of them absurd and false.— *Introduction to Catalogue of Turners at Marlborough House.*

112. THE "BABYLON" OF TURNER.—Ten miles away, down the Euphrates, where it gleams last along the plain, he gives us a drift of dark elongated vapour, melting beneath into a dim haze which embraces the hills on the horizon. It is exhausted with its own motion, and broken up by the wind in its own mass into numberless groups of billowy and tossing fragments, which, beaten by the weight of storm down to the earth, are just lifting themselves again on wearied wings, and perishing in the effort. Above these, and far beyond them, the eye goes back to a broad sea of white illuminated mist, or rather cloud melted into rain, and absorbed again before that rain has fallen, but penetrated throughout, whether it be vapour or whether it be dew, with soft sunshine,

turning it as white as snow. Gradually, as it rises, the rainy fusion ceases. You cannot tell where the film of blue on the left begins, but it is deepening, deepening still; and the cloud, with its edge first invisible, then all but imaginary, then just felt when the eye is *not* fixed on it, and lost when it is, at last rises, keen from excessive distance, but soft and mantling in its body as a swan's bosom fretted by faint wind; heaving fitfully against the delicate deep blue, with white waves, whose forms are traced by the pale lines of opalescent shadow, shade only because the light is within it, and not upon it, and which break with their own swiftness into a driven line of level spray, winnowed into threads by the wind, and flung before the following vapour like those swift shafts of arrowy water which a great cataract shoots into the air beside it, trying to find the earth. Beyond these, again, rises a colossal mountain of gray cumulus, through whose shadowed sides the sunbeams penetrate in dim, sloping, rain-like shafts; and over which they fall in a broad burst of streaming light, sinking to the earth, and showing through their own visible radiance the three successive ranges of hills which connect its desolate plain with space. Above, the edgy summit of the cumulus, broken into fragments, recedes into the sky, which is peopled in its serenity with quiet multitudes of the white, soft, silent cirrus; and, under these, again, drift near the zenith disturbed and impatient shadows of a darker spirit, seeking rest and finding none.—*M. P.*, I. II. iii. 3, § 16.

113. TURNER'S SERMON OF SALISBURY PLAIN.—On that plain of Salisbury, he had been struck first by its widely-spacious pastoral life; and secondly, by its monuments of the two great religions of England—Druidical and Christian.

He was not a man to miss the possible connection of these impressions. He treats the shepherd life as a type of the ecclesiastical; and composes his two drawings so as to illustrate both.

In the drawing of Salisbury, the plain is swept by rapid but not distressful rain. The cathedral occupies the centre of the picture, towering high over the city, of which the houses (made on purpose smaller than they really are) are scattered about it like a flock of sheep. The cathedral is surrounded by a great light. The storm gives way at first in a subdued gleam over a distant parish church, then bursts down again, breaks away into full light about the cathedral, and passes over the city, in various sun and shade. In the foreground stands a shepherd leaning on his staff, watching his flock;—bareheaded: he has given his cloak to a group of children, who have covered themselves up with it, and are shrinking from the rain; his dog crouches under a bank; his sheep, for the most part, are resting quietly, some coming up the slope of the bank towards him.

The rain-clouds in this picture are wrought with a care which I have never seen equalled in any other sky of the same kind. It is the rain of blessing—abundant, but full of brightness; golden gleams are flying across the wet grass, and fall softly on the lines of willows in the valley—willows by the watercourses; the little brooks flash out here and there between them and the fields. Turn now to the Stonehenge. That, also, stands in great light; but it is the Gorgon light—the sword of Chrysaor is bared against it. The cloud of judgment hangs above. The rock pillars seem to reel before its slope, pale beneath the lightning. And nearer, in the darkness, the shepherd lies dead, his flock scattered.—*M. P.*, V. VII. 4, § 19, 20.

114. TURNER'S FACILITY.—The truly noble works are those in which, without effort, he has expressed his thoughts as they came, and forgotten himself; and in these the outpouring of invention is not less miraculous than the swiftness and obedience of the mighty hand that expresses it. Any one who examines the drawings may see the evidence of this facility, in the strange freshness and sharpness of every touch of colour; but when the multitude of

delicate touches, with which all the aërial tones are worked, is taken into consideration, it would still appear impossible that the drawing could have been completed with *ease*, unless we had direct evidence on the matter: fortunately, it is not wanting. There is a drawing in Mr. Fawkes's collection of a man-of-war taking in stores: it is of the usual size of those of the England series, about 16 inches by 11 : it does not appear one of the most highly finished, but it is still farther removed from slightness. The hull of a first-rate occupies nearly one half of the picture on the right, her bows towards the spectator, seen in sharp perspective from stem to stern, with all her port-holes, guns, anchors, and lower rigging elaborately detailed ; there are two other ships of the line in the middle distance, drawn with equal precision ; a noble breezy sea dancing against their broad bows, full of delicate drawing in its waves ; a store-ship beneath the hull of the larger vessel, and several other boats, and a complicated cloudy sky. It might appear no small exertion of mind to draw the detail of all this shipping down to the smallest ropes, from memory, in the drawing-room of a mansion in the middle of Yorkshire, even if considerable time had been given for the effort. But Mr. Fawkes sat beside the painter from the first stroke to the last. Turner took a piece of blank paper one morning after breakfast, outlined his ships, finished the drawing in three hours, and went out to shoot.—*Pre-Raphaelitism* (*O. R.*, I., § 220).

115. THE SLAVE SHIP.—I think, the noblest sea that Turner has ever painted, and, if so, the noblest certainly ever painted by man, is that of the Slave Ship, the chief Academy picture of the Exhibition of 1840. It is a sunset on the Atlantic, after prolonged storm; but the storm is partially lulled, and the torn and streaming rain-clouds are moving in scarlet lines to lose themselves in the hollow of the night. The whole surface of sea included in the picture is divided into two ridges of enormous swell, not high, nor local, but a low broad heaving of the whole ocean, like the lifting of its bosom by deep-drawn breath after the torture of the storm. Between these two ridges the fire of the sunset falls along the trough of the sea, dyeing it with an awful but glorious light, the intense and lurid splendour which burns like gold, and bathes like blood. Along this fiery path and valley, the tossing waves, by which the swell of the sea is restlessly divided, lift themselves in dark, indefinite, fantastic forms, each casting a faint and ghastly shadow behind it along the illumined foam. They do not rise everywhere, but three or four together in wild groups, fitfully and furiously, as the under strength of the swell

compels or permits them; leaving between them
treacherous spaces of level and whirling water,
now lighted with green and lamp-like fire, now
flashing back the gold of the declining sun, now
fearfully dyed from above with the indistinguish-
able images of the burning clouds, which fall
upon them in flakes of crimson and scarlet, and
give to the reckless waves the added motion
of their own fiery flying. Purple and blue,
the lurid shadows of the hollow breakers are
cast upon the mist of night, which gathers cold
and low, advancing like the shadow of death
upon the guilty ship as it labours amidst the
lightning of the sea, its thin masts written upon
the sky in lines of blood, girded with condemnation in that fearful hue which signs the sky with
horror and mixes its flaming flood with the sunlight, and, cast far along the desolate heave of
the sepulchral waves, incarnadines the multitudinous sea.—*M. P.*, I. II. v. 3, § 39.

116. TURNER'S COLOUR.—Claude and Cuyp
had painted the sun*shine*, Turner alone, the sun
colour.

Observe this accurately. Those easily understood effects of afternoon light, gracious and
sweet so far as they reach, are produced by the
softly warm or yellow rays of the sun falling
through mist. They are low in tone, even in
nature, and disguise the colours of objects. They

are imitable even by persons who have little or
no gift of colour, if the tones of the picture are
kept low and in true harmony, and the reflected
lights warm. But they never could be painted by
great colourists. The fact of blue and crimson
being effaced by yellow and gray, puts such
effect at once out of the notice or thought of a
colourist, unless he has some special interest in
the motive of it. You might as well ask a
musician to compose with only three notes, as
Titian to paint without crimson and blue. Accordingly the colourists in general, feeling that
no other than this yellow sunshine was imitable,
refused it, and painted in twilight, when the
colour was full. Therefore, from the imperfect
colourists,—from Cuyp, Claude, Both, Wilson,
we get deceptive effect of sunshine; never
from the Venetians, from Rubens, Reynolds, or
Velasquez. From these we get only conventional substitutions for it, Rubens being especially daring in frankness of symbol.

Turner, however, as a landscape painter, had
to represent sunshine of one kind or another.
He went steadily through the subdued golden
chord, and painted Cuyp's favourite effect, "sun
rising through vapour," for many a weary year.
But this was not enough for him. He must
paint the sun in his strength, the sun rising
not through vapour. If you glance at that
Apollo slaying the Python, you will see there

is rose colour and blue on the clouds, as well as gold; and if then you turn to the Apollo in the Ulysses and Polyphemus—his horses are rising beyond the horizon,—you see he is not "rising through vapour," but above it;—gaining somewhat of a victory over vapour, it appears. . . .

The peculiar innovation of Turner was the perfection of the colour chord by means of *scarlet*. Other painters had rendered the golden tones, and the blue tones, of sky; Titian especially the last, in perfectness. But none had dared to paint, none seem to have seen, the scarlet and purple.

Nor was it only in seeing this colour in vividness when it occurred in full light, that Turner differed from preceding painters. His most distinctive innovation as a colourist was his discovery of the scarlet *shadow*. "True, there is a sunshine whose light is golden, and its shadow gray; but there is another sunshine, and that the purest, whose light is white, and its shadow scarlet." This was the essentially offensive, inconceivable thing, which he could not be believed in. There was some ground for the incredulity, because no colour is vivid enough to express the pitch of light of pure white sunshine, so that the colour given without the true intensity of light *looks* false. Nevertheless, Turner could not but report of the colour truly. "I must indeed be lower in the key, but that is no reason why I should be false in the note. Here is sunshine which glows even when subdued ; it has not cool shade, but fiery shade." This is the glory of sunshine.—*M. P.*, V. IX. II, § 3, 4, 6.

117. TURNER'S ST. GOTHARD.—Turner was always from his youth fond of stones. Whether large or small, loose or embedded, hewn into cubes or worn into boulders, he loved them as much as William Hunt loves pineapples and plums. So that this great litter of fallen stones, which to any one else would have been simply disagreeable, was to Turner much the same as if the whole valley had been filled with plums and pineapples, and delighted him exceedingly, much more than even the gorge of Dazio Grande just above. But that gorge had its effect upon him also, and was still not well out of his head when the diligence stopped at the bottom of the hill, just at that turn of the road on the right of the bridge ; which favourable opportunity Turner seized to make what he called a "memorandum" of the place, composed of a few pencil scratches on a bit of thin paper, that would roll up with others of the sort and go into his pocket afterwards. These pencil scratches he put a few blots of colour upon (I suppose at Bellinzona the same evening, certainly *not* upon the spot), and showed me this blotted sketch when he came home. I asked him to make me a drawing of

it, which he did, and casually told me afterwards (a rare thing for him to do) that he liked the drawing he had made.

The whole place is altered in scale, and brought up to the general majesty of the higher forms of the Alps. There are a few trees rooted in the rock on this side of the gallery, showing, by comparison, that it is not above four or five hundred feet high. These trees Turner cuts away, and gives the rock a height of about a thousand feet, so as to imply more power and danger in the avalanche coming down the couloir.

Next, he raises, in a still greater degree, all the mountains beyond, putting three or four ranges instead of one, but uniting them into a single massy bank at their base, which he makes overhang the valley, and thus reduces it nearly to such a chasm as that which he had just passed through above, so as to unite the expression of this ravine with that of the stony valley. The few trees, in the hollow of the glen, he feels to be contrary in spirit to the stones, and fells them, as he did the others; so also he feels the bridge in the foreground, by its slenderness, to contradict the aspect of violence in the torrent; he thinks the torrent and avalanches should have it all their own way hereabouts; so he strikes down the nearer bridge, and restores the one farther off, where the force of the stream may be supposed less. Next, the bit of road on the right, above the bank, is not built on a wall, nor on arches high enough to give the idea of an Alpine road in general; so he makes the arches taller, and the bank steeper, introducing, as we shall see presently, a reminiscence from the upper part of the pass.

I say, he "*thinks*" this, and "introduces" that. But, strictly speaking, he does not think at all. If he thought, he would instantly go wrong; it is only the clumsy and uninventive artist who thinks. All these changes come into his head involuntarily; an entirely imperative dream, crying, "Thus it must be," has taken possession of him; he can see, and do, no otherwise than as the dream directs.

This is especially to be remembered with respect to the next incident—the introduction of figures. Most persons to whom I have shown the drawing, and who feel its general character, regret that there is any living thing in it; they say it destroys the majesty of its desolation. But the dream said not so to Turner. The dream insisted particularly upon the great fact of its having come by the road. The torrent was wild, the stones were wonderful; but the most wonderful thing of all was how we ourselves, the dream and I, ever got here. By our feet we could not—by the clouds we could not—by any ivory gates we could not—in no other wise could we have come than by the coach road. One of

I.

U

the great elements of sensation, all the day long, has been that extraordinary road, and its goings on, and gettings about; here, under avalanches of stones, and among insanities of torrents, and overhangings of precipices, much tormented and driven to all manner of makeshifts and coils to this side and the other, still the marvellous road persists in going on, and that so smoothly and safely, that it is not merely great diligences, going in a caravannish manner, with whole teams of horses, that can traverse it, but little postchaises with small post-boys, and a pair of ponies. And the dream declared that the full essence and soul of the scene, and consummation of all the wonderfulness of the torrents and Alps, lay in a postchaise with small ponies and post-boy, which accordingly it insisted upon Turner's inserting, whether he liked it or not, at the turn of the road.—*M. P.*, IV. V. 2, § 13–15.

118. TURNER'S HEYSHAM.—The subject is a simple north-country village, on the shore of Morecambe Bay; not in the common sense a picturesque village; there are no pretty bow-windows, or red roofs, or rocky steps of entrance to the rustic doors, or quaint gables; nothing but a single street of thatched and chiefly clay-built cottages, ranged in a somewhat monotonous line, the roofs so green with moss that at first we

hardly discern the houses from the fields and trees. The village street is closed at the end by a wooden gate, indicating the little traffic there is on the road through it, and giving it something the look of a large farmstead, in which a right of way lies through the yard. The road which leads to this gate is full of ruts, and winds down a bad bit of hill between two broken banks of moor ground, succeeding immediately to the few enclosures which surround the village; they can hardly be called gardens: but a decayed fragment or two of fencing fill the gaps in the bank; a clothes-line, with some clothes on it, striped blue and red, and a smock-frock, is stretched between the trunks of some stunted willows; a *very* small haystack and pig-stye being seen at the back of the cottage beyond. An empty, two-wheeled, lumbering cart, drawn by a pair of horses with huge wooden collars, the driver sitting lazily in the sun, sideways on the leader, is going slowly home along the rough road, it being about country dinner-time. At the end of the village there is a better house, with three chimneys and a dormer window in its roof, and the roof is of stone shingle instead of thatch, but very rough. This house is no doubt the clergyman's: there is some smoke from one of its chimneys, none from any other in the village; this smoke is from the lowest chimney at the back, evidently that of the kitchen, and it is rather thick, the fire not

having been long lighted. A few hundred yards
from the clergyman's house, nearer the shore, is
the church, discernible from the cottages only by
its low two-arched belfry, a little neater than one
would expect in such a village; perhaps lately
built by the Puseyite incumbent: and beyond
the church, close to the sea, are two fragments
of a border war-tower, standing on their circular
mound, worn on its brow deep into edges and
furrows by the feet of the village children. On
the bank of moor, which forms the foreground,
are a few cows, the carter's dog barking at a
vixenish one: the milkmaid is feeding another,
a gentle white one, which turns its head to her,
expectant of a handful of fresh hay, which she
has brought for it in her blue apron, fastened up
round her waist; she stands with her pail on her
head, evidently the village coquette, for she has
a neat bodice, and pretty striped petticoat under
the blue apron, and red stockings. Nearer us,
the cowherd, bare-footed, stands on a piece of
the limestone rock (for the ground is thistly and
not pleasurable to bare feet);—whether boy or
girl we are not sure: it may be a boy, with a
girl's wornout bonnet on, or a girl with a pair of
ragged trowsers on; probably the first, as the
old bonnet is evidently useful to keep the sun out
of our eyes when we are looking for strayed cows
among the moorland hollows, and helps us at
present to watch (holding the bonnet's edge down)

the quarrel of the vixenish cow with the dog,
which, leaning on our long stick, we allow to proceed without any interference. A little to the right
the hay is being got in, of which the milkmaid
has just taken her apronful to the white cow;
but the hay is very thin, and cannot well be
raked up because of the rocks; we must glean
it like corn, hence the smallness of our stack
behind the willows; and a woman is pressing
a bundle of it hard together, kneeling against
the rock's edge, to carry it safely to the hay-cart
without dropping any. Beyond the village is a
rocky hill, deep set with brushwood, a square
crag or two of limestone emerging here and there,
with pleasant turf on their brows, heaved in russet
and mossy mounds against the sky, which, clear
and calm, and as golden as the moss, stretches
down behind it towards the sea. A single cottage
just shows its roof over the edge of the hill,
looking seawards: perhaps one of the village
shepherds is a sea captain now, and may have
built it there, that his mother may first see the
sails of his ship whenever it runs into the bay.
Then under the hill, and beyond the border
tower, is the blue sea itself, the waves flowing
in over the sand in long curved lines slowly;
shadows of cloud, and gleams of shallow water
on white sand alternating—miles away; but no
sail is visible, not one fisher-boat on the beach,
not one dark speck on the quiet horizon. Beyond

all are the Cumberland mountains, clear in the sun, with rosy light on all their crags.

I should think the reader cannot but feel the kind of harmony there is in this composition; the entire purpose of the painter to give us the impression of wild, yet gentle, country life, monotonous as the succession of the noiseless waves, patient and enduring as the rocks; but peaceful, and full of health and quiet hope, and sanctified by the pure mountain air and baptismal dew of heaven, falling softly between days of toil and nights of innocence.—*E. D.*, III., § 244, 245.

119. THE TRAGIC FEELING OF TURNER.— Turner's sense of beauty was perfect; deeper, therefore, far than Byron's; only that of Keats and Tennyson being comparable with it. And Turner's love of truth was as stern and patient as Dante's; so that when over these great capacities come the shadows of despair, the wreck is infinitely sterner and more sorrowful. With no sweet home for his childhood,—friendless in youth, loveless in manhood,—and hopeless in death, Turner was what Dante might have been, without the "bello ovile," without Casella, without Beatrice, and without Him who gave them all, and took them all away. Through all the remainder of his life, wherever he looked, he saw ruin.

Ruin, and twilight. What was the distinctive

effect of light which he introduced, such as no
man had painted before ? Brightness, indeed, he
gave, as we have seen, because it was true and
right; but in this he only perfected what others
had attempted. His own favourite light is not
Æglé, but Hesperid Æglé. Fading of the last
rays of sunset. Faint breathing of the sorrow
of night.

And fading of sunset, note also, on ruin. I
cannot but wonder that this difference between
Turner's work and previous art-conception has
not been more observed. None of the great
early painters draw ruins, except compulsorily.
The shattered buildings introduced by them are
shattered artificially, like models. There is no
real sense of decay; whereas Turner only
momentarily dwells on anything else than ruin.
Take up the Liber Studiorum, and observe how
this feeling of decay and humiliation gives solemnity to all its simplest subjects; even to his view
of daily labour. I have marked its tendency in
examining the design of the Mill and Lock, but
observe its continuance through the book. There
is no exultation in thriving city, or mart, or in
happy rural toil, or harvest gathering. Only the
grinding at the mill, and patient striving with
hard conditions of life. Observe the two disordered and poor farm-yards, cart, and plough-
share, and harrow rotting away : note the pastoral
by the brook side, with its neglected stream and

haggard trees, and bridge with the broken rail, and decrepit children—fever-struck—one sitting stupidly by the stagnant stream, the other in rags, and with an old man's hat on, and lame, leaning on a stick. Then the "Hedging and Ditching," with its bleak sky and blighted trees —hacked, and bitten, and starved by the clay soil into something between trees and fire-wood; its meanly-faced, sickly labourers—pollard labourers, like the willow trunk they hew; and the slatternly peasant-woman, with worn cloak and battered bonnet—an English Dryad. Then the Watermill, beyond the fallen steps, over-grown with the thistle: itself a ruin, mud-built at first, now propped on both sides;—the planks torn from its cattle-shed; a feeble beam, splintered at the end, set against the dwelling-house from the ruined pier of the watercourse; the old mill-stone—useless for many a day—half buried in slime, at the bottom of the wall; the listless children, listless dog, and the poor gleaner bring-ing her single sheaf to be ground. Then the "Peat Bog," with its cold, dark rain, and danger-ous labour. And last and chief, the mill in the valley of the Chartreuse. Another than Turner would have painted the convent: but he had no sympathy with the hope, no mercy for the in-dolence of the monk. He painted the mill in the valley. Precipice overhanging it, and wildness of dark forest round; blind rage and strength of

mountain torrent rolled beneath it,—calm sunset
above, but fading from the glen, leaving it to its
roar of passionate waters and sighing of pine-
branches in the night.

Such is his view of human labour. Of human
pride, see what records. Morpeth tower, roofless
and black; gate of old Winchelsea wall, the flock
of sheep driven *round* it, not through it; and
Rievaulx choir, and Kirkstall crypt; and Dun-
stanborough, wan above the sea; and Chepstow,
with arrowy light through traceried windows;
and Lindisfarne, with failing height of wasted
shaft and wall; and last and sweetest, Raglan,
in utter solitude, amidst the wild wood of its own
pleasance; the towers rounded with ivy, and the
forest roots choked with undergrowth, and the
brook languid amidst lilies and sedges. Legends
of gray knights and enchanted ladies keeping the
woodman's children away at the sunset.

These are his types of human pride. Of human
love: Procris, dying by the arrow; Hesperie, by
the viper's fang; and Rizpah, more than dead,
beside her children.—*M. P.*, V. IX. 11, § 26–29.

120. TURNER'S AGE AND DEATH.—Imagine
what it was for a man to live seventy years in
this hard world, with the kindest heart, and
the noblest intellect of his time, and never to
meet with a single word or ray of sympathy,
until he felt himself sinking into the grave.

From the time he knew his true greatness all
the world was turned against him : he held his
own; but it could not be without roughness
of bearing, and hardening of the temper, if not
of the heart.   No one understood him, no one
trusted him, and every one cried out against
him.   Imagine, any of you, the effect upon your
own minds, if every voice that you heard from
the human beings around you were raised, year
after year, through all your lives, only in condemnation of your efforts, and denial of your
success.   This may be borne, and borne easily,
by men who have fixed religious principles, or
supporting domestic ties.   But Turner had no
one to teach him in his youth, and no one to
love him in his old age.   Respect and affection,
if they came at all, came unbelieved, or came
too late.   Naturally irritable, though kind—
naturally suspicious, though generous—the gold
gradually became dim, and the most fine gold
changed, or, if not changed, overcast and clouded.
The deep heart was still beating, but it was
beneath a dark and melancholy mail, between
whose joints, however, sometimes the slightest
arrows found entrance, and power of giving pain.
He received no consolation in his last years,
nor in his death.   Cut off in great part from
all society—first, by labour, and at last by sick-
ness—hunted to his grave by the malignities
of small critics, and the jealousies of hopeless

rivalry, he died in the house of a stranger—
one companion of his life, and one only, staying
with him to the last. The window of his death-
chamber was turned towards the west, and the
sun shone upon his face in its setting, and rested
there, as he expired.—*L. A. P.*, III., § 106.

121. TURNER'S PLACE IN HISTORY.—This
man, this Turner, of whom you have known so
little while he was living among you, will one
day take his place beside Shakespere and Verulam, in the annals of the light of England.

Yes: beside Shakespere and Verulam, a third
star in that central constellation, round which,
in the astronomy of intellect, all other stars
make their circuit. By Shakespere, humanity
was unsealed to you; by Verulam, the *principles*
of Nature; and by Turner, her *aspect*. All these
were sent to unlock one of the gates of light,
and to unlock it for the first time. But of all
the three, though not the greatest, Turner was
the most unprecedented in his work. Bacon
did what Aristotle had attempted; Shakespere
did perfectly what Æschylus did partially; but
none before Turner had lifted the veil from the
face of nature; the majesty of the hills and
forests had received no interpretation, and the
clouds passed unrecorded from the face of the
heaven which they adorned, and of the earth
to which they ministered.—*L. A. P.*, III., § 101.

122. SAMUEL PROUT.—There is not a landscape of recent times in which the treatment of the architectural features has not been affected, however unconsciously, by principles which were first developed by Prout. Of those principles the most original were his familiarisation of the sentiment, while he elevated the subject, of the picturesque. That character had been sought, before his time, either in solitude or in rusticity; it was supposed to belong only to the savageness of the desert or the simplicity of the hamlet; it lurked beneath the brows of rocks, and the eaves of cottages; to seek it in a city would have been deemed an extravagance, to raise it to the height of a cathedral, a heresy. Prout did both, and both simultaneously; he found and proved, in the busy shadows and sculptured gables of the Continental street, sources of picturesque delight as rich and as interesting as those which had been sought amidst the darkness of thickets and the eminence of rocks; and he contrasted with the familiar circumstances of urban life, the majesty and the aërial elevation of the most noble architecture, expressing its details in more splendid accumulation, and with a more patient love than ever had been reached or manifested before his time by any artist who introduced such subjects as members of a general composition. He thus became the interpreter of a great period of the world's history, of that in which

age and neglect had cast the interest of ruin over the noblest ecclesiastical structures of Europe, and in which there had been born at their feet a generation other in its feelings and thoughts than that to which they owed their existence, a generation which understood not their meaning, and regarded not their beauty, and which yet had a character of its own, full of vigour, animation, and originality, which rendered the grotesque association of the circumstances of its ordinary and active life with the solemn memorialism of the elder building, one which rather pleased by the strangeness than pained by the violence of its contrast.—*Art Journal,* March 1849 (*O. R.,* I., § 147).

123. PEASANT BOYS OF MURILLO AND WILLIAM HUNT.—Go into the Dulwich Gallery, and meditate for a little over that much celebrated picture of the two beggar boys, one eating, lying on the ground, the other standing beside him. We have among our own painters one who cannot indeed be set beside Murillo as a painter of Madonnas, for he is a pure Naturalist, and, never having seen a Madonna, does not paint any ; but who, as a painter of beggar or peasant boys, may be set beside Murillo, or any one else,—W. Hunt. He loves peasant boys, because he finds them more roughly and picturesquely dressed, and more healthily coloured,

than others. And he paints all that he sees in
them fearlessly; all the health and humour,
and freshness and vitality, together with such
awkwardness and stupidity, and what else of
negative or positive harm there may be in the
creature; but yet so that on the whole we love
it, and find it perhaps even beautiful, or, if not,
at least we see that there is capability of good
in it, rather than of evil; and all is lighted up
by a sunshine and sweet colour that makes the
smock frock as precious as cloth of gold. But
look at those two ragged and vicious vagrants
that Murillo has gathered out of the street.
You smile at first, because they are eating so
naturally, and their roguery is so complete.
But is there anything else than roguery there,
or was it well for the painter to give his time to
the painting of those repulsive and wicked children? Do you feel moved with any charity
towards children as you look at them? Are we
the least more likely to take any interest in
ragged schools, or to help the next pauper child
that comes in our way, because the painter has
shown us a cunning beggar feeding greedily?
Mark the choice of the act. He might have
shown hunger in other ways, and given interest
to even this act of eating, by making the face
wasted, or the eye wistful. But he did not care
to do this. He delighted merely in the disgusting manner of eating, the food filling the cheek;

the boy is not hungry, else he would not turn round to talk and grin as he eats.

But observe another point in the lower figure. It lies so that the sole of the foot is turned towards the spectator; not because it would have lain less easily in another attitude, but that the painter may draw, and exhibit, the gray dust engrained in the foot. Do not call this the painting of nature: it is mere delight in foulness. The lesson, if there be any, in the picture, is not one whit the stronger. We all know that a beggar's bare foot cannot be clean; there is no need to thrust its degradation into the light, as if no human imagination were vigorous enough for its conception.—*S. V.*, II. VI., § 60.

124. WILLIAM HUNT'S HOMELINESS.—A certain portion of this divine spirit is visible even in the lower examples of all the true men; it is, indeed, perhaps, the clearest test of their belonging to the true and great group, that they are continually touching what to the multitude appear vulgarities. The higher a man stands, the more the word "vulgar" becomes unintelligible to him. Vulgar? what, that poor farmer's girl of William Hunt's, bred in the stable, putting on her Sunday gown, and pinning her best cap out of the green and red pin-cushion! Not so; she may be straight on the road to those high heavens, and may shine hereafter as one of the stars in the

firmament for ever. Nay, even that lady in the satin bodice with her arm laid over a balustrade to show it, and her eyes turned up to heaven to show them ; and the sportsman waving his rifle for the terror of beasts, and displaying his perfect dress for the delight of men, are kept, by the very misery and vanity of them, in the thoughts of a great painter, at a sorrowful level, somewhat above vulgarity. It is only when the minor painter takes them on his easel, that they become things for the universe to be ashamed of.

We may dismiss this matter of vulgarity in plain and few words, at least as far as regards art. There is never vulgarity in a *whole* truth, however commonplace. It may be unimportant or painful. It cannot be vulgar. Vulgarity is only in concealment of truth, or in affectation.— *M. P.*, III. IV. 7, § 9.

125. BRETT'S "VAL D'AOSTA."—If any simple-minded, quietly-living person, indisposed towards railroad stations or crowded inns, cares to know in an untroublous and uncostly way what a Piedmontese valley is like in July, there it is for him. Rocks overlaid with velvet and fur to stand on, in the first place. If you look close into the velvet you will find it is jewelled and set with stars in a stately way. White poplars by the roadside, shaking silvery in the wind. I regret to say, the wind is apt to come up the

Val d' Aosta in an ill-tempered and rude manner,
turning leaves thus the wrong side out; but it
will be over in a moment. Beyond the poplars
you may see the slopes of arable and vineyard
ground such as give the wealth and life to Italy
which she idly trusts in. Ground laid ages ago
in wreaths, like new cut hay by the mountain
streams, now terraced and trimmed into all
gentle service. If you want to know what vines
look like under Italian training (far from the best),
that is the look of them—the dark spots and
irregular cavities, seen through the broken green
of their square-set ranks, distinguishing them
at any distance from the continuous pale fields
of low set staff and leaf, divided by no gaps of
gloom, which clothe a true *vine* country. There,
down in the mid valley, you see what pasture
and meadow-land we have, we Piedmontese, with
our hamlet and cottage life, and groups of
glorious wood. Just beyond the rock are two
splendid sweet chestnut trees, with forming
fruit, good for making bread of, no less than
maize; lower down, far to the left, a furlong or
two of the main stream with its white shore and
alders: not beautiful, for it has come down into
all this fair country from the Cormayeur glaciers,
and is yet untamed, cold, and furious, incapable
of rest. But above, there is rest, where the sunshine streams into iridescence through branches
of pine, and turns the pastures into strange

golden clouds, half grass, half dew; for the
shadows of the great hills have kept the dew
there since morning. Rest also, calm enough
among the ridges of rock and forest that heap
themselves into that purple pyramid, high on
the right. Look well into the making of it,—it
is indeed so, that a great mountain is built and
bears itself, and its forest fringes, and village
jewels—for those white spots far up the ravine
are villages—and peasant dynasties are hidden
among the film of blue. And above all are other
more desolate dynasties—the crowns that cannot
shake—of jagged rock; they also true and right,
even to their finest serration. So it is, that the
snow lies on those dark diadems for ever. A
notable picture, truly; a possession of much,
within a few feet square.—*Academy Notes:
No. V.*

126. A PRE-RAPHAELITE MASTERPIECE.—
I speak of the picture called "The Light of the
World," by Mr. Holman Hunt. Standing by
it yesterday for upwards of an hour, I watched
the effect it produced upon the passers-by. Few
stopped to look at it, and those who did almost
invariably with some contemptuous expression,
founded on what appeared to them the absurdity
of representing the Saviour with a lantern in
His hand. Now, it ought to be remembered that,
whatever may be the faults of a Pre-Raphaelite

picture, it must at least have taken much time; and therefore it may not unwarrantably be presumed that conceptions which are to be laboriously realised are not adopted in the first instance without some reflection. So that the spectator may surely question with himself whether the objections which now strike every one in a moment might not possibly have occurred to the painter himself, either during the time devoted to the design of the picture, or the months of labour required for its execution; and whether, therefore, there may not be some reason for his persistence in such an idea, not discoverable at the first glance.

Mr. Hunt has never explained his work to me. I give what appears to me its palpable interpretation.

The legend beneath it is the beautiful verse :— "Behold I stand at the door and knock. If any man hear my voice, and open the door, I will come in to him, and will sup with him, and he with me."—Rev. iii. 20. On the left-hand side of the picture is seen this door of the human soul. It is fast barred : its bars and nails are rusty ; it is knitted and bound to its stanchions by creeping tendrils of ivy, showing that it has never been opened. A bat hovers about it ; its threshold is overgrown with brambles, nettles, and fruitless corn,—the wild grass " whereof the mower filleth not his hand, nor he that bindeth the sheaves his bosom." Christ approaches it in the night time,—Christ in His everlasting offices, of prophet, priest, and king. He wears the white robe, representing the power of the Spirit upon Him; the jewelled robe and breast-plate, representing the sacerdotal investiture; the rayed crown of gold, inwoven with the crown of thorns; not dead thorns, but now bearing soft leaves, for the healing of the nations.

Now, when Christ enters any human heart, He bears with Him a two-fold light: first, the light of conscience, which displays past sin, and afterwards the light of peace, the hope of salva-tion. The lantern, carried in Christ's left hand, is this light of conscience. Its fire is red and fierce; it falls only on the closed door, on the weeds which encumber it, and on an apple shaken from one of the trees of the orchard, thus marking that the entire awakening of the conscience is not merely to committed, but to hereditary guilt.

The light is suspended by a chain, wrapt about the wrist of the figure, showing that the light which reveals sin appears to the sinner also to chain the hand of Christ.

The light which proceeds from the head of the figure, on the contrary, is that of the hope of salvation; it springs from the crown of thorns, and, though itself sad, subdued, and full of softness, is yet so powerful that it entirely melts into the glow of it the forms of the leaves and boughs, which it crosses, showing that every earthly object must be hidden by this light, where its sphere extends.

I believe there are very few persons on whom the picture, thus justly understood, will not produce a deep impression. For my own part, I think it one of the very noblest works of sacred art ever produced in this or any other age.— *Letter to the " Times "* (*A. C.*, I., p. 98–101).

V.

ARCHITECTURE AND SCULPTURE.

127. TWO FINE ARTS ONLY.—There are only two fine arts possible to the human race, sculpture and painting. What we call architecture is only the association of these in noble masses, or the placing them in fit places. All architecture other than this is, in fact, mere *building;* and though it may sometimes be graceful, as in the groinings of an abbey roof; or sublime, as in the battlements of a border tower; there is, in such examples of it, no more exertion of the powers of high art, than in the gracefulness of a well-ordered chamber, or the nobleness of a well-built ship of war.

All high art consists in the carving or painting natural objects, chiefly figures: it has always subject and meaning, never consisting solely in arrangement of lines, or even of colours. It always paints or carves something that it sees or believes in; nothing ideal or uncredited. For the most part, it paints and carves the men and things that are visible around it. And as soon as we possess a body of sculptors able, and willing, and having leave from the English public, to carve on the façades of our cathedrals portraits of the living bishops, deans, canons, and choristers, who are to minister in the said cathedrals; and on the façades of our public buildings, portraits of the men chiefly moving or acting in the same; and on our buildings, generally, the birds and flowers which are singing and budding in the fields around them, we shall have a school of English architecture. Not till then.—*S. L. A.*, Preface, original ed. (app. I., ed. of 1880).

128. THE FUNCTION OF ARCHITECTURE.— We are forced, for the sake of accumulating our power and knowledge, to live in cities: but such advantage as we have in association with each other is in great part counterbalanced by our loss of fellowship with Nature. We cannot all have our gardens now, nor our pleasant fields to meditate in at eventide. Then the function of our architecture is, as far as may be, to replace these; to tell us about Nature; to possess us with memories of her quietness; to be solemn and full of tenderness, like her, and rich in portraitures of her; full of delicate imagery of the flowers we can no more gather, and of the living creatures now far away from us in their own solitude. If ever you felt or found this in a London street,—if ever it furnished you with one serious thought, or one ray of true and gentle

pleasure,—if there is in your heart a true delight in its grim railings and dark casements, and wasteful finery of shops, and feeble coxcombry of club-houses,—it is well: promote the building of more like them. But if they never taught you anything, and never made you happier as you passed beneath them, do not think they have any mysterious goodness nor occult sublimity. Have done with the wretched affectation, the futile barbarism, of pretending to enjoy; for, as surely as you know that the meadow grass, meshed with fairy rings, is better than the wood pavement, cut into hexagons; and as surely as you know the fresh winds and sunshine of the upland are better than the choke-damp of the vault, or the gas-light of the ball-room, you may know, as I told you that you should, that the good architecture, which has life, and truth, and joy in it, is better than the bad architecture, which has death, dishonesty, and vexation of heart in it, from the beginning to the end of time.—*S. V.*, I. xxx., § 6.

129. THE SIGNIFICANCE OF ARCHITECTURE. —We take pleasure, or *should* take pleasure, in architectural construction altogether as the manifestation of an admirable human intelligence; it is not the strength, not the size, not the finish of the work which we are to venerate: rocks are always stronger, mountains always larger, all

natural objects more finished; but it is the intelligence and resolution of man in overcoming
physical difficulty which are to be the source
of our pleasure and subject of our praise. And
again, in decoration or beauty, it is less the actual
loveliness of the thing produced, than the choice
and invention concerned in the production, which
are to delight us; the love and the thoughts of
the workman more than his work: his work
must always be imperfect, but his thoughts and
affections may be true and deep.—*S. V.*, I.
II., § 4.

130. THE SUBLIME IN ARCHITECTURE.—
Besides this expression of living authority and
power, there is, however, a sympathy in the
forms of noble building, with what is most
sublime in natural things; and it is the governing Power directed by this sympathy, whose
operation I shall at present endeavour to trace,
abandoning all inquiry into the more abstract
fields of Invention: for this latter faculty, and the
questions of proportion and arrangement connected with its discussion, can only be rightly
examined in a general view of all the arts; but
its sympathy, in architecture, with the vast con-
trolling powers of Nature herself, is special, and
may shortly be considered; and that with the
more advantage, that it has, of late, been little
felt or regarded by architects. I have seen, in

recent efforts, much contest between two schools,
one affecting originality, and the other legality—
many attempts at beauty of design—many ingenious adaptations of construction; but I have
never seen any aim at the expression of abstract
power; never any appearance of a consciousness
that, in this primal art of man, there is room for
the marking of his relations with the mightiest,
as well as the fairest, works of God; and that
those works themselves have been permitted, by
their Master and his, to receive an added glory
from their association with earnest efforts of
human thought.   In the edifices of Man there
should be found reverent worship and following,
not only of the spirit which rounds the pillars
of the forest, and arches the vault of the avenue
—which gives veining to the leaf, and polish to
the shell, and grace to every pulse that agitates
animal organisation,—but of that also which
reproves the pillars of the earth, and builds up
her barren precipices into the coldness of the
clouds, and lifts her shadowy cones of mountain
purple into the pale arch of the sky; for these,
and other glories more than these, refuse not to
connect themselves, in his thoughts, with the
work of his own hand; the gray cliff loses not its
nobleness when it reminds us of some Cyclopean
waste of mural stone; the pinnacles of the rocky
promontory arrange themselves, undegraded, into
fantastic semblances of fortress towers; and even

the awful cone of the far-off mountain has a
melancholy mixed with that of its own solitude,
which is cast from the images of nameless tumuli
on white sea-shores, and of the heaps of reedy
clay, into which chambered cities melt in their
mortality.—*S. L. A.*, III., § 3.

131. THE SYMPHONY OF ARCHITECTURE.—
When you buy a print, the enjoyment of it is
confined to yourself and to your friends.   But if
you carve a piece of stone, and put it on the
outside of your house, it will give pleasure to
every person who passes along the street—to an
innumerable multitude, instead of a few.

Nay, but, you say, we ourselves shall not be
benefited by the sculpture on the outsides of our
houses.   Yes, you will, and in an extraordinary
degree;   for, observe farther, that architecture
differs from painting peculiarly in being an art
of *accumulation*.   The prints bought by your
friends, and hung up in their houses, have no
collateral effect with yours : they must be separately examined, and if ever they were hung side
by side, they would rather injure than assist each
other's effect.   But the sculpture on your friend's
house unites in effect with that on your own.
The two houses form one grand mass—far grander
than either separately;   much more if a third be
added—and a fourth;   much more if the whole
street—if the whole city—join in the solemn

harmony of sculpture. Your separate possessions of pictures and prints are to you as if you sang pieces of music with your single voices in your own houses. But your architecture would be as if you all sang together in one mighty choir. In the separate picture, it is rare that there exists any very high source of sublime emotion; but the great concerted music of the streets of the city, when turret rises over turret, and casement frowns beyond casement, and tower succeeds to tower along the farthest ridges of the inhabited hills,—this is a sublimity of which you can at present form no conception; and capable, I believe, of exciting almost the deepest emotion that art can ever strike from the bosoms of men.

And justly the deepest: for it is a law of God and of Nature, that your pleasures—as your virtues—shall be enhanced by mutual aid. As, by joining hand in hand, you can sustain each other best, so, hand in hand, you can delight each other best.—*L. A. P.*, II., § 49.

132. CHURCH BUILDING.—I am no advocate for meanness of private habitation. I would fain introduce into it all magnificence, care, and beauty, where they are possible; but I would not have that useless expense in unnoticed fineries or formalities; cornicing of ceilings and graining of doors, and fringing of curtains, and thousands such; things which have become

foolishly and apathetically habitual—things on whose common appliance hang whole trades, to which there never yet belonged the blessing of giving one ray of real pleasure, or becoming of the remotest or most contemptible use—things which cause half the expense of life, and destroy more than half its comfort, manliness, respectability, freshness, and facility. I speak from experience : I know what it is to live in a cottage with a deal floor and roof, and a hearth of mica slate ; and I know it to be in many respects healthier and happier than living between a Turkey carpet and gilded ceiling, beside a steel grate and polished fender. I do not say that such things have not their place and propriety; but I say this, emphatically, that the tenth part of the expense which is sacrificed in domestic vanities if not absolutely and meaninglessly lost in domestic discomforts and incumbrances, would, if collectively offered and wisely employed, build a marble church for every town in England ; such a church as it should be a joy and a blessing even to pass near in our daily ways and walks, and as it would bring the light into the eyes to see from afar, lifting its fair height above the purple crowd of humble roofs.

I have said for every town : I do not want a marble church for every village ; nay, I do not want marble churches at all for their own sake, but for the sake of the spirit that would build them. The church has no need of any visible splendours; her power is independent of them, her purity is in some degree opposed to them. The simplicity of a pastoral sanctuary is lovelier than the majesty of an urban temple; and it may be more than questioned whether, to the people, such majesty has ever been the source of any increase of effective piety; but to the builders it has been, and must ever be. It is not the church we want, but the sacrifice; not the emotion of admiration, but the act of adoration; not the gift, but the giving.—*S. L. A.*, I., § 7, 8.

133. Two Broad Divisions of Architecture.—Of the many broad divisions under which architecture may be considered, none appear to me more significant than that into buildings whose interest is in their walls, and those whose interest is in the lines dividing their walls. In the Greek temple the wall is as nothing; the entire interest is in the detached columns and the frieze they bear; in French Flamboyant, and in our detestable Perpendicular, the object is to get rid of the wall surface, and keep the eye altogether on tracery of line; in Romanesque work and Egyptian, the wall is a confessed and honoured member, and the light is often allowed to fall on large areas of it, variously decorated. Now, both these principles are admitted by Nature, the one

in her woods and thickets, the other in her plains, and cliffs, and waters; but the latter is pre-eminently the principle of power, and, in some sense, of beauty also. For, whatever infinity of fair form there may be in the maze of the forest, there is a fairer, as I think, in the surface of the quiet lake; and I hardly know that association of shaft or tracery, for which I would exchange the warm sleep of sunshine on some smooth, broad, human-like front of marble. Nevertheless, if breadth is to be beautiful, its substance must in some sort be beautiful; and we must not hastily condemn the exclusive resting of the Northern architects in divided lines, until at least we have remembered the difference between a blank surface of Caen stone, and one mixed from Genoa and Carrara, of serpentine with snow: but as regards abstract power and awfulness, there is no question; without breadth of surface it is in vain to seek them, and it matters little, so that the surface be wide, bold, and unbroken, whether it be of brick or of jasper; the light of heaven upon it, and the weight of earth in it, are all we need: for it is singular how forgetful the mind may become both of material and workmanship, if only it have space enough over which to range, and to remind it, however feebly, of the joy that it has in contemplating the flatness and sweep of great plains and broad seas. And it is a noble thing for men to do this with their cut stone or moulded clay, and to make the face of a wall look infinite, and its edge against the sky like an horizon : or even if less than this be reached, it is still delightful to mark the play of passing light on its broad surface, and to see by how many artifices and gradations of tinting and shadow, time and storm will set their wild signatures upon it ; and how in the rising or declining of the day the unbroken twilight rests long and luridly on its high lineless forehead, and fades away untraceably down its tiers of confused and countless stone.—*S. L. A.*, III., § 8.

134. THE ORIGIN OF GOTHIC.—The two orders, Doric and Corinthian, are the roots of all European architecture. You have, perhaps, heard of five orders : but there are only two real orders ; and there never can be any more until doomsday. On one of these orders the ornament is convex : those are Doric, Norman, and what else you recollect of the kind. On the other the ornament is concave : those are Corinthian, Early English, Decorated, and what else you recollect of that kind. The transitional form, in which the ornamental line is straight, is the centre or root of both. All other orders are varieties of these, or phantasms and grotesques, altogether indefinite in number and species.

This Greek architecture, then, with its two orders, was clumsily copied and varied by the

Romans with no particular result, until they began to bring the arch into extensive practical service; except only that the Doric capital was spoiled in endeavours to mend it, and the Corinthian much varied and enriched with fanciful, and often very beautiful imagery. And in this state of things came Christianity; seized upon the arch as her own: decorated it, and delighted in it: invented a new Doric capital to replace the spoiled Roman one: and all over the Roman Empire set to work, with such materials as were nearest at hand, to express and adorn herself as best she could. This Roman Christian architecture is the exact expression of the Christianity of the time, very fervid and beautiful—but very imperfect; in many respects ignorant, and yet radiant with a strong, childish light of imagination, which flames up under Constantine, illumines all the shores of the Bosphorus and the Ægean and the Adriatic Sea, and then gradually, as the people give themselves up to idolatry, becomes corpse-light. The architecture, like the religion it expressed, sinks into a settled form—a strange, gilded, and embalmed repose; and so would have remained for ever,—so does remain, where its languor has been undisturbed. But rough wakening was ordained for it.

This Christian art of the declining Empire is divided into two great branches, western and eastern; one centred at Rome, the other at

Byzantium, of which the one is the early Christian Romanesque, properly so called, and the other, carried to higher imaginative perfection by Greek workmen, is distinguished from it as Byzantine. But I wish the reader, for the present, to class these two branches of art together in his mind, they being, in points of main importance, the same; that is to say, both of them a true continuance and sequence of the art of old Rome itself, flowing uninterruptedly down from the fountain-head, and entrusted always to the best workmen who could be found —Latins in Italy and Greeks in Greece; and thus both branches may be ranged under the general term of Christian Romanesque, an architecture which had lost the refinement of Pagan art in the degradation of the Empire, but which was elevated by Christianity to higher aims, and by the fancy of the Greek workmen endowed with brighter forms. And this art the reader may conceive as extending in its various branches over all the central provinces of the Empire, taking aspects more or less refined, according to its proximity to the seats of government; dependent for all its power on the vigour and freshness of the religion which animated it; and as that vigour and purity departed, losing its own vitality, and sinking into nerveless rest, not deprived of its beauty, but benumbed, and incapable of advance or change.

Meantime there had been preparation for its renewal. While in Rome and Constantinople, and in the districts under their immediate influence, this Roman art of pure descent was practised in all its refinement, an impure form of it—a patois of Romanesque—was carried by inferior workmen into distant provinces; and still ruder imitations of this patois were executed by the barbarous nations on the skirts of the Empire. But these barbarous nations were in the strength of their youth; and while, in the centre of Europe, a refined and purely descended art was sinking into graceful formalism, on its confines a barbarous and borrowed art was organising itself into strength and consistency. The reader must therefore consider the history of the work of the period as broadly divided into two great heads: the one embracing the elaborately languid succession of the Christian art of Rome; and the other, the imitations of it executed by nations in every conceivable phase of early organisation, on the edges of the Empire, or included in its now merely nominal extent.

Some of the barbaric nations were, of course, not susceptible of this influence; and, when they burst over the Alps, appear like the Huns, as scourges only, or mix, as the Ostrogoths, with the enervated Italians, and give physical strength to the mass with which they mingle, without materially affecting its intellectual character. But others, both south and north of the Empire, had felt its influence, back to the beach of the Indian Ocean on the one hand, and to the ice creeks of the North Sea on the other. On the north and west the influence was of the Latins; on the south and east, of the Greeks. Two nations, pre-eminent above all the rest, represent to us the force of derived mind on either side. As the central power is eclipsed, the orbs of reflected light gather into their fulness; and when sensuality and idolatry had done their work, and the religion of the Empire was laid asleep in a glittering sepulchre, the living light rose upon both horizons, and the fierce swords of the Lombard and Arab were shaken over its golden paralysis.

The work of the Lombard was to give hardihood and system to the enervated body and enfeebled mind of Christendom; that of the Arab was to punish idolatry, and to proclaim the spirituality of worship. The Lombard covered every church which he built with the sculptured representations of bodily exercises—hunting and war. The Arab banished all imagination of creature form from his temples, and proclaimed from their minarets, " There is no god but God." Opposite in their character and mission, alike in their magnificence of energy, they came from the North and from the South, the glacier torrent and the lava stream: they met and contended over the wreck of the Roman Empire; and the very centre of the struggle, the point of pause of both, the dead water of the opposite eddies, charged with embayed fragments of the Roman wreck, is VENICE.

The Ducal Palace of Venice contains the three elements in exactly equal proportions—the Roman, Lombard, and Arab. It is the central building of the world.—*S. V.*, I. i., § 19–24.

135. THE NATURALISM OF GOTHIC.—There is one direction in which the Naturalism of the Gothic workmen is peculiarly manifested; and this direction is even more characteristic of the school than the Naturalism itself; I mean their peculiar fondness for the forms of Vegetation. In rendering the various circumstances of daily life, Egyptian and Ninevite sculpture is as frank and as diffuse as the Gothic. From the highest pomps of state or triumphs of battle, to the most trivial domestic arts and amusements, all is taken advantage of to fill the field of granite with the perpetual interest of a crowded drama; and the early Lombardic and Romanesque sculpture is equally copious in its description of the familiar circumstances of war and the chase. But in all the scenes portrayed by the workmen of these nations, vegetation occurs only as an explanatory accessory; the reed is introduced to mark the course of the river, or the tree to

mark the covert of the wild beast, or the ambush
of the enemy, but there is no especial interest
in the forms of the vegetation strong enough to
induce them to make it a subject of separate and
accurate study. Again, among the nations who
followed the arts of design exclusively, the forms
of foliage introduced were meagre and general,
and their real intricacy and life were neither
admired nor expressed. But to the Gothic workman the living foliage became a subject of intense affection, and he struggled to render all its
characters with as much accuracy as was compatible with the laws of his design and the nature
of his material, not unfrequently tempted in his
enthusiasm to transgress the one and disguise
the other.—*S. V.*, II. VI., § 68.

136. VARIETY IN ARCHITECTURE.—Change
or variety is as much a necessity to the human
heart and brain in buildings as in books; there
is no merit, though there is some occasional
use, in monotony; and we must no more expect
to derive either pleasure or profit from an architecture whose ornaments are of one pattern, and
whose pillars are of one proportion, than we
should out of a universe in which the clouds
were all of one shape, and the trees all of one
size.

And this we confess in deeds, though not in
words. All the pleasure which the people of

the nineteenth century take in art, is in pictures, sculpture, minor objects of virtù, or mediæval architecture, which we enjoy under the term picturesque: no pleasure is taken anywhere in modern buildings, and we find all men of true feeling delighting to escape out of modern cities into natural scenery: hence that peculiar love of landscape which is characteristic of the age. It would be well, if, in all other matters, we were as ready to put up with what we dislike, for the sake of compliance with established law, as we are in architecture.

How so debased a law ever came to be established, we shall see when we come to describe the Renaissance schools: here we have only to note, as the second most essential element of the Gothic spirit, that it broke through that law wherever it found it in existence; it not only dared, but delighted in, the infringement of every servile principle; and invented a series of forms of which the merit was, not merely that they were new, but that they were *capable of perpetual novelty*. The pointed arch was not merely a bold variation from the round, but it admitted of millions of variations in itself; for the proportions of a pointed arch are changeable to infinity, while a circular arch is always the same. The grouped shaft was not merely a bold variation from the single one, but it admitted of millions of variations in its grouping, and in the proportions resultant from its grouping. The introduction of tracery was not only a startling change in the treatment of window lights, but admitted endless changes in the interlacement of the tracery bars themselves. So that, while in all living Christian architecture the love of variety exists, the Gothic schools exhibited that love in culminating energy; and their influence, wherever it extended itself, may be sooner and farther traced by this character than by any other; the tendency to the adoption of Gothic types being always first shown by greater irregularity and richer variation in the forms of the architecture it is about to supersede, long before the appearance of the pointed arch or of any other recognisable *outward* sign of the Gothic mind.

We must, however, herein note carefully what distinction there is between a healthy and a diseased love of change; for as it was in healthy love of change that the Gothic architecture rose, it was partly in consequence of diseased love of change that it was destroyed.—*S. V.*, II. vi., § 29–32.

137. GOTHIC A DOMESTIC STYLE.—It needs but little inquiry into the spirit of the past, to ascertain what, once for all, I would desire here clearly and forcibly to assert, that wherever Christian church architecture has been good and lovely, it has been merely the perfect development

of the common dwelling-house architecture of the period; that when the pointed arch was used in the street, it was used in the church; when the round arch was used in the street, it was used in the church; when the pinnacle was set over the garret window, it was set over the belfry tower; when the flat roof was used for the drawing-room, it was used for the nave. There is no sacredness in round arches, nor in pointed; none in pinnacles, nor in buttresses; none in pillars, nor in traceries. Churches were larger than most other buildings, because they had to hold more people; they were more adorned than most other buildings, because they were safer from violence, and were the fitting subjects of devotional offering: but they were never built in any separate, mystical, and religious style; they were built in the manner that was common and familiar to everybody at the time. The flamboyant traceries that adorn the façade of Rouen Cathedral had once their fellows in every window of every house in the market-place; the sculptures that adorn the porches of St. Mark's had once their match on the walls of every palace on the Grand Canal; and the only difference between the church and the dwelling-house was, that there existed a symbolical meaning in the distribution of the parts of all buildings meant for worship, and that the painting or sculpture was, in the one case, less frequently of profane

subject than in the other. A more severe
distinction cannot be drawn : for secular history
was constantly introduced into church architecture ; and sacred history or allusion generally
formed at least one half of the ornament of the
dwelling-house. . . . I do not mean that every
dwelling-house of mediæval cities was as richly
adorned and as exquisite in composition as the
fronts of their cathedrals, but that they presented
features of the same kind, often in parts quite
as beautiful ; and that the churches were not
separated by any change of style from the buildings round them, as they are now, but were
merely more finished and full examples of a
universal style, rising out of the confused streets
of the city as an oak tree does out of an oak
copse, not differing in leafage, but in size and
symmetry. Of course the quainter and smaller
forms of turret and window necessary for domestic
service, the inferior materials, often wood instead
of stone, and the fancy of the inhabitants, which
had free play in the design, introduced oddnesses,
vulgarities, and variations into house architecture,
which were prevented by the traditions, the
wealth, and the skill of the monks and free-
masons ; while, on the other hand, conditions of
vaulting, buttressing, and arch and tower building,
were necessitated by the mere size of the cathedral, of which it would be difficult to find examples
elsewhere.—*S. V.*, II. IV., § 53, 54.

138. THE CAMPANILE OF GIOTTO AT FLORENCE.—The characteristics of Power and Beauty occur more or less in different buildings, some in one and some in another. But all together, and all in their highest possible relative degrees, they exist, as far as I know, only in one building in the world, the Campanile of Giotto at Florence.

In its first appeal to the stranger's eye there is something unpleasing; a mingling, as it seems to him, of over severity with over minuteness. But let him give it time, as he should to all other consummate art. I remember well how, when a boy, I used to despise that Campanile, and think it meanly smooth and finished. But I have since lived beside it many a day, and looked out upon it from my windows by sunlight and moonlight, and I shall not soon forget how profound and gloomy appeared to me the savageness of the Northern Gothic, when I afterwards stood, for the first time, beneath the front of Salisbury. The contrast is indeed strange, if it could be quickly felt, between the rising of those grey walls out of their quiet swarded space, like dark and barren rocks out of a green lake, with their rude, mouldering, rough-grained shafts, and triple lights, without tracery or other ornament than the martins' nests in the height of them, and that bright, smooth, sunny surface of glowing jasper, those spiral shafts and fairy traceries, so white, so faint, so crystalline, that their slight shapes are hardly traced in darkness on the pallor of the Eastern sky, that serene height of mountain alabaster, coloured like a morning cloud, and chased like a sea-shell. And if this be, as I believe it, the model and mirror of perfect architecture, is there not something to be learned by looking back to the early life of him who raised it? I said that the Power of human mind had its growth in the Wilderness; much more must the love and the conception of that beauty, whose every line and hue we have seen to be, at the best, a faded image of God's daily work, and an arrested ray of some star of creation, be given chiefly in the places which He has gladdened by planting there the fir-tree and the pine. Not within the walls of Florence, but among the far away fields of her lilies, was the child trained who was to raise that headstone of Beauty above her towers of watch and war. Remember all that he became; count the sacred thoughts with which he filled the heart of Italy; ask those who followed him what they learned at his feet; and when you have numbered his labours, and received their testimony, if it seem to you that God had verily poured out upon this His servant no common nor restrained portion of His Spirit, and that he was indeed a king among the children of men, remember also that the legend upon his crown was that of David's :—" I took thee from the sheepcote,

and from following the sheep."—*S. L. A.*,
IV., § 43.

139. REDUNDANT ORNAMENT OF GOTHIC.
—In the most characteristic buildings, a certain
portion of their effect depends upon accumulation
of ornament ; and many of those which have most
influence on the minds of men, have attained it by
means of this attribute alone.   And although, .
by careful study of the school, it is possible to
arrive at a condition of taste which shall be better
contented by a few perfect lines than by a whole
façade covered with fretwork, the building which
only satisfies such a taste is not to be considered
the best.   For the very first requirement of Gothic
architecture being, as we saw above, that it shall
both admit the aid, and appeal to the admiration,
of the rudest as well as the most refined minds,
the richness of the work is, paradoxical as the
statement may appear, a part of its humility.
No architecture is so haughty as that which is
simple ; which refuses to address the eye, except
in a few clear and forceful lines ; which implies,
in offering so little to our regards, that all it
has offered is perfect ; and disdains, either by
the complexity or the attractiveness of its features, to embarrass our investigation or betray us
into delight.   That humility, which is the very
life of the Gothic school, is shown not only in
the imperfection, but in the accumulation, of

ornament. The inferior rank of the workman is often shown as much in the richness, as the roughness, of his work; and if the co-operation of every hand, and the sympathy of every heart, are to be received, we must be content to allow the redundance which disguises the failure of the feeble, and wins the regard of the inattentive. There are, however, far nobler interests mingling, in the Gothic heart, with the rude love of decorative accumulation: a magnificent enthusiasm, which feels as if it never could do enough to reach the fulness of its ideal; an unselfishness of sacrifice, which would rather cast fruitless labour before the altar than stand idle in the market; and, finally, a profound sympathy with the fulness and wealth of the material universe, rising out of that Naturalism whose operation we have already endeavoured to define. The sculptor who sought for his models among the forest leaves, could not but quickly and deeply feel that complexity need not involve the loss of grace, nor richness that of repose; and every hour which he spent in the study of the minute and various works of Nature, made him feel more forcibly the barrenness of what was best in that of man: nor is it to be wondered at, that, seeing her perfect and exquisite creations poured forth in a profusion which conception could not grasp nor calculation sum, he should think that it ill became him to be niggardly of his own rude craftsmanship;

and where he saw throughout the universe a faultless beauty lavished on measureless spaces of broidered field and blooming mountain, to grudge his poor and imperfect labour to the few stones that he had raised one upon another for habitation or memorial. The years of his life passed away before his task was accomplished; but generation succeeded generation with unwearied enthusiasm, and the cathedral front was at last lost in the tapestry of its traceries, like a rock among the thickets and herbage of Spring. —*S. V.*, II. VI., § 78.

140. THE DECLINE OF GOTHIC.—The life of a nation is usually, like the flow of a lava stream, first bright and fierce, then languid and covered, at last advancing only by the tumbling over and over of its frozen blocks. And that last condition is a sad one to look upon. All the steps are marked most clearly in the arts, and in Architecture more than in any other; for it, being especially dependent, as we have just said, on the warmth of the true life, is also peculiarly sensible of the hemlock cold of the false: and I do not know anything more oppressive, when the mind is once awakened to its characteristics, than the aspect of a dead architecture. The feebleness of childhood is full of promise and of interest,—the struggle of imperfect knowledge full of energy and continuity—but to see impotence

and rigidity settling upon the form of the developed man; to see the types which once had the die of thought struck fresh upon them, worn flat by over use; to see the shell of the living creature in its adult form, when its colours are faded, and its inhabitant perished,—this is a sight more humiliating, more melancholy, than the vanishing of all knowledge, and the return to confessed and helpless infancy.

Nay, it is to be wished that such return were always possible. There would be hope if we could change palsy into puerility; but I know not how far we *can* become children again, and renew our lost life.—*S. L. A.*, V., § 3.

141. THE CINQUE-CENTO. — Against this degraded Gothic, then, came up the Renaissance armies; and their first assault was in the requirement of universal perfection. For the first time since the destruction of Rome, the world had seen, in the work of the greatest artists of the fifteenth century,—in the painting of Ghirlandajo, Masaccio, Francia, Perugino, Pinturicchio, and Bellini; in the sculpture of Mino da Fiesole, of Ghiberti, and Verrocchio,—a perfection of execution and fulness of knowledge which cast all previous art into the shade, and which, being in the work of those men united with all that was great in that of former days, did indeed justify the utmost enthusiasm with which their

efforts were, or could be, regarded. But when this perfection had once been exhibited in anything, it was required in everything; the world could no longer be satisfied with less exquisite execution, or less disciplined knowledge. The first thing that it demanded in all work was, that it should be done in a consummate and learned way; and men altogether forgot that it was possible to consummate what was contemptible, and to know what was useless. Imperatively requiring dexterity of touch, they gradually forgot to look for tenderness of feeling; imperatively requiring accuracy of knowledge, they gradually forgot to ask for originality of thought. The thought and the feeling which they despised departed from them, and they were left to felicitate themselves on their small science and their neat fingering. This is the history of the first attack of the Renaissance upon the Gothic schools, and of its rapid results; more fatal and immediate in architecture than in any other art, because there the demand for perfection was less reasonable, and less consistent with the capabilities of the workman; being utterly opposed to that rudeness or savageness on which, as we saw above, the nobility of the elder schools in great part depends. But, inasmuch as the innovations were founded on some of the most beautiful examples of art, and headed by some of the greatest men that the world ever saw, and as

I.

the Gothic with which they interfered was corrupt
and valueless, the first appearance of the Renaissance feeling had the appearance of a healthy movement. A new energy replaced whatever weariness
or dulness had affected the Gothic mind; an
exquisite taste and refinement, aided by extended
knowledge, furnished the first models of the new
school; and over the whole of Italy a style arose,
generally now known as cinque-cento, which in
sculpture and painting, as I just stated, produced
the noblest masters whom the world ever saw,
headed by Michael Angelo, Raphael, and Leonardo; but which failed of doing the same in
architecture, because, as we have seen above,
perfection is therein not possible, and failed more
totally than it would otherwise have done, because
the classical enthusiasm had destroyed the best
types of architectural form.

For, observe here very carefully, the Renaissance principle, as it consisted in a demand for
universal perfection, is quite distinct from the
Renaissance principle as it consists in a demand
for classical and Roman *forms* of perfection.
And if I had space to follow out the subject as
I should desire, I would first endeavour to
ascertain what might have been the course of
the art of Europe if no manuscripts of classical
authors had been recovered, and no remains of
classical architecture left, in the fifteenth century;
so that the executive perfection to which the

efforts of all great men had tended for five
hundred years, and which now at last was
reached, might have been allowed to develop
itself in its own natural and proper form, in
connection with the architectural structure of
earlier schools. This refinement and perfection
had indeed its own perils, and the history of
later Italy, as she sank into pleasure and thence
into corruption, would probably have been the
same whether she had ever learned again to
write pure Latin or not. Still the inquiry into
the probable cause of the enervation which might
naturally have followed the highest exertion of
her energies, is a totally distinct one from that
into the particular form given to this enervation
by her classical learning; and it is matter of
considerable regret to me that I cannot treat
these two subjects separately: I must be content
with marking them for separation in the mind
of the reader.

The effect, then, of the sudden enthusiasm for
classical literature, which gained strength during
every hour of the fifteenth century, was, as far
as respected architecture, to do away with the
entire system of Gothic science. The pointed
arch, the shadowy vault, the clustered shaft, the
heaven-pointing spire, were all swept away;
and no structure was any longer permitted but
that of the plain cross-beam from pillar to pillar,
over the round arch, with square or circular

shafts, and a low-gabled roof and pediment : two elements of noble form, which had fortunately existed in Rome, were, however, for that reason, still permitted ; the cupola, and, internally, the waggon vault.

These changes in form were all of them unfortunate ; and it is almost impossible to do justice to the occasionally exquisite ornamentation of the fifteenth century, on account of its being placed upon edifices of the cold and meagre Roman outline. There is, as far as I know, only one Gothic building in Europe, the Duomo of Florence, in which, though the ornament be of a much earlier school, it is so exquisitely finished as to enable us to imagine what might have been the effect of the perfect workmanship of the Renaissance, coming out of the hands of men like Verrocchio and Ghiberti, had it been employed on the magnificent framework of Gothic structure. This is the question which we ought to set ourselves practically to solve in modern times.

The changes effected in form, however, were the least part of the evil principles of the Renaissance. As I have just said, its main mistake, in its early stages, was the unwholesome demand for *perfection*, at any cost. I hope enough has been advanced, in the chapter on the Nature of Gothic, to show the reader that perfection is *not* to be had from the general workman, but at the cost of everything,—of his whole life, thought, and energy. And Renaissance Europe thought this a small price to pay for manipulative perfection. Men like Verrocchio and Ghiberti were not to be had every day, nor in every place ; and to require from the common workman execution or knowledge like theirs, was to require him to become their copyist. Their strength was great enough to enable them to join science with invention, method with emotion, finish with fire ; but in them the invention and the fire were first, while Europe saw in them only the method and the finish. This was new to the minds of men, and they pursued it to the neglect of everything else. "This," they cried, "we must have in all our work henceforward :" and they were obeyed. The lower workman secured method and finish, and lost, in exchange for them, his soul.

Now, therefore, do not let me be misunderstood when I speak generally of the evil spirit of the Renaissance. The reader may look through all I have written, from first to last, and he will not find one word but of the most profound reverence for those mighty men who could wear the Renaissance armour of proof, and yet not feel it encumber their living limbs,— Leonardo and Michael Angelo, Ghirlandajo and Masaccio, Titian and Tintoret. But I speak of the Renaissance as an evil time, because, when it saw those men go burning forth into the battle, it mistook their armour for their strength; and forthwith encumbered with the painful panoply every stripling who ought to have gone forth only with his own choice of three smooth stones of the brook.

This, then, the reader must always keep in mind when he is examining for himself any examples of cinque-cento work. When it has been done by a truly great man, whose life and strength could not be suppressed, and who turned to good account the whole science of his day, nothing is more exquisite. I do not believe, for instance, that there is a more glorious work of sculpture existing in the world than that equestrian statue of Bartolommeo Colleone. But when the cinque-cento work has been done by those meaner men, who, in the Gothic times, though in a rough way, would yet have found some means of speaking out what was in their hearts, it is utterly inanimate,—a base and helpless copy of more accomplished models; or, if not this, a mere accumulation of technical skill, in gaining which the workman had surrendered all other powers that were in him.

There is, therefore, of course, an infinite gradation in the art of the period, from the Sistine Chapel down to modern upholstery; but, for the most part, since in architecture the workman must be of an inferior order, it will be found that this cinque-cento painting and higher religious sculpture is noble, while the cinque-cento architecture, with its subordinate sculpture, is universally bad; sometimes, however, assuming forms in which the consummate refinement almost atones for the loss of force.—*S. V.*, III. I., § 16–22.

142. BUILD FOR POSTERITY.—God has lent us the earth for our life; it is a great entail. It belongs as much to those who are to come after us, and whose names are already written in the book of creation, as to us; and we have no right, by anything that we do or neglect, to involve them in unnecessary penalties, or deprive them of benefits which it was in our power to bequeath. And this the more, because it is one of the appointed conditions of the labour of men that, in proportion to the time between the seed-sowing and the harvest, is the fulness of the fruit; and that generally, therefore, the farther off we place our aim, and the less we desire to be ourselves the witnesses of what we have laboured for, the more wide and rich will be the measure of our success. Men cannot benefit those that are with them as they can benefit those who come after them; and of all the pulpits from which human voice is ever sent forth, there is none from which it reaches so far as from the grave.

Nor is there, indeed, any present loss, in such respect for futurity. Every human action gains

in honour, in grace, in all true magnificence, by
its regard to things that are to come. It is the
far sight, the quiet and confident patience, that,
above all other attributes, separate man from
man, and near him to his Maker; and there is
no action nor art, whose majesty we may not
measure by this test. Therefore, when we build,
let us think that we build for ever. Let it not
be for present delight, nor for present use alone;
let it be such work as our descendants will thank
us for, and let us think, as we lay stone on stone,
that a time is to come when those stones will
be held sacred because our hands have touched
them, and that men will say as they look upon
the labour and wrought substance of them, "See!
this our fathers did for us." For, indeed, the
greatest glory of a building is not in its stones,
nor in its gold. Its glory is in its Age, and in
that deep sense of voicefulness, of stern watching, of mysterious sympathy, nay, even of ap-
proval or condemnation, which we feel in walls
that have long been washed by the passing waves
of humanity. It is in their lasting witness against
men, in their quiet contrast with the transitional
character of all things, in the strength which,
through the lapse of seasons and times, and the
decline and birth of dynasties, and the changing
of the face of the earth, and of the limits of the
sea, maintains its sculptured shapeliness for a
time insuperable, connects forgotten and following

ages with each other, and half constitutes the identity, as it concentrates the sympathy, of nations ; it is in that golden stain of time, that we are to look for the real light, and colour, and preciousness of architecture ; and it is not until a building has assumed this character, till it has been entrusted with the fame, and hallowed by the deeds of men, till its walls have been witnesses of suffering, and its pillars rise out of the shadows of death, that its existence, more lasting as it is than that of the natural objects of the world around it, can be gifted with even so much as these possess of language and of life.—*S. L. A.*, VI., § 9, 10.

143. RESTORATION.—Neither by the public, nor by those who have the care of public monuments, is the true meaning of the word *restoration* understood. It means the most total destruction which a building can suffer: a destruction out of which no remnants can be gathered: a destruction accompanied with false description of the thing destroyed. Do not let us deceive ourselves in this important matter ; it is *impossible*, as impossible as to raise the dead, to restore anything that has ever been great or beautiful in architecture. That which I have insisted upon as the life of the whole, that spirit which is given only by the hand and eye of the workman, never can be recalled. Another

spirit may be given by another time, and it is then a new building; but the spirit of the dead workman cannot be summoned up, and commanded to direct other hands, and other thoughts. And as for direct and simple copying, it is palpably impossible. What copying can there be of surfaces that have been worn half an inch down? The whole finish of the work was in the half inch that is gone; if you attempt to restore that finish, you do it conjecturally; if you copy what is left, granting fidelity to be possible, (and what care, or watchfulness, or cost can secure it), how is the new work better than the old?

There was yet in the old *some* life, some mysterious suggestion of what it had been, and of what it had lost; some sweetness in the gentle lines which rain and sun had wrought. There can be none in the brute hardness of the new carving. . . . The first step to restoration, (I have seen it, and that again and again, seen it on the Baptistery of Pisa, seen it on the Casa d' Oro at Venice, seen it on the Cathedral of Lisieux,) is to dash the old work to pieces; the second is usually to put up the cheapest and basest imitation which can escape detection, but in all cases, however careful, and however laboured, an imitation still, a cold model of such parts as *can* be modelled, with conjectural supplements; and my experience has as yet

furnished me with only one instance, that of the
Palais de Justice at Rouen, in which even this,
the utmost degree of fidelity which is possible,
has been attained, or even attempted.

Do not let us talk then of restoration. The
thing is a Lie from beginning to end. You may
make a model of a building as you may of a
corpse, and your model may have the shell of the
old walls within it as your cast might have the
skeleton, with what advantage I neither see nor
care: but the old building is destroyed, and that
more totally and mercilessly than if it had sunk
into a heap of dust, or melted into a mass of clay:
more has been gleaned out of desolated Nineveh
than ever will be out of re-built Milan.

But, it is said, there may come a necessity for
restoration! Granted. Look the necessity full
in the face, and understand it on its own terms.
It is a necessity for destruction. Accept it as
such, pull the building down, throw its stones
into neglected corners, make ballast of them, or
mortar, if you will; but do it honestly, and do
not set up a Lie in their place. And look that
necessity in the face before it comes, and you
may prevent it. The principle of modern times,
(a principle which, I believe, at least in France,
to be *systematically acted on by the masons*, in
order to find themselves work, as the Abbey
of St. Ouen was pulled down by the magistrates
of the town by way of giving work to some

vagrants,) is to neglect buildings first, and restore
them afterwards. Take proper care of your
monuments, and you will not need to restore
them. A few sheets of lead put in time upon
the roof, a few dead leaves and sticks swept in
time out of a water-course, will save both roof
and walls from ruin. Watch an old building
with an anxious care; guard it as best you may,
and at *any* cost, from every influence of dilapida-
tion. Count its stones as you would jewels of
a crown; set watches about it as if at the gates
of a besieged city; bind it together with iron
where it loosens; stay it with timber where it
declines; do not care about the unsightliness
of the aid: better a crutch than a lost limb; and
do this tenderly, and reverently, and continually,
and many a generation will still be born and
pass away beneath its shadow. Its evil day
must come at last; but let it come declaredly
and openly, and let no dishonouring and false
substitute deprive it of the funeral offices of
memory.

Of more wanton or ignorant ravage it is vain
to speak; my words will not reach those who
commit them, and yet, be it heard or not, I
must not leave the truth unstated, that it is
again no question of expediency or feeling
whether we shall preserve the buildings of
past times or not. *We have no right whatever
to touch them.* They are not ours. They belong

partly to those who built them, and partly to all the generations of mankind who are to follow us. The dead have still their right in them : that which they laboured for, the praise of achievement or the expression of religious feeling, or whatsoever else it might be which in those buildings they intended to be permanent, we have no right to obliterate. What we have ourselves built, we are at liberty to throw down ; but what other men gave their strength and wealth and life to accomplish, their right over does not pass away with their death : still less is the right to the use of what they have left vested in us only. It belongs to all their successors. It may hereafter be a subject of sorrow, or a cause of injury, to millions, that we have consulted our present convenience by casting down such buildings as we choose to dispense with. That sorrow, that loss we have no right to inflict.—*S. L. A.*, VI., § 18, 19.

144. ORIGINALITY.—A day never passes without our hearing our English architects called upon to be original, and to invent a new style : about as sensible and necessary an exhortation as to ask of a man who has never had rags enough on his back to keep out cold, to invent a new mode of cutting a coat. Give him a whole coat first, and let him concern himself about the fashion of it afterwards. We want no new style

of architecture. Who wants a new style of painting or sculpture? But we want *some* style. It is of marvellously little importance, if we have a code of laws and they be good laws, whether they be new or old, foreign or native, Roman or Saxon, or Norman, or English laws. But it is of considerable importance that we should have a code of laws of one kind or another, and that code accepted and enforced from one side of the island to another, and not one law made ground of judgment at York and another in Exeter. And in like manner it does not matter one marble splinter whether we have an old or new architecture, but it matters everything whether we have an architecture truly so called or not; that is, whether an architecture whose laws might be taught at our schools from Cornwall to Northumberland, as we teach English spelling and English grammar, or an architecture which is to be invented fresh every time we build a workhouse or a parish school. There seems to me to be a wonderful misunderstanding among the majority of architects of the present day as to the very nature and meaning of originality, and of all wherein it consists. Originality in expression does not depend on invention of new words; nor originality in poetry on invention of new measures; nor, in painting, on invention of new colours, or new modes of using them. The chords of music, the harmonies of colour, the

general principles of the arrangement of sculp-
tural masses, have been determined long ago,
and, in all probability, cannot be added to any
more than they can be altered.   Granting that
they may be, such additions or alterations are
much more the work of time and of multitudes
than of individual inventors.   We may have one
Van Eyck, who will be known as the introducer
of a new style once in ten centuries, but he himself will trace his invention to some accidental
by-play or pursuit; and the use of that invention
will depend altogether on the popular necessities
or instincts of the period.   Originality depends
on nothing of the kind.   A man who has the gift
will take up any style that is going, the style of
his day, and will work in that, and be great in
that, and make everything that he does in it look
as fresh as if every thought of it had just come
down from heaven.   I do not say that he will
not take liberties with his materials, or with his
rules: I do not say that strange changes will not
sometimes be wrought by his efforts, or his
fancies, in both.   But those changes will be
instructive, natural, facile, though sometimes
marvellous; they will never be sought after as
things necessary to his dignity or to his independence; and those liberties will be like the
liberties that a great speaker takes with the
language, not a defiance of its rules for the sake
of singularity; but inevitable, uncalculated, and

brilliant consequences of an effort to express
what the language, without such infraction, could
not. . . .

Neither originality, nor change, good though
both may be, and this is commonly a most
merciful and enthusiastic supposition with respect to either, is ever to be sought in itself, or
can ever be healthily obtained by any struggle
or rebellion against common laws. We want
neither the one nor the other. The forms of
architecture already known are good enough for
us, and for far better than any of us; and it
will be time enough to think of changing them
for better when we can use them as they are.
—*S. L. A.*, VII., § 4, 5.

145. THE USE OF SCULPTURE.—I believe
that the elevation of all arts in England to their
true dignity depends principally on our recovering
that unity of purpose in sculptors and architects,
which characterised the designers of all great
Christian buildings. Sculpture, separated from
architecture, always degenerates into effeminacies
and conceits; architecture, stripped of sculpture,
is at best a convenient arrangement of dead
walls; associated, they not only adorn, but
reciprocally exalt each other, and give to all the
arts of the country in which they thus exist, a
correspondent tone of majesty.

But I would plead for the enrichment of this

doorway by portrait sculpture, not so much even on any of these important grounds, as because it would be the first example in modern English architecture of the real value and right place of commemorative statues. We seem never to know at present where to put such statues. In the midst of the blighted trees of desolate squares, or at the crossings of confused streets, or balanced on the pinnacles of pillars, or riding across the tops of triumphal arches, or blocking up the aisles of cathedrals,—in none of these positions, I think, does the portrait statue answer its purpose. It may be a question whether the erection of such statues is honourable to the erectors, but assuredly it is not honourable to the persons whom it pretends to commemorate : nor is it in any wise matter of exultation to a man who has deserved well of his country, to reflect that he may one day encumber a crossing, or disfigure a park gate. But there is no man of worth or heart, who would not feel it a high and priceless reward that his statue should be placed where it might remind the youth of England of what had been exemplary in his life, or useful in his labours, and might be regarded with no empty reverence, no fruitless pensiveness, but with the emulative, eager, unstinted passionateness of honour, which youth pays to the dead leaders of the cause it loves, or discoverers of the light by which it lives. To be buried under weight of marble, or with

I. 2 A

splendour of ceremonial, is still no more than burial; but to be remembered daily, with profitable tenderness, by the activest intelligences of the nation we have served, and to have power granted even to the shadows of the poor features, sunk into dust, to animate, to command, as the father's brow rules and exalts the toil of his children—this is not burial, but immortality. —*The Oxford Museum*, 1859 (*A. C.*, I., p. 204–206).

146. DECORATIVE ART.—The only essential distinction between Decorative and other art is the being fitted for a fixed place; and in that place, related, either in subordination or in command, to the effect of other pieces of art. And all the greatest art which the world has produced is thus fitted for a place, and subordinated to a purpose. There is no existing highest-order art but is decorative. The best sculpture yet produced has been the decoration of a temple front—the best painting, the decoration of a room. Raphael's best doing is merely the wall-colouring of a suite of apartments in the Vatican, and his cartoons were made for tapestries. Correggio's best doing is the decoration of two small church cupolas at Parma; Michael Angelo's, of a ceiling in the Pope's private chapel; Tintoret's, of a ceiling and side wall belonging to a charitable society at Venice; while Titian and Veronese threw out

their noblest thoughts, not even on the inside, but on the outside of the common brick and plaster walls of Venice.

Get rid, then, at once of any idea of Decorative art being a degraded or a separate kind of art. Its nature or essence is simply its being fitted for a definite place ; and, in that place, forming part of a great and harmonious whole, in companionship with other art ; and so far from this being a degradation to it—so far from Decorative art being inferior to other art because it is fixed to a spot—on the whole it may be considered as rather a piece of degradation that it should be portable. Portable art—independent of all place—is for the most part ignoble art. Your little Dutch landscape, which you put over your sideboard to-day, and between the windows to-morrow, is a far more contemptible piece of work than the extents of field and forest with which Benozzo has made green and beautiful the once melancholy arcade of the Campo Santo at Pisa ; and the wild boar of silver which you use for a seal, or lock into a velvet case, is little likely to be so noble a beast as the bronze boar who foams forth the fountain from under his tusks in the market-place of Florence. It is, indeed, possible that the portable picture or image may be first-rate of its kind, but it is not first-rate because it is portable ; nor are Titian's frescoes less than first-rate because they are fixed; nay, very frequently the highest compliment you can pay to a cabinet picture is to say —"It is as grand as a fresco."—*The Two Paths*, III., § 73, 74.

147. THE LAW OF TECHNICAL CONDITIONS. —Of all the various principles of art which, in modern days, we have defied or forgotten, none are more indisputable, and few of more practical importance than this:—

"All art, working with given materials, must propose to itself the objects which, with those materials, are most perfectly attainable; and becomes illegitimate and debased if it propose to itself any other objects better attainable with other materials."

Thus, great slenderness, lightness, or intricacy of structure,—as in ramifications of trees, detached folds of drapery, or wreaths of hair,— is easily and perfectly expressible in metal-work or in painting, but only with great difficulty and imperfectly expressible in sculpture. All sculpture, therefore, which professes as its chief end the expression of such characters, is debased; and if the suggestion of them be accidentally required of it, that suggestion is only to be given to an extent compatible with perfect ease of execution in the given material,—not to the utmost possible extent. For instance: some of the most delightful drawings of our own water-colour painter, Hunt, have been of bird's nests; of which, in painting, it is perfectly possible to represent the intricate fibrous or mossy structure; therefore, the effort is a legitimate one, and the art is well employed. But to carve a bird's nest out of marble would be physically impossible, and to reach any approximate expression of its structure would require prolonged and intolerable labour. Therefore, all sculpture which set itself to carving bird's nests as an end, or which, if a bird's nest were required of it, carved it to the utmost possible point of realisation, would be debased. Nothing but the general form, and as much of the fibrous structure as could be with perfect ease represented, ought to be attempted at all.

But more than this. The workman has not done his duty, and is not working on safe principles, unless he even so far *honours* the materials with which he is working as to set himself to bring out their beauty, and to recommend and exalt, as far as he can, their peculiar qualities. If he is working in marble, he should insist upon and exhibit its transparency and solidity; if in iron, its strength and tenacity; if in gold, its ductility; and he will invariably find the material grateful, and that his work is all the nobler for being eulogistic of the substance of which it is made.—*S. V.*, II., *App.* 12.

148. The Raison d'Être of Conventional Art.—The highest art, in all kinds, is that which conveys the most truth; and the best ornamentation possible would be the painting of interior walls with frescoes by Titian, representing perfect Humanity, in colour; and the sculpture of exterior walls by Phidias, representing perfect Humanity, in form. Titian and Phidias are precisely alike in their conception and treatment of nature—everlasting standards of the right.

Beneath ornamentation such as men like these could bestow, falls in various rank, according to its subordination to vulgar uses or inferior places, what is commonly conceived as ornamental art. The lower its office, and the less tractable its material, the less of nature it should contain, until a zigzag becomes the best ornament for the hem of a robe, and a mosaic of bits of glass the best design for a coloured window. But all these forms of lower art are to be conventional only because they are subordinate:—not because conventionalism is in itself a good or desirable thing. All right conventionalism is a wise acceptance of, and compliance with, conditions of restraint or inferiority;—it may be inferiority of our knowledge or power—as in the art of a semi-savage nation; or restraint by reason of material—as in the way the glass-painter should restrict himself to transparent hue, and a sculptor deny himself the eyelash and its film of flowing hair, which he cannot cut in marble;—but in all cases whatever, right conventionalism is either a wise acceptance of an inferior place, or a noble display of power under accepted limitation: it is *not* an improvement of natural form into something better or purer than Nature herself.—*The Oxford Museum*, 1859 (*A. C.*, I., p. 209–210).

149. CONVENTION A NECESSITY IN ARCHITECTURE.—The architect has no right to require of us a picture of Titian's in order to complete his design; neither has he the right to calculate on the co-operation of perfect sculptors, in subordinate capacities. Far from this; his business is to dispense with such aid altogether, and to devise such a system of ornament as shall be capable of execution by uninventive and even unintelligent workmen; for supposing that he required noble sculpture for his ornament, how far would this at once limit the number and the scale of possible buildings? Architecture is the work of nations; but we cannot have nations of great sculptors. Every house in every street of every city ought to be good architecture, but we cannot have Chantrey or Thorwaldsen at work upon it: nor, even if we chose only to devote ourselves to our public buildings, could the mass and majesty of them be great, if we required all to be executed by great men: greatness is not to be had in the required quantity. Giotto may design a

campanile, but he cannot carve it; he can only carve one or two of the bas-reliefs at the base of it. And with every increase of your fastidiousness in the execution of your ornament, you diminish the possible number and grandeur of your buildings. Do not think you can educate your workmen, or that the demand for perfection will increase the supply: educated imbecility and finessed foolishness are the worst of all imbecilities and foolishnesses; and there is no free-trade measure which will ever lower the price of brains,—there is no California of common sense. Exactly in the degree in which you require your decoration to be wrought by able men, you diminish the extent and number of architectural works. Your business as an architect, is to calculate only on the co-operation of inferior men, to think for them, and to indicate for some of them at least such expressions of your thoughts as the weakest capacity can comprehend and the feeblest hand can execute. This is the definition of the purest architectural abstractions. They are the deep and laborious thoughts of the greatest men, put into such easy letters that they can be written by the simplest. *They are expressions of the mind of manhood by the hands of childhood.*—*S. V.*, I. XXI., § 11.

150. TWO VIRTUES OF ARCHITECTURE.— The first thing we have to ask of the decoration

is that it should indicate strong liking, and that honestly. It matters not so much what the thing is, as that the builder should really love it and enjoy it, and say so plainly. The architect of Bourges Cathedral liked hawthorns; so he has covered his porch with hawthorn,—it is a perfect Niobe of May. Never was such hawthorn; you would try to gather it forthwith, but for fear of being pricked. The old Lombard architects liked hunting; so they covered their work with horses and hounds, and men blowing trumpets two yards long. The base Renaissance architects of Venice liked masquing and fiddling; so they covered their work with comic masks and musical instruments. Even that was better than our English way of liking nothing, and professing to like triglyphs.

But the second requirement in decoration, is that it should show we like the right thing. And the right thing to be liked is God's work, which He made for our delight and contentment in this world. And all noble ornamentation is the expression of man's delight in God's work.

So, then, these are the two virtues of building: first, the signs of man's own good work; secondly, the expression of man's delight in better work than his own.—*S. V.*, I. II., § 13–15.

151. THE NATURE OF ORNAMENT.—All ornament is base which takes for its subject

human work, it is utterly base,—painful to every
rightly-toned mind, without perhaps immediate
sense of the reason, but for a reason palpable
enough when we *do* think of it. For to carve
our own work, and set it up for admiration, is
a miserable self-complacency, a contentment in
our own wretched doings, when we might have
been looking at God's doings.   And all noble
ornament is the exact reverse of this.   It is the
expression of man's delight in God's work.

For observe, the function of ornament is to
make you happy.   Now in what are you rightly
happy ?   Not in thinking of what you have done
yourself; not in your own pride; not your own
birth ; not in your own being, or your own will,
but in looking at God ; watching what He does;
what He is; and obeying His law, and yielding
yourself to His will.

You are to be made happy by ornaments;
therefore they must be the expression of all this.
Not copies of your own handiwork; not boast-
ings of your own grandeur; not heraldries; not
king's arms, nor any creature's arms, but God's
arm, seen in His work.   Not manifestation of
your delight in your own laws, or your own
liberties, or your own inventions; but in divine
laws, constant, daily, common laws;—not Com-
posite laws, nor Doric laws, nor laws of the five
orders, but of the Ten Commandments.

Then the proper material of ornament will be

whatever God has created ; and its proper treatment, that which seems in accordance with or
symbolical of His laws.—*S. V.*, I. xx., § 15–17.

152. VARIETY IN ORNAMENT.—Now let us
consider for an instant what would be the effect
of continually repeating an expression of a beautiful thought to any other of the senses at times
when the mind could not address that sense to
the understanding of it. Suppose that in time
of serious occupation, of stern business, a companion should repeat in our ears continually some
favourite passage of poetry, over and over again
all day long. We should not only soon be utterly
sick and weary of the sound of it, but that sound
would at the end of the day have so sunk into
the habit of the ear that the entire meaning of
the passage would be dead to us, and it would
ever thenceforward require some effort to fix and
recover it. The music of it would not mean-
while have aided the business in hand, while its
own delightfulness would thenceforward be in a
measure destroyed. It is the same with every
other form of definite thought. If you violently
present its expression to the senses, at times
when the mind is otherwise engaged, that expression will be ineffective at the time, and will
have its sharpness and clearness destroyed for
ever. Much more if you present it to the mind
at times when it is painfully affected or disturbed,

or if you associate the expression of pleasant thought with incongruous circumstances, you will affect that expression thenceforward with a painful colour for ever.

Apply this to expressions of thought received by the eye. Remember that the eye is at your mercy more than the ear. "The eye, it cannot choose but see." Its nerve is not so easily numbed as that of the ear, and it is often busied in tracing and watching forms when the ear is at rest. Now if you present lovely forms to it when it cannot call the mind to help it in its work, and among objects of vulgar use and unhappy position, you will neither please the eye nor elevate the vulgar object. But you will fill and weary the eye with the beautiful form, and you will infect that form itself with the vulgarity of the thing to which you have violently attached it. It will never be of much use to you any more; you have killed, or defiled it; its freshness and purity are gone. You will have to pass it through the fire of much thought before you will cleanse it, and warm it with much love before it will revive.—*S. L. A.*, IV., § 17, 18.

153. The Place of Ornament.—Must not beauty, then, it will be asked, be sought for in the forms which we associate with our every-day life? Yes, if you do it consistently, and in places where it can be calmly seen; but not if you use

the beautiful form only as a mask and covering of the proper conditions and uses of things, nor if you thrust it into the places set apart for toil. Put it in the drawing-room, not into the work-shop; put it upon domestic furniture, not upon tools of handicraft. All men have sense of what is right in this matter, if they would only use and apply that sense; every man knows where and how beauty gives him pleasure, if he would only ask for it when it does so, and not allow' it to be forced upon him when he does not want it. Ask any one of the passengers over London Bridge at this instant whether he cares about the forms of the bronze leaves on its lamps, and he will tell you, No. Modify these forms of leaves to a less scale, and put them on his milk-jug at breakfast, and ask him whether he likes them, and he will tell you, Yes. People have no need of teaching if they could only think and speak truth, and ask for what they like and want, and for nothing else : nor can a right dis-position of beauty be ever arrived at except by this common sense, and allowance for the circum-stances of the time and place. It does not follow, because bronze leafage is in bad taste on the lamps of London Bridge, that it would be so on those of the Ponte della Trinità; nor, because it would be a folly to decorate the house fronts of Gracechurch Street, that it would be equally so to adorn those of some quiet provincial town.

The question of greatest external or internal decoration depends entirely on the conditions of probable repose. It was a wise feeling which made the streets of Venice so rich in external ornament, for there is no couch of rest like the gondola. So, again, there is no subject of street ornament so wisely chosen as the fountain, where it is a fountain of use; for it is just there that perhaps the happiest pause takes place in the labour of the day, when the pitcher is rested on the edge of it, and the breath of the bearer is drawn deeply, and the hair swept from the forehead, and the uprightness of the form declined against the marble ledge, and the sound of the kind word or light laugh mixes with the trickle of the falling water, heard shriller and shriller as the pitcher fills. What pause is so sweet as that—so full of the depth of ancient days, so softened with the calm of pastoral solitude?— *S. L. A.*, IV., § 23.

154. LUXURIANCE OF ORNAMENT.—It is one of the affectations of architects to speak of overcharged ornament. Ornament cannot be overcharged if it be good, and is always overcharged when it is bad. . . . It is not less the boast of some styles that they can bear ornament, than of others that they can do without it; but we do not often enough reflect that those very styles, of so haughty simplicity, owe part of their

pleasurableness to contrast, and would be wearisome if universal. They are but the rests and monotones of the art; it is to its far happier, far higher, exaltation that we owe those fair fronts of variegated mosaic, charged with wild fancies and dark hosts of imagery, thicker and quainter than ever filled the depth of midsummer dream; those vaulted gates, trellised with close leaves; those window-labyrinths of twisted tracery and starry light; those misty masses of multitudinous pinnacle and diademed tower; the only witnesses, perhaps, that remain to us of the faith and fear of nations. All else for which the builders sacrificed, has passed away—all their living interests, and aims, and achievements. We know not for what they laboured, and we see no evidence of their reward. Victory, wealth, authority, happiness—all have departed, though bought by many a bitter sacrifice. But of them, and their life and their toil upon the earth, one reward, one evidence, is left to us in those gray heaps of deep-wrought stone. They have taken with them to the grave their powers, their honours, and their errors; but they have left us their adoration.—*S. L. A.*, I., § 15.

As regards quantity of ornament, I have already said, again and again, you cannot have too much if it be good; that is, if it be thoroughly united and harmonised by the laws hitherto insisted

upon. But you may easily have too much, if
you have more than you have sense to manage.
For with every added order of ornament increases
the difficulty of discipline.   It is exactly the same
as in war ; you cannot, as an abstract law, have
too many soldiers, but you may easily have more
than the country is able to sustain, or than your
generalship is competent to command.   And every
regiment which you cannot manage will, on the
day of battle, be in your way, and encumber the
movements it is not in disposition to sustain.—
S. V., I. xxi., § 35.

155. Use of Colour in Architectural
Ornament.—I do not feel able to speak with
any confidence respecting the touching of *sculpture*
with colour.   I would only note one point, that
sculpture is the representation of an idea, while
architecture is itself a real thing.   The idea may,
as I think, be left colourless, and coloured by the
beholder's mind : but a reality ought to have
reality in all its attributes : its colour should be
as fixed as its form.   I cannot, therefore, consider
architecture as in any wise perfect without colour.
Farther, I think the colours of architecture should
be those of natural stones ; partly because more
durable, but also because more perfect and graceful.   For to conquer the harshness and deadness
of tones laid upon stone or on gesso, needs the
management and discretion of a true painter ;

and on this co-operation we must not calculate in laying down rules for general practice. If Tintoret or Giorgione are at hand, and ask us for a wall to paint, we will alter our whole design for their sake, and become their servants; but we must, as architects, expect the aid of the common workman only; and the laying of colour by a mechanical hand, and its toning under a vulgar eye, are far more offensive than rudeness in cutting the stone. The latter is imperfection only; the former deadness or discordance. At the best, such colour is so inferior to the lovely and mellow hues of the natural stone, that it is wise to sacrifice some of the intricacy of design, if by so doing we may employ the nobler material. And if, as we looked to Nature for instruction respecting form, we look to her also to learn the management of colour, we shall, perhaps, find that this sacrifice of intricacy is for other causes expedient.

First, then, I think that in making this reference we are to consider our building as a kind of organised creature; in colouring which we must look to the single and separately organised creatures of Nature, not to her landscape combinations. Our building, if it is well composed, is *one thing*, and is to be coloured as Nature would colour *one thing*—a shell, a flower, or an animal; not as she colours groups of things.— *S. L. A.*, IV., § 35, 36.

156. IMITATIONS OF MARBLE AND WOOD.
—There is not a meaner occupation for the
human mind than the imitation of the stains and
striæ of marble and wood. When engaged in any
easy and simple mechanical occupation, there
is still some liberty for the mind to leave the
literal work; and the clash of the loom or the
activity of the fingers will not always prevent the
thoughts from some happy expatiation in their
own domains. But the grainer must think of
what he is doing; and veritable attention and
care, and occasionally considerable skill, are consumed in the doing of a more absolute nothing
than I can name in any other department of
painful idleness. I know not anything so humiliating as to see a human being, with arms and
limbs complete, and apparently a head, and
assuredly a soul, yet into the hands of which
when you have put a brush and pallet, it cannot
do anything with them but imitate a piece of
wood. It cannot colour, it has no ideas of
colour; it cannot draw, it has no ideas of form;
it cannot caricature, it has no ideas of humour.
It is incapable of anything beyond knots. All
its achievement, the entire result of the daily
application of its imagination and immortality,
is to be such a piece of texture as the sun
and dew are sucking up out of the muddy
ground, and weaving together, far more finely,
in millions of millions of growing branches, over

every rood of waste woodland and shady hill.
—*S. V.*, III. I., § 46.

157. MACHINE-MADE ORNAMENT.—There
are two reasons, both weighty, against the sub-
stitution of cast or machine work for that of the
hand : one, that all cast and machine work is bad,
as work ; the other, that it is dishonest. Of its
badness I shall speak in another place, that being
evidently no efficient reason against its use when
other cannot be had. Its dishonesty, however,
which, to my mind, is of the grossest kind, is, I
think, a sufficient reason to determine absolute
and unconditional rejection of it.

Ornament, as I have often before observed, has
two entirely distinct sources of agreeableness :
one, that of the abstract beauty of its forms, which,
for the present, we will suppose to be the same
whether they come from the hand or the machine ;
the other, the sense of human labour and care
spent upon it. How great this latter influence
we may perhaps judge, by considering that there
is not a cluster of weeds growing in any cranny
of ruin which has not a beauty in all respects
nearly equal, and, in some, immeasurably superior,
to that of the most elaborate sculpture of its stones :
and that all our interest in the carved work, our
sense of its richness, though it is tenfold less rich
than the knots of grass beside it ; of its delicacy,
though it is a thousandfold less delicate ; of its

admirableness, though a millionfold less admirable; results from our consciousness of its being the work of poor, clumsy, toilsome man. Its true delightfulness depends on our discovering in it the record of thoughts, and intents, and trials, and heart-breakings—of recoveries and joyfulnesses of success: all this *can* be traced by a practised eye; but, granting it even obscure, it is presumed or understood; and in that is the worth of the thing, just as much as the worth of anything else we call precious. The worth of a diamond is simply the understanding of the time it must take to look for it before it is found; and the worth of an ornament is the time it must take before it can be cut. It has an intrinsic value besides, which the diamond has not; (for a diamond has no more real beauty than a piece of glass;) but I do not speak of that at present; I place the two on the same ground; and I suppose that hand-wrought ornament can no more be generally known from machine work, than a diamond can be known from paste; nay, that the latter may deceive, for a moment, the mason's, as the other the jeweller's, eye; and that it can be detected only by the closest examination. Yet exactly as a woman of feeling would not wear false jewels, so would a builder of honour disdain false ornaments. The using of them is just as downright and inexcusable a lie. You use that which pretends to a worth which it has not; which pretends to have cost, and to be, what it did not, and is not; it is an imposition, a vulgarity, an impertinence, and a sin. Down with it to the ground, grind it to powder, leave its ragged place upon the wall, rather; you have not paid for it, you have no business with it, you do not want it. Nobody wants ornaments in this world, but everybody wants integrity. All the fair devices that ever were fancied, are not worth a lie. Leave your walls as bare as a planed board, or build them of baked mud and chopped straw, if need be ; but do not rough-cast them with falsehood.—*S. L. A.*, II., § 19.

158. TRUE VALUE OF FINISH.—Never demand an exact finish, when it does not lead to a noble end. For observe, I have only dwelt upon the rudeness of Gothic, or any other kind of imperfectness, as admirable, where it was impossible to get design or thought without it. If you are to have the thought of a rough and untaught man, you must have it in a rough and untaught way ; but from an educated man, who can without effort express his thoughts in an educated way, take the graceful expression, and be thankful. Only *get* the thought, and do not silence the peasant because he cannot speak good grammar, or until you have taught him his grammar. Grammar and refinement are good things, both ; only be sure of the better

thing first. And thus in art, delicate finish is desirable from the greatest masters, and is always given by them. In some places Michael Angelo, Leonardo, Phidias, Perugino, Turner, all finished with the most exquisite care; and the finish they give always leads to the fuller accomplishment of their noble purposes. But lower men than these cannot finish, for it requires consummate knowledge to finish consummately, and then we must take their thoughts as they are able to give them. So the rule is simple. Always look for invention first, and after that, for such execution as will help the invention, and as the inventor is capable of without painful effort, and *no more*. Above all, demand no refinement of execution where there is no thought, for that is slaves' work, unredeemed. Rather choose rough work than smooth work, so only that the practical purpose be answered, and never imagine there is reason to be proud of anything that may be accomplished by patience and sand-paper.

I shall only give one example, which however will show the reader what I mean, from the manufacture of glass. Our modern glass is exquisitely clear in its substance, true in its form, accurate in its cutting. We are proud of this. We ought to be ashamed of it. The old Venice glass was muddy, inaccurate in all its forms, and clumsily cut, if at all. And the old Venetian was justly proud of it.   For there is this difference between the English and Venetian workman, that the former thinks only of accurately matching his patterns, and getting his curves perfectly true and his edges perfectly sharp, and becomes a mere machine for rounding curves and sharpening edges; while the old Venetian cared not a whit whether his edges were sharp or not, but he invented a new design for every glass that he made, and never moulded a handle or a lip without a new fancy in it.   And therefore, though some Venetian glass is ugly and clumsy enough, when made by clumsy and uninventive workmen, other Venetian glass is so lovely in its forms that no price is too great for it; and we never see the same form in it twice.   Now you cannot have the finish and the varied form too.   If the workman is thinking about his edges, he cannot be thinking of his design; if of his design, he cannot think of his edges.   Choose whether you will pay for the lovely form or the perfect finish, and choose at the same moment whether you will make the worker a man or a grindstone.

Nay, but the reader interrupts me,—"If the workman can design beautifully, I would not have him kept at the furnace.   Let him be taken away and made a gentleman, and have a studio, and design his glass there, and I will have it blown and cut for him by common workmen, and so I will have my design and my finish too."

All ideas of this kind are founded upon two mistaken suppositions: the first, that one man's thoughts can be, or ought to be, executed by another man's hands; the second, that manual labour is a degradation, when it is governed by intellect.—*S. V.*, II. VI., § 19–21.

159. FINISH IN SCULPTURE.—I cannot too often repeat, it is not coarse cutting, it is not blunt cutting, that is necessarily bad; but it is *cold* cutting—the look of equal trouble everywhere—the smooth, diffused tranquillity of heartless pains—the regularity of a plough in a level field. The chill is more likely, indeed, to show itself in finished work than in any other—men cool and tire as they complete: and if completeness is thought to be vested in polish, and to be attainable by help of sand-paper, we may as well give the work to the engine-lathe at once. But *right* finish is simply the full rendering of the intended impression; and *high* finish is the rendering of a well intended and vivid impression; and it is oftener got by rough than fine handling. I am not sure whether it is frequently enough observed that sculpture is not the mere cutting of the *form* of any thing in stone; it is the cutting of the *effect* of it. Very often the true form, in the marble, would not be in the least like itself. The sculptor must paint with his chisel: half his touches are not to realise,

but to put power into, the form : they are touches
of light and shadow; and raise a ridge, or sink
a hollow, not to represent an actual ridge or
hollow, but to get a line of light, or a spot of
darkness.—*S. L. A.*, V., § 21.

160. CHIAROSCURO IN ARCHITECTURE.—
Rembrandtism is a noble manner in architecture,
though a false one in painting; and I do not
believe that ever any building was truly great,
unless it had mighty masses, vigorous and deep,
of shadow mingled with its surface. And among
the first habits that a young architect should
learn, is that of thinking in shadow, not looking
at a design in its miserable liny skeleton; but
conceiving it as it will be when the dawn lights
it, and the dusk leaves it; when its stones will
be hot, and its crannies cool; when the lizards
will bask on the one, and the birds build in
the other. Let him design with the sense of
cold and heat upon him; let him cut out the
shadows, as men dig wells in unwatered plains;
and lead along the lights, as a founder does his
hot metal; let him keep the full command of
both, and see that he knows how they fall, and
where they fade. His paper lines and proportions are of no value : all that he has to do
must be done by spaces of light and darkness;
and his business is to see that the one is broad
and bold enough not to be swallowed up by

twilight, and the other deep enough not to be dried like a shallow pool by a noon-day sun.

And, that this may be, the first necessity is that the quantities of shade or light, whatever they may be, shall be thrown into masses, either of something like equal weight, or else large masses of the one relieved with small of the other; but masses of one or other kind there must be. No design that is divided at all, and is not divided into masses, can ever be of the smallest value: this great law respecting breadth, precisely the same in architecture and painting, is so important, that the examination of its two principal applications will include most of the conditions of majestic design on which I would at present insist.—*S. L. A.*, III., § 13.

161. THE LIMITS OF ART-EDUCATION.— Such, then, are a few of the great principles, by the enforcement of which you may hope to promote the success of the modern student of design; but remember, none of these principles will be useful at all, unless you understand them to be, in one profound and stern sense, useless.

That is to say, unless you feel that neither you nor I, nor any one, can, in the great ultimate sense, teach anybody how to make a good design.

If designing *could* be taught, all the world would learn; as all the world reads, or calculates.

But designing is not to be spelled, nor summed. My men continually come to me, in my drawing class in London, thinking I am to teach them what is instantly to enable them to gain their bread. "Please, sir, show us how to design." "Make designers of us." And you, I doubt not, partly expect me to tell you to-night how to make designers of your Bradford youths. Alas! I could as soon tell you how to make or manufacture an ear of wheat, as to make a good artist of any kind. I can analyse the wheat very learnedly for you, and tell you there is starch in it, and carbon, and silex. I can give you starch, and charcoal, and flint; but you are as far from your ear of wheat as you were before. All that can possibly be done for any one who wants ears of wheat is to show them where to find grains of wheat, and how to sow them; and then, with patience, in Heaven's time, the ears will come—or will perhaps come,—ground and weather permitting. So in this matter of making artists; first you must find your artist in the grain; then you must plant him; fence and weed the field about him; and with patience, ground and weather permitting, you may get an artist out of him—not otherwise.—*T. P.*, III., § 86.

162. THE CONDITIONS OF ART-CRAFTSMANSHIP.—Do you suppose Gothic decoration is an easy thing, or that it is to be carried out with

a certainty of success at the first trial, under new
and difficult conditions?   The system of the
Gothic decorations took eight hundred years to
mature, gathering its power by undivided inheritance of traditional method, and unbroken acces-
sion of systematic power; from its culminating
point in the Sainte Chapelle, it faded through four
hundred years of splendid decline; now for two
centuries it has lain dead,—and more than so—
buried; and more than so—forgotten, as a dead
man out of mind: do you expect to revive it out
of those retorts and furnaces of yours, as the
cloud-spirit of the Arabian sea rose from beneath
the seals of Solomon?   Perhaps I have been
myself faultfully answerable for this too eager
hope in your mind (as well as in that of others)
by what I have urged so often respecting the
duty of bringing out the power of subordinate
workmen in decorative design.   But do you think
I meant workmen trained (or untrained) in the
way that ours have been until lately, and then
cast loose on a sudden, into unassisted conten-
tions with unknown elements of style?   I meant
the precise contrary of this; I meant workmen
as we have yet to create them: men inheriting
the instincts of their craft through many generations, rigidly trained in every mechanical art that
bears on their materials, and familiarised from
infancy with every condition of their beautiful
and perfect treatment; informed and refined in

manhood, by constant observation of all natural
fact and form; then classed, according to their
proved capacities, in ordered companies, in which
every man shall know his part, and take it calmly
and without effort or doubt—indisputably well,—
unaccusably accomplished—mailed and weaponed
cap-à-pie for his place and function.   Can you
lay your hand on such men? or do you think
that mere natural good-will and good-feeling can
at once supply their place?   Not so—and the
more faithful and earnest the minds you have to
deal with, the more careful you should be not
to urge them towards fields of effort, in which,
too early committed, they can only be put to
unserviceable defeat.— *The Oxford Museum*, 1859
(*A. C.*, I., p. 198–200).

163. ARTISTS AND CRAFTSMEN.—On a large
scale, and in work determinable by line and rule,
it is indeed both possible and necessary that the
thoughts of one man should be carried out by
the labour of others; in this sense I have already
defined the best architecture to be the expression
of the mind of manhood by the hands of childhood.   But on a smaller scale, and in a design
which cannot be mathematically defined, one
man's thoughts can never be expressed by
another: and the difference between the spirit of
touch of the man who is inventing and of the
man who is obeying directions, is often all the

difference between a great and a common work of art. How wide the separation is between original and second-hand execution, I shall endeavour to show elsewhere; it is not so much to our purpose here as to mark the other and more fatal error of despising manual labour when governed by intellect; for it is no less fatal an error to despise it when thus regulated by intellect, than to value it for its own sake. We are always in these days endeavouring to separate the two; we want one man to be always thinking, and another to be always working, and we call one a gentleman, and the other an operative; whereas the workman ought often to be thinking, and the thinker often to be working, and both should be gentlemen, in the best sense. As it is, we make both ungentle, the one envying, the other despising, his brother; and the mass of society is made up of morbid thinkers, and miserable workers. Now it is only by labour that thought can be made healthy, and only by thought that labour can be made happy, and the two cannot be separated with impunity. It would be well if all of us were good handicraftsmen in some kind, and the dishonour of manual labour done away with altogether; so that though there should still be a trenchant distinction of race between nobles and commoners, there should not, among the latter, be a trenchant distinction of employment, as between idle and working men, or between men of liberal and illiberal professions. All professions should be liberal, and there should be less pride felt in peculiarity of employment, and more in excellence of achievement. And yet more, in each several profession, no master should be too proud to do its hardest work. The painter should grind his own colours; the architect work in the mason's yard with his men; the master manufacturer be himself a more skilful operative than any man in his mills; and the distinction between one man and another be only in experience and skill, and the authority and wealth which these must naturally and justly obtain.—*S. V.*, II. VI., § 21.

164. FOR ART'S SAKE.—Is your art first with you? Then you are artists; you may be, after you have made your money, misers and usurers; you may be, after you have got your fame, jealous, and proud, and wretched, and base:— but yet, *as long as you won't spoil your work*, you are artists. On the other hand—Is your money first with you, and your fame first with you? Then, you may be very charitable with your money, and very graceful in the way you wear your reputation, and very courteous to those beneath you, and very acceptable to those above you; but you are *not artists*. You are mechanics, and drudges.—*T. P.*, IV., § 135.

165. How to get Good Art.—There's no way of getting good Art, I repeat, but one—at once the simplest and most difficult—namely, to enjoy it. Examine the history of nations, and you will find this great fact clear and unmistakable on the front of it—that good Art has only been produced by nations who rejoiced in it; fed themselves with it, as if it were bread; basked in it, as if it were sunshine; shouted at the sight of it; danced with the delight of it; quarrelled for it; fought for it; starved for it; did, in fact, precisely the opposite with it of what we want to do with it—they made it to keep, and we to sell.

And truly this is a serious difficulty for us as a commercial nation. The very primary motive with which we set about the business, makes the business impossible. The first and absolute condition of the thing's ever becoming saleable is, that we shall make it without wanting to sell it; nay, rather with a determination not to sell it at any price, if once we get hold of it. Try to make your Art popular, cheap—a fair article for your foreign market; and the foreign market will always show something better. But make it only to please yourselves, and even be resolved that you won't let anybody else have any; and forthwith you will find everybody else wants it.—*Inaugural Address, Cambridge School of Art* (*O. R.,* I., § 299–300).

166. STUDIES FOR THE ARCHITECT.—An architect should live as little in cities as a painter. Send him to our hills, and let him study there what nature understands by a buttress, and what by a dome. There was something in the old power of architecture, which it had from the recluse more than from the citizen. The buildings of which I have spoken with chief praise, rose, indeed, out of the war of the piazza, and above the fury of the populace; and Heaven forbid that for such cause we should ever have to lay a larger stone, or rivet a firmer bar, in our England! But we have other sources of power, in the imagery of our iron coasts and azure hills; of power more pure, nor less serene, than that of the hermit spirit which once lighted with white lines of cloisters the glades of the Alpine pine, and raised into ordered spires the wild rocks of the Norman sea; which gave to the temple gate the depth and darkness of Elijah's Horeb cave; and lifted out of the populous city, gray cliffs of lonely stone, into the midst of sailing birds and silent air.—*S. L. A.*. III., § 24.

VI.

ETHICAL AND DIDACTIC.

167. KNOWLEDGE.—The real animating power of knowledge is only in the moment of its being first received, when it fills us with wonder and joy; a joy for which, observe, the previous ignorance is just as necessary as the present knowledge. That man is always happy who is in the presence of something which he cannot know to the full, which he is always going on to know. This is the necessary condition of a finite creature with divinely rooted and divinely directed intelligence; this, therefore, its happy state,—but observe, a state, not of triumph or joy in what it knows, but of joy rather in the continual discovery of new ignorance, continual self-abasement, continual astonishment. Once thoroughly our own, the knowledge ceases to give us pleasure. It may be practically useful to us, it may be good for others, or good for usury to obtain more; but, in itself, once let it be thoroughly familiar, and it is dead. The wonder is gone from it, and all the fine colour which it had when first we drew it up out of the infinite sea. . . . All men feel this,

though they do not think of it, nor reason out its consequences. They look back to the days of childhood as of greatest happiness, because those were the days of greatest wonder, greatest simplicity, and most vigorous imagination. And the whole difference between a man of genius and other men, it has been said a thousand times, and most truly, is that the first remains in great part a child, seeing with the large eyes of children, in perpetual wonder, not conscious of much knowledge,—conscious, rather, of infinite ignorance, and yet infinite power; a fountain of eternal admiration, delight, and creative force within him, meeting the ocean of visible and governable things around him.—*S. V.*, III. II., § 28.

168. LIMBS OF THE MIND.—As our bodies, to be in health, must be *generally* exercised, so our minds, to be in health, must be *generally* cultivated. You would not call a man healthy who had strong arms, but was paralytic in his feet; nor one who could walk well, but had no use of his hands; nor one who could see well, if he could not hear. You would not voluntarily reduce your bodies to any such partially developed state. Much more, then, you would not, if you could help it, reduce your minds to it. Now, your minds are endowed with a vast number of gifts of totally different uses—limbs of mind as it were, which, if you

don't exercise, you cripple. One is curiosity; that is a gift, a capacity of pleasure in knowing; which if you destroy, you make yourselves cold and dull. Another is sympathy; the power of sharing in the feelings of living creatures, which if you destroy, you make yourselves hard and cruel. Another of your limbs of mind is admiration; the power of enjoying beauty or ingenuity, which if you destroy, you make yourselves base and irreverent. Another is wit; or the power of playing with the lights on the many sides of truth; which if you destroy, you make yourselves gloomy, and less useful and cheering to others than you might be. So that in choosing your way of work it should be your aim, as far as possible, to bring out all these faculties, as far as they exist in you; not one merely, nor another, but all of them. And the way to bring them out, is simply to concern yourselves attentively with the subjects of each faculty. To cultivate sympathy you must be among living creatures, and thinking about them; and to cultivate admiration, you must be among beautiful things and looking at them.—*T. P.*, IV., § 110.

169. EDUCATION.—It might be matter of dispute what processes have the greatest effect in developing the intellect; but it can hardly be disputed what facts it is most advisable that a man entering into life should accurately know.

I believe, in brief, that he ought to know three things :—

First, Where he is :

Secondly, Where he is going :

Thirdly, What he had best do under those circumstances.

First, Where he is.—That is to say, what sort of a world he has got into; how large it is; what kind of creatures live in it, and how; what it is made of, and what may be made of it.

Secondly, Where he is going.—That is to say, what chances or reports there are of any other world besides this; what seems to be the nature of that other world; and whether, for information respecting it he had better consult the Bible, Koran, or Council of Trent.

Thirdly, What he had best do under those circumstances.—That is to say, what kind of faculties he possesses; what are the present state and wants of mankind; what is his place in Society; and what are the readiest means in his power of attaining happiness and diffusing it. The man who knows these things, and who has had his will so subdued in the learning them, that he is ready to do what he knows he ought, I should call educated ; and the man who knows them not,—uneducated, though he could talk all the tongues of Babel. . . .

The great leading error of modern times is the mistaking erudition for education. I call it the

leading error, for I believe that, with little difficulty, nearly every other might be shown to have
root in it; and, most assuredly, the worst that
are fallen into on the subject of art.

Education then, briefly, is the leading human
souls to what is best, and making what is best
out of them; and these two objects are always
attainable together, and by the same means;
the training which makes men happiest in themselves also makes them most serviceable to others.
True education, then, has respect, first to the
ends which are proposable to the man, or attainable by him; and, secondly, to the material of
which the man is made. So far as it is able,
it chooses the end according to the material:
but it cannot always choose the end, for the
position of many persons in life is fixed by
necessity; still less can it choose the material;
and, therefore, all it can do is to fit the one to
the other as wisely as may be.

But the first point to be understood is that
the material is as various as the ends; that not
only one man is unlike another, but *every* man
is essentially different from *every* other, so that
no training, no forming, nor informing, will ever
make two persons alike in thought or in power.
Among all men, whether of the upper or lower
orders, the differences are eternal and irrecon-
cilable, between one individual and another, born
under absolutely the same circumstances. One

man is made of agate, another of oak ; one of
slate, another of clay. The education of the first
is polishing ; of the second, seasoning ; of the
third, rending ; of the fourth, moulding. It is
of no use to season the agate ; it is vain to try
to polish the slate ; but both are fitted, by the
qualities they possess, for services in which they
may be honoured.

Now the cry for the education of the lower
classes, which is heard every day more widely
and loudly, is a wise and a sacred cry, provided
it be extended into one for the education of *all*
classes, with definite respect to the work each
man has to do, and the substance of which he
is made. But it is a foolish and vain cry, if it
be understood, as in the plurality of cases it is
meant to be, for the expression of mere craving
after knowledge, irrespective of the simple purposes of the life that now is, and blessings of that
which is to come.

One great fallacy into which men are apt to
fall when they are reasoning on this subject is :
that light, as such, is always good ; and darkness,
as such, always evil. Far from it. Light un-
tempered would be annihilation. It is good to
them that sit in darkness and in the shadow of
death ; but to those that faint in the wilderness,
so also is the shadow of the great rock in a
weary land. If the sunshine is good, so also
is the cloud of the latter rain. Light is only

beautiful, only available for life, when it is tempered with shadow; pure light is fearful, and unendurable by humanity. And it is not less ridiculous to say that the light, as such, is good in itself, than to say that the darkness is good in itself. Both are rendered safe, healthy, and useful by the other; the night by the day, the day by the night; and we could just as easily live without the dawn as without the sunset, so long as we are human. Of the celestial city we are told there shall be "no night there," and then we shall know even as also we are known: but the night and the mystery have both their service here; and our business is not to strive to turn the night into day, but to be sure that we are as they that watch for the morning.

Therefore, in the education either of lower or upper classes, it matters not the least how much or how little they know, provided they know just what will fit them to do their work, and to be happy in it. What the sum or the nature of their knowledge ought to be at a given time or in a given case, is a totally different question: the main thing to be understood is, that a man is not educated, in any sense whatsoever, because he can read Latin, or write English, or can behave well in a drawing-room; but that he is only educated if he is happy, busy, beneficent, and effective in the world; that millions of peasants are therefore at this moment better

educated than most of those who call themselves
gentlemen ; and that the means taken to "educate" the lower classes in any other sense may
very often be productive of a precisely opposite
result.

Observe, I do not say, nor do I believe, that
the lower classes ought not to be better educated,
in millions of ways, than they are. I believe
*every man in a Christian kingdom ought to be
equally well educated.* But I would have it education to purpose ; stern, practical, irresistible,
in moral habits, in bodily strength and beauty, in
all faculties of mind capable of being developed
under the circumstances of the individual, and
especially in the technical knowledge of his own
business ; but yet, infinitely various in its effort,
directed to make one youth humble, and another
confident ; to tranquillise this mind, to put some
spark of ambition into that ; now to urge, and
now to restrain : and in the doing of all this, considering knowledge as one only out of myriads
of means in its hands, or myriads of gifts at its
disposal ; and giving it or withholding it as a good
husbandman waters his garden, giving the full
shower only to the thirsty plants, and at times
when they are thirsty; whereas at present we
pour it upon the heads of our youth as the snow
falls on the Alps, on one and another alike, till
they can bear no more, and then take honour to
ourselves because here and there a river descends

from their crests into the valleys, not observing that we have made the loaded hills themselves barren for ever.—*S. V.*, III., *App. 7.*

170. ON BOOKS AND READING.—Your judgment will be, of course, much affected by your taste in literature. Indeed, I know many persons who have the purest taste in literature, and yet false taste in art, and it is a phenomenon which puzzles me not a little; but I have never known any one with false taste in books, and true taste in pictures. It is also of the greatest importance to you, not only for art's sake, but for all kinds of sake, in these days of book deluge, to keep out of the salt swamps of literature, and live on a little rocky island of your own, with a spring and a lake in it, pure and good. I cannot, of course, suggest the choice of your library to you: every several mind needs different books; but there are some books which we all need, and assuredly, if you read Homer, Plato, Æschylus, Herodotus, Dante, Shakespere, and Spenser, as much as you ought, you will not require wide enlargement of shelves to right and left of them for purposes of perpetual study. Among modern books, avoid generally magazine and review literature. Sometimes it may contain a useful abridgement or a wholesome piece of criticism; but the chances are ten to one it will either waste your time or mislead you. If you

want to understand any subject whatever, read
the best book upon it you can hear of: not a
review of the book. If you don't like the first
book you try, seek for another; but do not hope
ever to understand the subject without pains,
by a reviewer's help. Avoid especially that
class of literature which has a knowing tone;
it is the most poisonous of all. Every good book,
or piece of book, is full of admiration and awe;
it may contain firm assertion or stern satire,
but it never sneers coldly, nor asserts haughtily,
and it always leads you to reverence or love
something with your whole heart. It is not
always easy to distinguish the satire of the
venomous race of books from the satire of the
noble and pure ones; but in general you may
notice that the cold-blooded, Crustacean and
Batrachian books will sneer at sentiment; and
the warm-blooded, human books, at sin. . . .

Read little at a time, trying to feel interest in
little things, and reading not so much for the sake
of the story as to get acquainted with the pleasant
people into whose company these writers bring
you. A common book will often give you much
amusement, but it is only a noble book which will
give you dear friends. Remember, also, that it
is of less importance to you in your earlier years,
that the books you read should be clever than
that they should be right. I do not mean oppressively or repulsively instructive; but that the

thoughts they express should be just, and the feelings they excite generous. . . .

Certainly at present, and perhaps through all your life, your teachers are wisest when they make you content in quiet virtue, and that literature and art are best for you which point out, in common life, and in familiar things, the objects for hopeful labour, and for humble love.—*E. D., App.* 2.

171. MANUAL TRAINING.—All youths, of whatever rank, ought to learn some manual trade thoroughly; for it is quite wonderful how much a man's views of life are cleared by the attainment of the capacity of doing any one thing well with his hands and arms. For a long time, what right life there was in the upper classes of Europe depended in no small degree on the necessity which each man was under of learning to fence; at this day, the most useful things which boys learn at public schools are, I believe, riding, rowing, and cricketing. But it would be far better that members of Parliament should be able to plough straight, and make a horseshoe, than only to feather oars neatly or point their toes prettily in stirrups.—*Political Economy of Art, Addenda* (*J. E.*, § 128).

172. GREAT MEN INDUSTRIOUS.—If we were to be asked abruptly, and required to answer

briefly, what qualities chiefly distinguish great artists from feeble artists, we should answer, I suppose, first, their sensibility and tenderness; secondly, their imagination; and thirdly, their industry. Some of us might, perhaps, doubt the justice of attaching so much importance to this last character, because we have all known clever men who were indolent, and dull men who were industrious. But though you may have known clever men who were indolent, you never knew a *great* man who was so; and, during such investigation as I have been able to give to the lives of the artists whose works are in all points noblest, no fact ever looms so large upon me—no law remains so steadfast in the universality of its application, as the fact and law that they are all great workers: nothing concerning them is matter of more astonishment than the quantity they have accomplished in the given length of their life; and when I hear a young man spoken of, as giving promise of high genius, the first question I ask about him is always—

Does he work?

But though this quality of industry is essential to an artist, it does not in any wise make an artist; many people are busy, whose doings are little worth. Neither does sensibility make an artist; since, as I hope, many can feel both strongly and nobly, who yet care nothing about art. But the gifts which distinctively mark the artist—*without* which he must be feeble in life, forgotten in death—*with* which he may become one of the shakers of the earth, and one of the signal lights in heaven—are those of sympathy and imagination.—*T. P.*, IV., § 98, 99.

173. EFFORT AND SUCCESS.—How many pangs would be spared to thousands, if this great truth and law were but once sincerely, humbly understood—that if a great thing can be done at all, it can be done easily; that, when it is needed to be done, there is perhaps only one man in the world who can do it; but *he* can do it without any trouble—without more trouble, that is, than it costs small people to do small things; nay, perhaps with less. And yet what truth lies more openly on the surface of all human phenomena? Is not the evidence of Ease on the very front of all the greatest works in existence? Do they not say plainly to us,—not, "there has been a great *effort* here," but "there has been a great *power* here"? . . .

Yet let me not be misunderstood, nor this great truth be supposed anywise resolvable into the favourite dogma of young men, that they need not work if they have genius. The fact is that a man of genius is always far more ready to work than other people, and gets so much more good from the work that he does, and is often so little conscious of the inherent divinity in himself, that he is very apt to ascribe all his capacity to his work, and to tell those who ask him how he came to be what he is, "If I *am* anything, which I much doubt, I made myself so merely by labour." This was Newton's way of talking, and I suppose it would be the general tone of men whose genius had been devoted to the physical sciences. Genius in the Arts must commonly be more self-conscious, but in whatever field, it will always be distinguished by its perpetual, steady, well-directed, happy, and faithful labour in accumulating and disciplining its powers, as well as by its gigantic, incommunicable facility in exercising them. Therefore, literally, it is no man's business whether he has genius or not: work he must, whatever he is; but quietly and steadily; and the natural and unforced results of such work will be always the things that God meant him to do, and will be his best. No agonies nor heart-rendings will enable him to do any better. If he be a great man, they will be great things; if a small man, small things; but always, if thus peacefully done, good and right; always, if restlessly and ambitiously done, false, hollow, and despicable.—*Pre-Raphaelitism* (*O. R.*, I., § 170, 171).

174. PRIZES.—I believe all emulation to be a false motive, and all giving of prizes a false means. All that you can depend upon in a boy,

as significative of true power, likely to issue in good fruit, is his will to work for the work's sake, not his desire to surpass his school-fellows; and the aim of the teaching you give him ought to be, to prove to him and strengthen in him his own separate gift, not to put him into swollen rivalry with those who are everlastingly greater than he: still less ought you to hang favours and ribands about the neck of the creature who is the greatest, to make the rest envy him. Try to make them love him and follow him, not struggle with him.

There must, of course, be examination to ascertain and attest both progress and relative capacity; but our aim should be to make the students rather look upon it as a means of ascertaining their own true positions and powers in the world, than as an arena in which to carry away a present victory.—*Political Economy of Art, Addenda (J. E., § 135, 136).*

175. EVIL OF PRIDE.—I have been more and more convinced, the more I think of it, that in general *pride is at the bottom of all great mistakes.* All the other passions do occasional good, but whenever pride puts in *its* word, everything goes wrong, and what it might really be desirable to do, quietly and innocently, it is mortally dangerous to do, proudly. Thus, while it is very often good for the artist to make *studies* of things, for the sake of knowing their forms, with their

high lights all white, the moment he does this in a haughty way, and thinks himself drawing in the great style, because he leaves high lights white, it is all over with him; and half the degradation of art in modern times has been owing to endeavours, much fostered by the metaphysical Germans, to see things without colour, as if colour were a vulgar thing, the result being, in most students, that they end by not being able to see anything at all; whereas the true and perfect way of studying any object is simply to look what its colour is in high light, and put that safely down, if possible; or, if you are making a chiaroscuro study, to take the gray answering to that colour, and cover the *whole* object at once with that gray, firmly resolving that no part of it shall be brighter than that; then look for the darkest part of it, and if, as is probable, its darkest part be still a great deal lighter than black, or than other things about it, assume a given shade, as dark as, with due reference to other things, you can have it, but no darker. Mark that for your extreme dark on the object, and between those limits get as much drawing as you can, by subtlety of gradation. That will tax your powers of drawing indeed; and you will find this, which seems a childish and simple way of going to work, requires verily a thousandfold more power to carry out than all the pseudo-scientific abstractions that ever were invented.—*M. P.*, IV. v. 3, § 22.

176. FIRST IMPRESSIONS.—Generally speaking, I find that when we first look at a subject, we get a glimpse of some of the greatest truths about it: as we look longer, our vanity, and false reasoning, and half-knowledge, lead us into various wrong opinions; but as we look longer still, we gradually return to our first impressions, only with a full understanding of their mystical and innermost reasons; and of much beyond and beside them, not then known to us, now added (partly as a foundation, partly as a corollary) to what at first we felt or saw. It is thus eminently in this matter of colour. Lay your hand over the page of this book,—any child or simple person looking at the hand and book, would perceive, as the main fact of the matter, that a brownish pink thing was laid over a white one. The grand artist comes and tells you that your hand is not pink, and your paper is not white. He shades your fingers and shades your book, and makes you see all manner of starting veins, and projecting muscles, and black hollows, where before you saw nothing but paper and fingers. But go a little farther, and you will get more innocent again; you will find that, when "science has done its worst, two and two still make four;" and that the main and most important facts about your hand, so seen, are, after all, that it has four fingers and a thumb —showing as brownish pink things on white paper.—*M. P.*, IV. V. 3, § 21.

177. As Little Children.—Everybody likes to do good; but not one in a hundred finds *this* out. Multitudes think they like to do evil; yet no man ever really enjoyed doing evil since God made the world.

So in this lesser matter of ornament. It needs some little care to try experiments upon yourself; it needs deliberate question and upright answer. But there is no difficulty to be overcome, no abstruse reasoning to be gone into; only a little watchfulness needed, and thoughtfulness, and so much honesty as will enable you to confess to yourself, and to all men, that you enjoy things, though great authorities say you should not.

This looks somewhat like pride; but it is true humility, a trust that you have been so created as to enjoy what is fitting for you, and a willingness to be pleased, as it was intended you should be. It is the child's spirit, which we are most happy when we most recover; remaining wiser than children in our gratitude that we can still be pleased with a fair colour, or a dancing light. And, above all, do not try to make all these pleasures reasonable, nor to connect the delight which you take in ornament with that which you take in construction or usefulness. They have no connection; and every effort that you make to reason from one to the other will blunt your sense of beauty, or confuse it with sensations altogether inferior to it. You were made for enjoyment, and the world was filled with things which you will enjoy, unless you are too proud to be pleased by them, or too grasping to care for what you cannot turn to other account than mere delight. Remember that the most beautiful things in the world are the most useless ; peacocks and lilies, for instance ; at least I suppose this quill I hold in my hand writes better than a peacock's would, and the peasants of Vevay, whose fields in spring time are as white with lilies as the Dent du Midi is with its snow, told me the hay was none the better for them.—*S. V.*, I. ii., § 16, 17.

178. NOVELTY.—The enormous influence of novelty—the way in which it quickens observation, sharpens sensation, and exalts sentiment—is not half enough taken note of by us, and is to me a very sorrowful matter. I think that what Wordsworth speaks of as a glory in the child, because it has come fresh from God's hands, is in reality nothing more than the freshness of all things to its newly opened sight. I find that by keeping long away from hills, I can in great part still restore the old childish feeling about them ; and the more I live and work among them, the more it vanishes.

This evil is evidently common to all minds ; Wordsworth himself mourning over it in the same poem :

> " Custom hangs upon us, with a weight
> Heavy as frost, and deep almost as life."

And if we grow impatient under it, and seek to recover the mental energy by more quickly repeated and brighter novelty, it is all over with our enjoyment. There is no cure for this evil, any more than for the weariness of the imagination already described, but in patience and rest: if we try to obtain perpetual change, change itself will become monotonous; and then we are reduced to that old despair, " If water chokes, what will you drink after it ? " And the two points of practical wisdom in this matter are, first, to be content with as little novelty as possible at a time; and, secondly, to preserve, as much as possible in the world, the sources of novelty.

I say, first, to be content with as little change as possible. If the attention is awake, and the feelings in proper train, a turn of a country road, with a cottage beside it, which we have not seen before, is as much as we need for refreshment; if we hurry past it, and take two cottages at a time, it is already too much : hence, to any person who has all his senses about him, a quiet walk along not more than ten or twelve miles of road a day, is the most amusing of all travelling; and all travelling becomes dull in exact proportion to its rapidity. Going by railroad I do not consider as travelling at all ; it is merely " being sent " to a place, and very little different from becoming a parcel; the next step to it would of course be

telegraphic transport, of which, however, I suppose it has been truly said by Octave Feuillet,

"*Il y aurait des gens assez bêtes* pour trouver çà amusant."

If we walk more than ten or twelve miles, it breaks
up the day too much; leaving no time for stopping
at the stream sides or shady banks, or for any
work at the end of the day; besides that the last
few miles are apt to be done in a hurry, and may
then be considered as lost ground. But if, advancing thus slowly, after some days we approach
any more interesting scenery, every yard of the
changeful ground becomes precious and piquant;
and the continual increase of hope, and of surrounding beauty, affords one of the most exquisite
enjoyments possible to the healthy mind; besides
that real knowledge is acquired of whatever it is
the object of travelling to learn, and a certain
sublimity given to all places, so attained, by the
true sense of the spaces of earth that separate
them. A man who really loves travelling would
as soon consent to pack a day of such happiness
into an hour of railroad, as one who loved eating
would agree, if it were possible, to concentrate
his dinner into a pill.

And, secondly, I say that it is wisdom to
preserve as much as possible the innocent *sources*
of novelty;—not definite inferiorities of one place
to another, if such can be done away; but differences of manners and customs, of language and

architecture. The greatest effort ought especially to be made by all wise and far-sighted persons, in the present crisis of civilisation, to enforce the distinction between wholesome reform, and heartless abandonment of ancestral custom; between kindly fellowship of nation with nation, and apelike adoption, by one, of the habits of another. It is ludicrously woeful to see the luxurious inhabitants of London and Paris rushing over the Continent (as they say, to *see* it), and transposing every place, as far as lies in their power, instantly into a likeness of Regent Street and the Rue de la Paix, which they need not certainly have come so far to see.—*M. P.*, III., IV. 17, § 22–25.

179. GOOD BREEDING.—Two great errors, colouring, or rather discolouring, severally, the minds of the higher and lower classes, have sown wide dissension, and wider misfortune, through the society of modern days. These errors are in our modes of interpreting the word "gentleman."

Its primal, literal, and perpetual meaning is "a man of pure race;" well bred, in the sense that a horse or dog is well bred.

The so-called higher classes, being generally of purer race than the lower, have retained the true idea, and the convictions associated with it; but are afraid to speak it out, and equivocate about it in public; this equivocation mainly proceeding from their desire to connect another meaning with it, and a false one;—that of "a man living in idleness on other people's labour;" —with which idea the term has nothing whatever to do.

The lower classes, denying vigorously, and with reason, the notion that a gentleman means an idler, and rightly feeling that the more any one works, the more of a gentleman he becomes, and is likely to become,—have nevertheless got little of the good they otherwise might, from the truth, because, with it, they wanted to hold a falsehood,—namely, that race was of no consequence. It being precisely of as much consequence in man as it is in any other animal.

The nation cannot truly prosper till both these errors are finally got quit of. Gentlemen have to learn that it is no part of their duty or privilege to live on other people's toil. They have to learn that there is no degradation in the hardest manual, or the humblest servile, labour, when it is honest. But that there *is* degradation, and that deep, in extravagance, in bribery, in indolence, in pride, in taking places they are not fit for, or in coining places for which there is no need. It does not disgrace a gentleman to become an errand boy, or a day labourer; but it disgraces him much to become a knave, or a thief. And knavery is not the less knavery because it involves large interests, nor theft the less theft because it is countenanced by usage, or accompanied by failure in undertaken duty. It is an incomparably less guilty form of robbery to cut a purse out of a man's pocket, than to take it out of his hand on the understanding that you are to steer his ship up channel, when you do not know the soundings.

On the other hand, the lower orders, and all orders, have to learn that every vicious habit and chronic disease communicates itself by descent; and that by purity of birth the entire system of the human body and soul may be gradually elevated, or, by recklessness of birth, degraded; until there shall be as much difference between the well-bred and ill-bred human creature (whatever pains be taken with their education) as between a wolf-hound and the vilest mongrel cur. And the knowledge of this great fact ought to regulate the education of our youth, and the entire conduct of the nation.—*M. P.*, V. IX. 7, § 1–3.

180. THE TRUE GENTLEMAN.—A gentleman's first characteristic is that fineness of structure in the body, which renders it capable of the most delicate sensation; and of structure in the mind which renders it capable of the most delicate sympathies—one may say, simply, "fineness of nature." This is, of course, compatible with heroic bodily strength and mental firmness; in

fact, heroic strength is not conceivable without such delicacy. Elephantine strength may drive its way through a forest and feel no touch of the boughs ; but the white skin of Homer's Atrides would have felt a bent rose-leaf, yet subdue its feeling in glow of battle, and behave itself like iron. I do not mean to call an elephant a vulgar animal ; but if you think about him carefully, you will find that his non-vulgarity consists in such gentleness as is possible to elephantine nature ; not in his insensitive hide, nor in his clumsy foot ; but in the way he will lift his foot if a child lies in his way ; and in his sensitive trunk, and still more sensitive mind, and capability of pique on points of honour.

And, though rightness of moral conduct is ultimately the great purifier of race, the sign of nobleness in not in this rightness of moral conduct, but in sensitiveness. When the make of the creature is fine, its temptations are strong, as well as its perceptions ; it is liable to all kinds of impressions from without in their most violent form ; liable therefore to be abused and hurt by all kinds of rough things which would do a coarser creature little harm, and thus to fall into frightful wrong if its fate will have it so. Thus David, coming of gentlest as well as royalest race, of Ruth as well as of Judah, is sensitiveness through all flesh and spirit ; not that his compassion will restrain him from murder when his terror urges him to it; nay, he is driven to the murder all the more by his sensitiveness to the shame which otherwise threatens him. But when his own story is told him under a disguise, though only a lamb is now concerned, his passion about it leaves him no time for thought. "The man shall die"—note the reason—"because he had no pity." He is so eager and indignant that it never occurs to him as strange that Nathan hides the name. This is true gentleman. A vulgar man would assuredly have been cautious, and asked "who it was?"

Hence it will follow that one of the probable signs of high-breeding in men generally, will be their kindness and mercifulness; these always indicating more or less fineness of make in the mind; and miserliness and cruelty the contrary; hence that of Isaiah: "The vile person shall no more be called liberal, nor the churl said to be bountiful." But a thousand things may prevent this kindness from displaying or continuing itself; the mind of the man may be warped so as to bear mainly on his own interests, and then all his sensibilities will take the form of pride, or fastidiousness, or revengefulness; and other wicked, but not ungentlemanly tempers; or, farther, they may run into utter sensuality and covetousness, if he is bent on pleasure, accompanied with quite infinite cruelty when the pride is wounded or the passions thwarted;—until your gentleman

becomes Ezzelin, and your lady, the deadly
Lucrece; yet still gentleman and lady, quite incapable of making anything else of themselves,
being so born.

A truer sign of breeding than mere kindness
is therefore sympathy;—a vulgar man may often
be kind in a hard way, on principle, and because
he thinks he ought to be; whereas, a highly-bred
man, even when cruel, will be cruel in a softer
way, understanding and feeling what he inflicts,
and pitying his victim. Only we must carefully
remember that the quantity of sympathy a gentleman feels can never be judged of by its outward
expression, for another of his chief characteristics
is apparent reserve. I say "apparent" reserve;
for the sympathy is real, but the reserve not: a
perfect gentleman is never reserved, but sweetly
and entirely open, so far as it is good for others,
or possible, that he should be. . . .

Self-command is often thought a characteristic
of high-breeding; and to a certain extent it is
so, at least it is one of the means of forming
and strengthening character; but it is rather a
way of imitating a gentleman than a characteristic of him; a true gentleman has no need of
self-command; he simply feels rightly on all
occasions; and desiring to express only so much
of his feeling as it is right to express, does not
need to command himself. Hence perfect ease
is indeed characteristic of him; but perfect ease

is inconsistent with self-restraint. Nevertheless gentlemen, so far as they fail of their own ideal, need to command themselves, and do so; while, on the contrary, to feel unwisely, and to be unable to restrain the expression of the unwise feeling, is vulgarity; and yet even then, the vulgarity, at its root, is not in the mistimed expression, but in the unseemly feeling; and when we find fault with a vulgar person for "exposing himself," it is not his openness, but clumsiness; and yet more the want of sensibility to his own failure, which we blame; so that still the vulgarity resolves itself into want of sensibility. Also, it is to be noted that great powers of self-restraint may be attained by very vulgar persons when it suits their purposes.—*M. P.*, V. IX. 7, § 5–8, 10.

181. SIGNS OF VULGARITY.—Another great sign of vulgarity is also, when traced to its root, another phase of insensibility, namely, the undue regard to appearances and manners, as in the households of vulgar persons, of all stations, and the assumption of behaviour, language, or dress unsuited to them, by persons in inferior stations of life. I say "undue" regard to appearances, because in the undueness consists, of course, the vulgarity. It is due and wise in some sort to care for appearances, in another sort undue and unwise. Wherein lies the difference?

At first one is apt to answer quickly: the

vulgarity is simply in pretending to be what you
are not. But that answer will not stand. A queen
may dress like a waiting-maid,—perhaps succeed,
if she chooses, in passing for one; but she will
not, therefore, be vulgar; nay, a waiting-maid
may dress like a queen, and pretend to be one,
and yet need not be vulgar, unless there is inherent vulgarity in her. In Scribe's very absurd
but very amusing *Reine d'un jour*, a milliner's
girl sustains the part of a .queen for a day. She
several times amazes and disgusts her courtiers by
her straightforwardness; and once or twice very
nearly betrays herself to her maids of honour by
an unqueenly knowledge of sewing; but she is
not in the least vulgar, for she is sensitive, simple,
and generous, and a queen could be no more.

Is the vulgarity, then, only in trying to play
a part you cannot play, so as to be continually
detected? No; a bad amateur actor may be continually detected in his part, but yet continually
detected to be a gentleman: a vulgar regard to
appearances has nothing in it necessarily of
hypocrisy. You shall know a man not to be a
gentleman by the perfect and neat pronunciation
of his words: but he does not pretend to pronounce accurately; he *does* pronounce accurately,
the vulgarity is in the real (not assumed) scrupu-
lousness.

It will be found on farther thought, that a vulgar
regard for appearances is, primarily, a selfish one,

resulting not out of a wish to give pleasure (as a wife's wish to make herself beautiful for her husband), but out of an endeavour to mortify others, or attract for pride's sake ;—the common "keeping up appearances" of society, being a mere selfish struggle of the vain with the vain. But the deepest stain of the vulgarity depends on this being done, not selfishly only, but stupidly, without understanding the impression which is really produced, nor the relations of importance between oneself and others, so as to suppose that their attention is fixed upon us, when we are in reality ciphers in their eyes—all which comes of insensibility. Hence pride simple is not vulgar (the looking down on others because of their true inferiority to us), nor vanity simple (the desire of praise), but conceit simple (the attribution to ourselves of qualities we have not), is always so. In cases of over-studied pronunciation, etc., there is insensibility, first, in the person's thinking more of himself than of what he is saying ; and, secondly, in his not having musical fineness of ear enough to feel that his talking is uneasy and strained.

Finally, vulgarity is indicated by coarseness of language or manners, only so far as this coarseness has been contracted under circumstances not necessarily producing it. The illiterateness of a Spanish or Calabrian peasant is not vulgar, because they had never an opportunity

of acquiring letters ; but the illiterateness of an
English school-boy is. So again, provincial dialect
is not vulgar ; but cockney dialect, the corruption,
by blunted sense, of a finer language continually
heard, is so in a deep degree ; and again, of this
corrupted dialect, that is the worst which consists,
not in the direct or expressive alteration of the
form of a word, but in an unmusical destruction
of it by dead utterance and bad or swollen formation of lip.   There is no vulgarity in—

> " Blythe, blythe, blythe was she,
>   Blythe was she, but and ben,
> And weel she liked a Hawick gill,
>   And leugh to see a tappit hen ; "

but much in Mrs. Gamp's inarticulate " bottle on
the chumleypiece, and let me put my lips to it
when I am so dispoged."

So also of personal defects, those only are
vulgar which imply insensibility or dissipation.

There is no vulgarity in the emaciation of
Don Quixote, the deformity of the Black Dwarf,
or the corpulence of Falstaff; but much in the
same personal characters, as they are seen in
Uriah Heep, Quilp, and Chadband. . . .

All the different impressions connected with
negligence or foulness depend, in like manner,
on the degree of insensibility implied.   Disorder
in a drawing-room is vulgar, in an antiquary's
study, not ; the black battle-stain on a soldier's

face is not vulgar, but the dirty face of a house-maid is.

And lastly, courage, so far as it is a sign of race, is peculiarly the mark of a gentleman or a lady: but it becomes vulgar if rude or insensitive, while timidity is not vulgar, if it be a characteristic of race or fineness of make. A fawn is not vulgar in being timid, nor a crocodile " gentle " because courageous.

Without following the inquiry into farther detail, we may conclude that vulgarity consists in a deadness of the heart and body, resulting from prolonged, and especially from inherited conditions of " degeneracy," or literally " un-racing ;" —gentlemanliness, being another word for an intense humanity. And vulgarity shows itself primarily in dulness of heart, not in rage or cruelty, but in inability to feel or conceive noble character or emotion. This is its essential, pure, and most fatal form. Dulness of bodily sense and general stupidity, with such forms of crime as peculiarly issue from stupidity, are its material manifestation.—*M. P.*, V. IX. 7, § 16-23.

182. FALSEHOOD.—Cunning signifies especially a habit or gift of over-reaching, accompanied with enjoyment and a sense of superiority. It is associated with small and dull conceit, and with an absolute want of sympathy or affection. Its essential connection with vulgarity may be

at once exemplified by the expression of the butcher's dog in Landseer's " Low Life." Cruik-shank's " Noah Claypole," in the illustrations to " Oliver Twist," in the interview with the Jew, is, however, still more characteristic. It is the intensest rendering of vulgarity absolute and utter with which I am acquainted.

The truthfulness which is opposed to cunning ought, perhaps, rather to be called the desire of truthfulness ; it consists more in unwillingness to deceive than in not deceiving,—an unwillingness implying sympathy with and respect for the person deceived ; and a fond observance of truth up to the possible point, as in a good soldier's mode of retaining his honour through a *ruse-de-guerre*. A cunning person seeks for opportunities to deceive ; a gentleman shuns them. A cunning person triumphs in deceiving ; a gentleman is humiliated by his success, or at least by so much of the success as is dependent merely on the false-hood, and not on his intellectual superiority.

The absolute disdain of all lying belongs rather to Christian chivalry than to mere high breeding ; as connected merely with this latter, and with general refinement and courage, the exact rela-tions of truthfulness may be best studied in the well-trained Greek mind. The Greeks believed that mercy and truth were co-relative virtues— cruelty and falsehood, co-relative vices. But they did not call necessary severity, cruelty ; nor

necessary deception, falsehood. It was needful
sometimes to slay men, and sometimes to deceive
them. When this had to be done, it should be
done well and thoroughly; so that to direct a
spear well to its mark, or a lie well to its end, was
equally the accomplishment of a perfect gentleman.
Hence, in the pretty diamond-cut-diamond scene
between Pallas and Ulysses, when she receives
him on the coast of Ithaca, the goddess laughs de-
lightedly at her hero's good lying, and gives him
her hand upon it;—showing herself then in her
woman's form, as just a little more than his
match. "Subtle would he be, and stealthy, who
should go beyond thee in deceit, even were he a
god, thou many-witted! What! here in thine
own land, too, wilt thou not cease from cheating?
Knowest thou not me, Pallas Athena, maid of
Jove, who am with thee in all thy labours, and
gave thee favour with the Phæacians, and keep
thee, and have come now to weave cunning with
thee?" But how completely this kind of cunning
was looked upon as a part of a man's power, and
not as a diminution of faithfulness, is perhaps
best shown by the single line of praise in which
the high qualities of his servant are summed up
by Chremulus in the Plutus—"Of all my house
servants, I hold you to be the faithfullest, and
the greatest cheat (or thief)."

Thus, the primal difference between honourable
and base lying in the Greek mind lay in honourable

purpose. A man who used his strength wantonly to hurt others was a monster; so, also, a man who used his cunning wantonly to hurt others. Strength and cunning were to be used only in self-defence, or to save the weak, and then were alike admirable. This was their first idea. Then the second, and perhaps the more essential, difference between noble and ignoble lying in the Greek mind, was that the honourable lie—or, if we may use the strange, yet just, expression, the true lie—knew and confessed itself for such—was ready to take the full responsibility of what it did. As the sword answered for its blow, so the lie for its snare. But what the Greeks hated with all their heart was the false lie;—the lie that did not know itself, feared to confess itself, which slunk to its aim under a cloak of truth, and sought to do liars' work, and yet not take liars' pay, excusing itself to the conscience by quibble and quirk. Hence the great expression of Jesuit principle by Euripides, "The tongue has sworn, but not the heart," was a subject of execration throughout Greece, and the satirists exhausted their arrows on it—no audience was ever tired of hearing (τὸ Εὐριπίδειον ἐκεῖνο) "that Euripidean thing" brought to shame.

And this is especially to be insisted on in the early education of young people. It should be pointed out to them with continual earnestness that the essence of lying is in deception, not in words; a lie may be told by silence, by equivocation, by the accent on a syllable, by a glance of the eye attaching a peculiar significance to a sentence; and all these kinds of lies are worse and baser by many degrees than a lie plainly worded; so that no form of blinded conscience is so far sunk as that which comforts itself for having deceived, because the deception was by gesture or silence, instead of utterance; and, finally, according to Tennyson's deep and trenchant line, "A lie which is half a truth is ever the worst of lies."—*M. P.*, V. IX. 7, § 11–14.

183. FRATERNITY.—In the various awkward and unfortunate efforts which the French have made at the development of a social system, they have at least stated one true principle, that of Fraternity or brotherhood. Do not be alarmed; they got all wrong in their experiments, because they quite forgot that this fact of fraternity implied another fact quite as important—that of paternity, or fatherhood. That is to say, if they were to regard the nation as one family, the condition of unity in that family consisted no less in their having a head, or a father, than in their being faithful and affectionate members, or brothers. . . .

Observe, I do not mean in the least that we ought to place such an authority in the hands of any one person, or of any class or body of persons. But I do mean to say that as an individual who conducts himself wisely must make laws for himself which at some time or other may appear irksome or injurious, but which, precisely at the time they appear most irksome, it is most necessary he should obey,—so a nation which means to conduct itself wisely must establish authority over itself, vested either in kings, councils, or laws, which it must resolve to obey, even at times when the law or authority appears irksome to the body of the people, or injurious to certain masses of it.   And this kind of national law has hitherto been only judicial; contented, that is, with an endeavour to prevent and punish violence and crime: but, as we advance in our social knowledge, we shall endeavour to make our government paternal as well as judicial; that is, to establish such laws and authorities as may at once direct us in our occupations, protect us against our follies, and visit us in our distresses: a government which shall have its soldiers of the plough-share as well as its soldiers of the sword, and which shall distribute more proudly its golden crosses of industry—golden as the glow of the harvest, than now it grants its bronze crosses of honour—bronzed with the crimson of blood. —*Political Economy of Art*, I. (*J. E.*, § 14, 15).

184. ON THE PROVERB, "DE MORTUIS."— If you are to put off your kindness until death, —why not, in God's name, put off also your

enmity? and if you choose to write your lingering affections upon stones, wreak also your delayed anger upon clay. This would be just, and, in the last case, little as you think it, generous. The true baseness is in the bitter reverse—the strange iniquity of our folly. Is a man to be praised, honoured, pleaded for? It might do harm to praise or plead for him while he lived. Wait till he is dead. Is he to be maligned, dishonoured, and discomforted? See that you do it while he is alive. It would be too ungenerous to slander him when he could feel malice no more; too contemptible to try to hurt him when he was past anguish. Make yourselves busy, ye unjust, ye lying, ye hungry for pain! Death is near. This is your hour, and the power of darkness. Wait, ye just, ye merciful, ye faithful in love! Wait but for a little while, for this is not your rest.

"Well, but," it is still answered, "is it not, indeed, ungenerous to speak ill of the dead, since they cannot defend themselves?"

Why should they? If you speak ill of them falsely, it concerns you, not them. Those lies of thine will "hurt a man as thou art," assuredly they will hurt thyself; but that clay, or the delivered soul of it, in no wise. Ajacean shield, seven-folded, never stayed lance-thrust as that turf will, with daisies pied. What you say of those quiet ones is wholly and utterly the world's affair and yours. The lie will, indeed, cost its proper price, and work its appointed work; you may ruin living myriads by it,—you may stop the progress of centuries by it,—you may have to pay your own soul for it,—but as for ruffling one corner of the folded shroud by it, think it not. The dead have none to defend them! Nay, they have two defenders, strong enough for the need —God, and the worm.—*M. P.*, IV., *App.* 1.

185. TOMBS.—Our respect for the dead, when they are *just* dead, is something wonderful, and the way we show it more wonderful still. We show it with black feathers and black horses; we show it with black dresses and bright heraldries; we show it with costly obelisks and sculptures of sorrow, which spoil half of our most beautiful cathedrals. We show it with frightful gratings and vaults, and lids of dismal stone, in the midst of the quiet grass; and last, and not least, we show it by permitting ourselves to tell any number of lies we think amiable or credible, in the epitaph. This feeling is common to the poor as well as the rich; and we all know how many a poor family will nearly ruin themselves, to testify their respect for some member of it in his coffin, whom they never much cared for when he was out of it; and how often it happens that a poor old woman will starve herself to death, in order that she may be respectably buried!

Now, this being one of the most complete and

special ways of wasting money;—no money being less productive of good, or of any percentage whatever, than that which we shake away from the ends of undertakers' plumes—it is of course the duty of all good economists, and kind persons, to prove and proclaim continually, to the poor as well as the rich, that respect for the dead is not really shown by laying great stones on them to tell us where they are laid : but by remembering where they are laid, without a stone to help us ; trusting them to the sacred grass and saddened flowers; and still more, that respect and love are shown to them, not by great monuments to them which we build with *our* hands, but by letting the monuments stand which they built with *their own.*— *Political Economy of Art*, Lect. 2 (*J. E.*, § 70, 71.)

186. HOME.—I cannot but think it an evil sign of a people when their houses ·are built to last for one generation only. There is a sanctity in a good man's house which cannot be renewed in every tenement that rises on its ruins ; and I believe that good men would generally feel this, and that having spent their lives happily and honourably, they would be grieved at the close of them to think that the place of their earthly abode, which had seen, and seemed almost to sympathise in, all their honour, their gladness, or their suffering,—that this, with all the record it bare of them, and all of material things that they

had loved and ruled over, and set the stamp of themselves upon—was to be swept away, as soon as there was room made for them in the grave; that no respect was to be shown to it, no affection felt for it, no good to be drawn from it by their children; that though there was a monument in the church, there was no warm monument in the hearth and house to them ; that all that they ever treasured was despised, and the places that had sheltered and comforted them were dragged down to the dust. I say that a good man would fear this; and that, far more, a good son, a noble descendant, would fear doing it to his father's house. I say that if men lived like men indeed, their houses would be temples—temples which we should hardly dare to injure, and in which it would make us holy to be permitted to live; and there must be a strange dissolution of natural affection, a strange unthankfulness for all that homes have given and parents taught, a strange consciousness that we have been unfaithful to our fathers' honour, or that our own lives are not such as would make our dwellings sacred to our children, when each man would fain build to himself, and build for the little revolution of his own life only. And I look upon those pitiful concretions of lime and clay which spring up in mildewed forwardness out of the kneaded fields about our capital—upon those thin, tottering, foundationless shells of splintered wood and imitated stone—upon those gloomy rows of formalised minuteness, alike without difference and without fellowship, as solitary as similar—not merely with the careless disgust of an offended eye, not merely with sorrow for a desecrated landscape, but with a painful foreboding that the roots of our national greatness must be deeply cankered when they are thus loosely struck in their native ground; that those comfortless and unhonoured dwellings are the signs of a great and spreading spirit of popular discontent; that they mark the time when every man's aim is to be in some more elevated sphere than his natural one, and every man's past life is his habitual scorn; when men build in the hope of leaving the places they have built, and live in the hope of forgetting the years that they have lived; when the comfort, the peace, the religion of home have ceased to be felt; and the crowded tenements of a struggling and restless population differ only from the tents of the Arab or the Gipsy by their less healthy openness to the air of heaven, and less happy choice of their spot of earth; by their sacrifice of liberty without the gain of rest, and of stability without the luxury of change. . . .

I would have, then, our ordinary dwelling-houses built to last, and built to be lovely: as rich and full of pleasantness as may be, within and without; with what degree of likeness to each other in style and manner, I will say presently, under another head; but, at all events, with such differences as might suit and express each man's character and occupation, and partly his history. This right over the house, I conceive, belongs to its first builder, and is to be respected by his children; and it would be well that blank stones should be left in places, to be inscribed with a summary of his life and of its experience, raising thus the habitation into a kind of monument, and developing, into more systematic instructiveness, that good custom which was of old universal, and which still remains among some of the Swiss and Germans, of acknowledging the grace of God's permission to build and possess a quiet resting-place.—*S. L. A.*, VI., § 3, 6.

187. MENTAL SLAVERY OF MODERN WORKMEN.—Reader, look round this English room of yours, about which you have been proud so often, because the work of it was so good and strong, and the ornaments of it so finished. Examine again all those accurate mouldings, and perfect polishings, and unerring adjustments of the seasoned wood and tempered steel. Many a time you have exulted over them, and thought how great England was, because her slightest work was done so thoroughly. Alas! if read rightly, these perfectnesses are signs of a slavery in our England a thousand times more bitter and more degrading than that of the scourged African or

helot Greek. Men may be beaten, chained, tormented, yoked liked cattle, slaughtered like summer flies, and yet remain in one sense, and the best sense, free. But to smother their souls within them, to blight and hew into rotting pollards the suckling branches of their human intelligence, to make the flesh and skin which, after the worm's work on it, is to see God, into leathern thongs to yoke machinery with,—this it is to be slave-masters indeed ; and there might be more freedom in England, though her feudal lords' lightest words were worth men's lives, and though the blood of the vexed husbandman dropped in the furrows of her fields, than there is while the animation of her multitudes is sent like fuel to feed the factory smoke, and the strength of them is given daily to be wasted into the fineness of a web, or racked into the exactness of a line.

And, on the other hand, go forth again to gaze upon the old Cathedral front, where you have smiled so often at the fantastic ignorance of the old sculptors ; examine once more those ugly goblins, and formless monsters, and stern statues, anatomiless and rigid ; but do not mock at them, for they are signs of the life and liberty of every workmen who struck the stone ; a freedom of thought, and rank in scale of being, such as no laws, no charters, no charities can secure ; but which it must be the first aim of all Europe at this day to regain for her children.

Let me not be thought to speak wildly or extravagantly. It is verily this degradation of the operative into a machine, which, more than any other evil of the times, is leading the mass of the nations everywhere into vain, incoherent, destructive struggling for a freedom of which they cannot explain the nature to themselves. Their universal outcry against wealth, and against nobility, is not forced from them either by the pressure of famine, or the sting of mortified pride. These do much, and have done much in all ages; but the foundations of society were never yet shaken as they are at this day. It is not that men are ill-fed, but that they have no pleasure in the work by which they make their bread, and therefore look to wealth as the only means of pleasure. It is not that men are pained by the scorn of the upper classes, but they cannot endure their own; for they feel that the kind of labour to which they are condemned is verily a degrading one, and makes them less than men. Never had the upper classes so much sympathy with the lower, or charity for them, as they have at this day, and yet never were they so much hated by them : for, of old, the separation between the noble and the poor was merely a wall built by law ; now it is a veritable difference in level of standing, a precipice between upper and lower grounds in the field of humanity, and there is pestilential air at the bottom of it. I

know not if a day is ever to come when the
nature of right freedom will be understood, and
when men will see that to obey another man, to
labour for him, yield reverence to him or to his
place, is not slavery. It is often the best kind
of liberty—liberty from care. The man who
says to one, Go, and he goeth, and to another,
Come, and he cometh, has, in most cases, more
sense of restraint and difficulty than the man
who obeys him. The movements of the one are
hindered by the burden on his shoulder; of the
other, by the bridle on his lips: there is no way
by which the burden may be lightened; but we
need not suffer from the bridle if we do not
champ at it. To yield reverence to another, to
hold ourselves and our lives at his disposal, is
not slavery; often, it is the noblest state in
which a man can live in this world. There is,
indeed, a reverence which is servile, that is to
say, irrational or selfish: but there is also noble
reverence, that is to say, reasonable and loving;
and a man is never so noble as when he is
reverent in this kind; nay, even if the feeling
pass the bounds of mere reason, so that it be
loving, a man is raised by it. Which had,
in reality, most of the serf nature in him,
—the Irish peasant who was lying in wait
yesterday for his landlord, with his musket
muzzle thrust through the ragged hedge; or
that old mountain servant, who, 200 years ago,

at Inverkeithing,* gave up his own life and the lives of his seven sons for his chief?—as each fell, calling forth his brother to the death, "Another for Hector!" And therefore, in all ages and all countries, reverence has been paid and sacrifice made by men to each other, not only without complaint, but rejoicingly; and famine, and peril, and sword, and all evil, and all shame, have been borne willingly in the causes of masters and kings; for all these gifts of the heart ennobled the men who gave, not less than the men who received them, and nature prompted, and God rewarded the sacrifice. But to feel their souls withering within them, unthanked; to find their whole being sunk into an unrecognised abyss; to be counted off into a heap of mechanism, numbered with its wheels, and weighed with its hammer strokes; this nature bade not,—this God blesses not,—this humanity for no long time is able to endure.

We have much studied and much perfected, of late, the great civilised invention of the division of labour; only we give it a false name. It is not, truly speaking, the labour that is divided; but the men:—Divided into mere segments of men—broken into small fragments and crumbs of life;

---

* "In the battle of Inverkeithing, between the Royalists and Oliver Cromwell's troops, a foster-father and seven brave sons are known to have sacrificed themselves for Sir Hector Maclean of Duart."—Preface to *The Fair Maid of Perth*.

so that all the little piece of intelligence that is left in a man is not enough to make a pin, or a nail, but exhausts itself in making the point of a pin, or the head of a nail. Now it is a good and desirable thing, truly, to make many pins in a day; but if we could only see with what crystal sand their points were polished,—sand of human soul, much to be magnified before it can be discerned for what it is,—we should think there might be some loss in it also. And the great cry that rises from all our manufacturing cities, louder than their furnace blast, is all in very deed for this,—that we manufacture everything there except men; we blanch cotton, and strengthen steel, and refine sugar, and shape pottery; but to brighten, to strengthen, to refine, or to form a single living spirit, never enters into our estimate of advantages. And all the evil to which that cry is urging our myriads can be met only in one way: not by teaching nor preaching, for to teach them is but to show them their misery, and to preach to them, if we do nothing more than preach, is to mock at it. It can be met only by a right understanding, on the part of all classes, of what kinds of labour are good for men, raising them, and making them happy; by a determined sacrifice of such convenience, or beauty, or cheapness as is to be got only by the degradation of the workman; and by equally determined demand for

I.   2 F

the products and results of healthy and ennobling labour.

And how, it will be asked, are these products to be recognised, and this demand to be regulated? Easily: by the observance of three broad and simple rules.

1. Never encourage the manufacture of any article not absolutely necessary, in the production of which *Invention* has no share.

2. Never demand an exact finish for its own sake, but only for some practical or noble end.

3. Never encourage imitation or copying of any kind, except for the sake of preserving record of great works.—*S. V.*, II. VI., § 13–17.

188. TRUE CHARITY.—You know how often it is difficult to be wisely charitable, to do good without multiplying the sources of evil. You know that to give alms is nothing unless you give thought also; and that therefore it is written, not "blessed is he that *feedeth* the poor," but, "blessed is he that *considereth* the poor." And you know that a little thought and a little kindness are often worth more than a great deal of money.

Now this charity of thought is not merely to be exercised towards the poor; it is to be exercised towards all men. There is assuredly no action of our social life, however unimportant, which, by kindly thought, may not be made to have a beneficial influence upon others; and it is impossible to spend the smallest sum of money, for any not absolutely necessary purpose, without a grave responsibility attaching to the manner of spending it. The object we ourselves covet may, indeed, be desirable and harmless, so far as we are concerned, but the providing us with it may, perhaps, be a very prejudicial occupation to some one else. And then it becomes instantly a moral question, whether we are to indulge ourselves or not. Whatever we wish to buy, we ought first to consider not only if the thing be fit for us, but if the manufacture of it be a wholesome and happy one; and if, on the whole, the sum we are going to spend will do as much good spent in this way as it would if spent in any other way. It may be said that we have not time to consider all this before we make a purchase. But no time could be spent in a more important duty; and God never imposes a duty without giving the time to do it. Let us, however, only acknowledge the principle;—once make up your mind to allow the consideration of the *effect* of your purchases to regulate the *kind* of your purchase, and you will soon easily find grounds enough to decide upon. The plea of ignorance will never take away our responsibilities. It is written, "If thou sayest, Behold, we knew it not; doth not He that pondereth the heart consider it? and He that keepeth thy soul, doth not He know it?"— *L. A. P.*, II., § 44, 45.

189. THE PATRONAGE OF LABOUR.—If you are a young lady, and employ a certain number of sempstresses for a given time, in making a given number of simple and serviceable dresses, suppose seven; of which you can wear one yourself for half the winter, and give six away to poor girls who have none, you are spending your money unselfishly. But if you employ the same number of sempstresses for the same number of days, in making four, or five, or six beautiful flounces for your own ball-dress—flounces which will clothe no one but yourself, and which you will yourself be unable to wear at more than one ball—you are employing your money selfishly. You have maintained, indeed, in each case, the same number of people; but in the one case you have directed their labour to the service of the community; in the other case you have consumed it wholly upon yourself. I don't say you are never to do so; I don't say you ought not sometimes to think of yourselves only, and to make yourselves as pretty as you can; only do not confuse coquettishness with benevolence, nor cheat yourselves into thinking that all the finery you can wear is so much put into the hungry mouths of those beneath you: it is not so; it is what you yourselves, whether you will or no, must sometimes instinctively feel it to be—it is what those who stand shivering in the streets, forming a line to watch you as you step out of your carriages,

know it to be; those fine dresses do not mean that so much has been put into their mouths, but that so much has been taken out of their mouths.

The real politico-economical signification of every one of those beautiful toilettes, is just this; that you have had a certain number of people put for a certain number of days wholly under your authority, by the sternest of slave-masters,— hunger and cold; and you have said to them, "I will feed you, indeed, and clothe you, and give you fuel for so many days; but during those days you shall work for me only: your little brothers need clothes, but you shall make none for them: your sick friend needs clothes, but you shall make none for her: you yourself will soon need another, and a warmer dress; but you shall make none for yourself. You shall make nothing but lace and roses for me; for this fortnight to come, you shall work at the patterns and petals, and then I will crush and consume them away in an hour." You will perhaps answer,—" It may not be particularly benevolent to do this, and we won't call it so; but at any rate we do no wrong in taking their labour when we pay them their wages: if we pay for their work we have a right to it."

No;—a thousand times no. The labour which you have paid for, does indeed become, by the act of purchase, your own labour: you have bought the hands and the time of those workers; they are, by right and justice, your own hands, your

own time. But have you a right to spend your
own time, to work with your own hands only for
your own advantage ?—much more, when, by
purchase, you have invested your own person
with the strength of others; and added to your
own life, a part of the life of others ? You may,
indeed, to a certain extent, use their labour for
your delight : remember I am making no general
assertions against splendour of dress, or pomp of
accessories of life; on the contrary, there are
many reasons for thinking that we do not at
present attach enough importance to beautiful
dress, as one of the means of influencing general
taste and character. But I *do* say, that you
must weigh the value of what you ask these
workers to produce for you in its own distinct
balance; that on its own worthiness or desirable-
ness rests the question of your kindness, and not
merely on the fact of your having employed people
in producing it ; and I say farther, that as long as
there are cold and nakedness in the land around
you, so long there can be no question at all but
that splendour of dress is a crime. In due time,
when we have nothing better to set people to work
at, it may be right to let them make lace and cut
jewels; but as long as there are any who have
no blankets for their beds and no rags for their
bodies, so long it is blanket-making and tailoring
we must set people to work at—not lace.

And it would be strange, if at any great

assembly which, while it dazzled the young and
the thoughtless, beguiled the gentler hearts that
beat beneath the embroidery, with a placid sensation of luxurious benevolence—as if by all that
they wore in waywardness of beauty, comfort has
been first given to the distressed, and aid to the
indigent; it would be strange, I say, if, for a
moment, the spirits of Truth and of Terror, which
walk invisibly among the masques of the earth,
would lift the dimness from our erring thoughts,
and show us how—inasmuch as the sums exhausted for that magnificence would have given
back the failing breath to many an unsheltered
outcast on moor and street—they who wear it have
literally entered into partnership with Death ; and
dressed themselves in his spoils.   Yes, if the veil
could be lifted not only from your thoughts, but
from your human sight, you would see—the angels
do see—on those gay white dresses of yours,
strange dark spots, and crimson patterns that you
knew not of—spots of the inextinguishable red that
all the seas cannot wash away ; yes, and among
the pleasant flowers that crown your fair heads,
and glow on your wreathed hair, you would see
that one weed was always twisted which no one
thought of—the grass that grows on graves.—
Political Economy of Art, Lect. I. (*J. E.*, § 50–53).

190. A POLITICAL PARABLE.—Fancy a farmer's wife, to whom one or two of her servants

should come at twelve o'clock at noon, crying that they had got nothing to do; that they did not know what to do next; and fancy, still farther, the said farmer's wife looking hopelessly about her rooms and yard, they being all the while considerably in disorder, not knowing where to set the spare handmaidens to work, and at last complaining bitterly that she had been obliged to give them their dinner for nothing. That's the type of the kind of political economy we practise too often in England. Would you not at once assert of such a mistress that she knew nothing of her duties? and would you not be certain, if the household were rightly managed, the mistress would be only too glad at any moment to have the help of any number of spare hands; that she would know in an instant what to set them to; —in an instant what part of to-morrow's work might be most serviceably forwarded, what part of next month's work most wisely provided for, or what new task of some profitable kind under-taken; and when the evening came, and she dis-missed her servants to their recreation or their rest, or gathered them to the reading round the work-table, under the eaves in the sunset, would you not be sure to find that none of them had been overtasked by her, just because none had been left idle; that everything had been accom-plished because all had been employed; that the kindness of the mistress had aided her presence of mind, and the slight labour had been entrusted to the weak, and the formidable to the strong; and that as none had been dishonoured by inactivity, so none had been broken by toil?—*Political Economy of Art*, I. (*J. E.*, § 11).

191. ECONOMY.—All economy, whether of states, households, or individuals, may be defined to be the art of managing labour. The world is so regulated by the laws of Providence, that a man's labour, well applied, is always amply sufficient to provide him during his life with all things needful to him, and not only with those, but with many pleasant objects of luxury; and yet farther, to procure him large intervals of healthful rest and serviceable leisure. And a nation's labour, well applied, is in like manner amply sufficient to provide its whole population with good food and comfortable habitation; and not with those only, but with good education besides, and objects of luxury, art treasures, such as these you have around you now. But by those same laws of Nature and Providence, if the labour of the nation or of the individual be misapplied, and much more if it be insufficient,—if the nation or man be indolent and unwise,—suffering and want result, exactly in proportion to the indolence and improvidence,—to the refusal of labour, or to the misapplication of it. Wherever you see want, or misery, or degradation, in this world about you,

there, be sure, either industry has been wanting or industry has been in error. It is not accident, it is not Heaven-commanded calamity, it is not the original and inevitable evil of man's nature, which fill your streets with lamentation, and your graves with prey. It is only that, when there should have been providence, there has been waste; when there should have been labour, there has been lasciviousness; and wilfulness, when there should have been subordination.

Now, we have warped the word "economy" in our English language into a meaning which it has no business whatever to bear. In our use of it, it constantly signifies merely sparing or saving; economy of money means saving money —economy of time, sparing time, and so on. But that is a wholly barbarous use of the word— barbarous in a double sense, for it is not English, and it is bad Greek; barbarous in a treble sense, for it is not English, it is bad Greek, and it is worse sense. Economy no more means saving money than it means spending money. It means, the administration of a house; its stewardship; spending or saving, that is, whether money or time, or anything else, to the best possible advantage. In the simplest and clearest definition of it, economy, whether public or private, means the wise management of labour; and it means this mainly in three senses: namely, first, *applying* your labour rationally; secondly, *preserving* its produce carefully ; lastly, *distributing* its produce seasonably.—*Political Economy of Art*, Lect. I. (*J. E.*, § 7, 8).

192. TOIL THE ONLY SOURCE OF WEALTH.— By far the greater part of the suffering and crime which exist at this moment in civilised Europe, arises simply from people not understanding this truism—not knowing that produce or wealth is eternally connected by the laws of heaven and earth with resolute labour ; but hoping in some way to cheat or abrogate this everlasting law of life, and to feed where they have not furrowed, and be warm where they have not woven.

I repeat, nearly all our misery and crime result from this one misapprehension. The law of nature is, that a certain quantity of work is necessary to produce a certain quantity of good, of any kind whatever. If you want knowledge, you must toil for it : if food, you must toil for it ; and if pleasure, you must toil for it. But men do not acknowledge this law, or strive to evade it, hoping to get their knowledge, and food, and pleasure for nothing ; and in this effort they either fail of getting them, and remain ignorant and miserable, or they obtain them by making other men work for their benefit ; and then they are tyrants and robbers. Yes, and worse than robbers. I am not one who in the least doubts or disputes the progress of this century in many

things useful to mankind; but it seems to me a
very dark sign respecting us that we look with so
much indifference upon dishonesty and cruelty in
the pursuit of wealth.　In the dream of Nebuchadnezzar it was only the *feet* that were part of iron
and part of clay; but many of us are now getting
so cruel in our avarice, that it seems as if, in us,
the *heart* were part of iron, part of clay.—
T. P., V., § 176.

193. MUTUAL RESPONSIBILITIES.—I wish to
plead for your several and future consideration of
this one truth, that the nation of Discipline and
Interference lies at the very root of all human
progress or power; that the "Let alone" principle
is, in all things which man has to do with, the
principle of death; that it is ruin to him, certain
and total, if he lets his land alone—if he lets his
fellow-men alone—if he lets his own soul alone;
that his whole life, on the contrary, must, if it is
a healthy life, be continually one of ploughing and
pruning, rebuking and helping, governing and
punishing; and that therefore it is only in the
concession of some great principle of restraint
and interference in national action that he can
ever hope to find the secret of protection against
national degradation.　I believe that the masses
have a right to claim education from their government; but only so far as they acknowledge the
duty of yielding obedience to their government.

I believe they have a right to claim employment from their governors; but only so far as they yield to the governor the direction and discipline of their labour; and it is only so far as they grant to the men whom they may set over them, the father's authority to check the childishnesses of national fancy, and direct the waywardnesses of national energy, that they have a right to ask that none of their distresses should be unrelieved, none of their weaknesses unwatched; and that no grief, nor nakedness, nor peril, should exist for them, against which the father's hand was not outstretched, or the father's shield uplifted.— *Political Economy of Art*, I. (*J. E.*, § 16).

194. STATE INTERVENTION.—When a peasant mother sees one of her careless children fall into a ditch, her first proceeding is to pull him out; her second, to box his ears; her third, ordinarily, to lead him carefully a little way by the hand, or send him home for the rest of the day. The child usually cries, and very often would clearly prefer remaining in the ditch; and if he understood any of the terms of politics would certainly express resentment at the interference with his individual liberty: but the mother has done her duty. Whereas the usual call of the mother nation to any of her children, under such circumstances, has lately been nothing more than the foxhunter's, —"Stay still there; I shall clear you." And if

we always *could* clear them, their requests to be left in muddy independence might be sometimes allowed by kind people, or their cries for help disdained by unkind ones. But we can't clear them. The whole nation is, in fact, bound together, as men are by ropes on a glacier : if one falls, the rest must either lift him, or drag him along with them as dead weight, not without much increase of danger to themselves. And the law of right being manifestly in this—as, whether manifestly or not, it is, always, the law of prudence, —the only question is, how this wholesome help and interference are to be administered.—*Political Economy of Art : Addenda (J. E.,* § 127).

195. QUIXOTISM, or Utopianism; that is another of the devil's pet words. I believe the quiet admission which we are all of us so ready to make, that, because things have long been wrong, it is impossible they should ever be right, is one of the most fatal sources of misery and crime from which this world suffers. Whenever you hear a man dissuading you from attempting to do well, on the ground that perfection is "Utopian," beware of that man. Cast the word out of your dictionary altogether. There is no need for it. Things are either possible or impossible—you can easily determine which, in any given state of human science. If the thing is impossible, you need not trouble yourselves about it ; if possible, try for it.

It is very Utopian to hope for the entire doing away with drunkenness and misery out of the Canongate; but the Utopianism is not our business—the *work* is.   It is Utopian to hope to give every child in this kingdom the knowledge of God from its youth; but the Utopianism is not our business—the *work* is.—*L. A. P.*, II., § 33.

196. WHAT TO DO.—We may at least labour for a system of greater honesty and kindness in the minor commerce of our daily life; since the great dishonesty of the great buyers and sellers is nothing more than the natural growth and outcome from the little dishonesty of the little buyers and sellers.   Every person who tries to buy an article for less than its proper value, or who tries to sell it at more than its proper value— every consumer who keeps a tradesman waiting for his money, and every tradesman who bribes a consumer to extravagance by credit, is helping forward, according to his own measure of power, a system of baseless and dishonourable commerce, and forcing his country down into poverty and shame.   And people of moderate means and average powers of mind would do far more real good by merely carrying out stern principles of justice and honesty in common matters of trade, than by the most ingenious schemes of extended philanthropy, or vociferous declarations of theological doctrine.   There are three weighty matters

of the law—justice, mercy, and truth; and of these the Teacher puts truth last, because that cannot be known but by a course of acts of justice and love. But men put, in all their efforts, truth first, because they mean by it their own opinions; and thus, while the world has many people who would suffer martyrdom in the cause of what they call truth, it has few who will suffer even a little inconvenience, in that of justice and mercy.—*Political Economy of Art : Addenda* (*J. E.,* § 152).

197. THE ASCETICISM OF MONEY MAKING. —Three principal forms of asceticism have existed in this weak world. Religious asceticism, being the refusal of pleasure and knowledge for the sake (as supposed) of religion; seen chiefly in the middle ages. Military asceticism, being the refusal of pleasure and knowledge for the sake of power; seen chiefly in the early days of Sparta and Rome. And monetary asceticism, consisting in the refusal of pleasure and knowledge for the sake of money; seen in the present days of London and Manchester.

"We do not come here to look at the mountains," said the Carthusian to me at the Grande Chartreuse. "We do not come here to look at the mountains," the Austrian generals would say, encamping by the shores of Garda. "We do not come here to look at the mountains," so the thriving manufacturers tell me, between Rochdale and Halifax.

All these asceticisms have their bright and their dark sides. I myself like the military asceticism best, because it is not so necessarily a refusal of general knowledge as the two others, but leads to acute and marvellous use of mind, and perfect use of body. Nevertheless, none of the three are a healthy or central state of man. There is much to be respected in each, but they are not what we should wish large numbers of men to become. A monk of La Trappe, a French soldier of the Imperial Guard, and a thriving mill-owner, supposing each a type, and no more than a type, of his class, are all interesting specimens of humanity, but narrow ones,—so narrow that even all the three together would not make up a perfect man. Nor does it appear in any way desirable that either of the three classes should extend itself so as to include a majority of the persons in the world, and turn large cities into mere groups of monastery, barracks, or factory. I do not say that it may not be desirable that one city, or one country, sacrificed for the good of the rest, should become a mass of barracks or factories. Perhaps, it may be well that this England should become the furnace of the world; so that the smoke of the island, rising out of the sea, should be seen from a hundred leagues away, as if it were a field of fierce volcanoes; and every kind of sordid, foul,

I. 2 G

or venomous work which, in other countries, men dreaded or disdained, it should become England's duty to do,—becoming thus the off-scourer of the earth, and taking the hyena instead of the lion upon her shield. I do not, for a moment, deny this; but, looking broadly, not at the destiny of England, nor of any country in particular, but of the world, this is certain—that men exclusively occupied either in spiritual reverie, mechanical destruction, or mechanical productive-ness, fall below the proper standard of their race, and enter into a lower form of being; and that the true perfection of the race, and, therefore, its power and happiness, are only to be attained by a life which is neither speculative nor productive; but essentially contemplative and protective, which (A) does not lose itself in the monk's vision or hope, but delights in seeing present and real things as they truly are; which (B) does not mortify itself for the sake of obtaining powers of destruction, but seeks the more easily attainable powers of affection, observance, and protection; which (C), finally, does not mortify itself with a view to productive accumulation, but delights itself in peace, with its appointed portion. So that the things to be desired for man in a healthy state, are that he should not see dreams, but realities; that he should not destroy life, but save it; and that he should be not rich, but content.

Towards which last state of contentment, I do not see that the world is at present approximating. There are, indeed, two forms of discontent: one laborious, the other indolent and complaining. We respect the man of laborious desire, but let us not suppose that his restlessness is peace, or his ambition meekness. It is because of the special connection of meekness with contentment that it is promised that the meek shall "inherit the earth." Neither covetous men, nor the Grave, can *inherit* anything; they can but consume. Only contentment can possess.—*M. P.*, V. IX. 11, § 17–19.

198. A PEASANT PEOPLE.—There has been much dispute respecting the character of the Swiss, arising out of the difficulty which other nations had to understand their simplicity. They were assumed to be either romantically virtuous, or basely mercenary, when in fact they were neither heroic nor base, but were true-hearted men, stubborn with more than any recorded stubbornness; not much regarding their lives, yet not casting them causelessly away; forming no high ideal of improvement, but never relaxing their grasp of a good they had once gained; devoid of all romantic sentiment, yet loving with a practical and patient love that neither wearied nor forsook; little given to enthusiasm in religion, but maintaining their faith in a purity which no

worldliness deadened, and no hypocrisy soiled;
neither chivalrously generous nor pathetically
humane, yet never pursuing their defeated enemies,
not suffering their poor to perish; proud, yet not
allowing their pride to prick them into unwary
or unworthy quarrel; avaricious, yet contentedly
rendering to their neighbour his due; dull, but
clear-sighted to all the principles of justice; and
patient, without ever allowing delay to be prolonged by sloth, or forbearance by fear.

This temper of Swiss mind, while it animated
the whole confederacy, was rooted chiefly in one
small district which formed the heart of their
country, yet lay not among its highest mountains.
Beneath the glaciers of Zermatt and Evolena, and
on the scorching slopes of the Valais, the peasants
remained in an aimless torpor, unheard of but as
the obedient vassals of the great Bishopric of Sion.
But where the lower ledges of calcareous rock
were broken by the inlets of the Lake of Lucerne,
and bracing winds penetrating from the north for-
bade the growth of the vine, compelling the peasantry to adopt an entirely pastoral life, was reared
another race of men. Their narrow domain should
be marked by a small green spot on every map of
Europe. It is about forty miles from east to west;
as many from north to south; yet on that shred
of rugged ground, while every kingdom of the
world around it rose or fell in fatal change, and
every multitudinous race mingled or wasted itself

in various dispersion and decline, the simple
shepherd dynasty remained changeless. . . .

Voluntarily placing themselves under the protection of the House of Hapsburg, they acknowledged its supremacy, but resisted its oppression;
and rose against the unjust governors it appointed
over them, not to gain, but to redeem, their liberties. Victorious in the struggle by the Lake of
Egeri, they stood the foremost standard-bearers
among the nations of Europe in the cause of loyalty
and life—loyalty in its highest sense, to the laws
of God's helpful justice, and of man's faithful and
brotherly fortitude.

You will find among them, as I said, no subtle
wit nor high enthusiasm, only an undeceivable
common sense, and an obstinate rectitude. They
cannot be persuaded into their duties, but they
feel them; they use no phrases of friendship, but
do not fail you at your need. Questions of creed,
which other nations sought to solve by logic or
reverie, these shepherds brought to practical tests;
sustained with tranquillity the excommunication of
abbots who wanted to feed their cattle on other
people's fields, and, halbert in hand, struck down
the Swiss Reformation, because the Evangelicals
of Zurich refused to send them their due supplies
of salt. Not readily yielding to the demands of
superstition, they were patient under those of
economy; they would purchase the remission of
taxes, but not of sins; and while the sale of

indulgences was arrested in the church of Einsie-
deln as boldly as at the gates of Wittenberg, the
inhabitants of the valley of Frutigen ate no meat
for seven years, in order peacefully to free themselves and their descendants from the scigniorial
claims of the Baron of Thurm.

What praise may be justly due to this modest
and rational virtue, we have perhaps no sufficient
grounds for defining. It must long remain questionable how far the vices of superior civilisation
may be atoned for by its achievements, and the
errors of more transcendental devotion forgiven
to its rapture. But, take it for what we may, the
character of this peasantry is, at least, serviceable
to others and sufficient for their own peace; and
in its consistency and simplicity, it stands alone
in the history of the human heart.—*M. P.*, V. VI.
9, § 12–15.

199. WAR.—You may, perhaps, be surprised
at my implying that war itself çan be right, or
necessary, or noble at all. Nor do I speak
of all war as necessary, nor of all war as
noble. Both peace and war are noble or ignoble
according to their kind and occasion. No man
has a profounder sense of the horror and guilt
of ignoble war than I have: I have personally
seen its effects, upon nations, of unmitigated
evil, on soul and body, with perhaps as much
pity, and as much bitterness of indignation, as

any of those whom you will hear continually declaiming in the cause of peace. But peace may be sought in two ways. One way is as Gideon sought it, when he built his altar in Ophrah, naming it, "God send peace," yet sought this peace that he loved, as he was ordered to seek it, and the peace was sent, in God's way :— "the country was in quietness forty years in the days of Gideon." And the other way of seeking peace is as Menahem sought it, when he gave the King of Assyria a thousand talents of silver, "that his hand might be with him." That is, you may either win your peace, or buy it :—win it, by resistance to evil ; buy it, by compromise with evil. You may buy your peace, with silenced consciences ; you may buy it, with broken vows,—buy it, with lying words,—buy it, with base connivances,—buy it with the blood of the slain, and the cry of the captive, and the silence of lost souls—over hemispheres of the earth, while you sit smiling at your serene hearths, lisping comfortable prayers evening and morning, and counting your pretty Protestant beads (which are flat, and of gold, instead of round, and of ebony, as the monks' ones were), and so mutter continually to yourselves, "Peace, peace," when there is No peace ; but only captivity and death, for you, as well as for those you leave unsaved ;—and yours darker than theirs.—*T. P.*, V., § 195.

200. ENGLAND'S STRENGTH—"LUFF BOY!"
—War with France? it may be; and they say
good ships are building at Cherbourg. War
with Russia? That also is conceivable; and the
Russians invent machines that explode under
water by means of knobs. War with the fiend
in ourselves? That may not so easily come to
pass, he and we being in close treaty hitherto,
yet perhaps in good time may be looked for.
And against enemies, foreign or internal, French,
Sclavonic, or dæmoniac, what arms have we to
count upon? I hear of good artillery practice
at Woolwich,—of new methods of sharpening
sabres invented by Sikhs,—of a modern condition
of the blood of Nessus, which sets sails on fire,
and makes an end of Herculean ships, like
Phœnixes. All which may perhaps be well, or
perhaps ill, for us. But, if our enemies want to
judge of our proved weapons and armour, let
them come and look here. Bare head, bare
fist, bare foot, and blue jacket. If these will not
save us, nothing will.—*Notes on the Academy
Pictures*, 1859.

201. MAN THE GREAT DESTROYER.—Nearly
every great and intellectual race of the world has
produced, at every period of its career, an art
with some peculiar and precious character about
it, wholly unattainable by any other race, and at
any other time; and the intention of Providence

concerning that art, is evidently that it should
all grow together into one mighty temple; the
rough stones and the smooth all finding their
place, and rising day by day, in richer and higher
pinnacles to heaven. Now, just fancy what a
position the world, considered as one great work-
room—one great factory in the form of a globe—
would have been in by this time, if it had in the
least understood this duty, or been capable of it.
Fancy what we should have had around us now,
if, instead of quarrelling and fighting over their
work, the nations had aided each other in their
work, or if even in their conquests, instead of
effacing the memorials of those they succeeded
and subdued, they had guarded the spoils of their
victories. Fancy what Europe would be now, if
the delicate statues and temples of the Greeks,
—if the broad roads and massy walls of the
Romans,—if the noble and pathetic architecture
of the middle ages, had not been ground to dust
by mere human rage. You talk of the scythe of
Time, and the tooth of Time: I tell you, Time
is scytheless and toothless; it is we who gnaw
like the worm—we who smite like the scythe.
It is ourselves who abolish—ourselves who consume: we are the mildew, and the flame; and
the soul of man is to its own work as the moth,
that frets when it cannot fly, and as the hidden
flame that blasts where it cannot illuminate. All
these lost treasures of human intellect have been

wholly destroyed by human industry of destruction ; the marble would have stood its two thousand years as well in the polished statue as in the Parian cliff; but we men have ground it to powder, and mixed it with our own ashes. The walls and the ways would have stood—it is we who have left not one stone upon another, and restored its pathlessness to the desert ; the great cathedrals of old religion would have stood —it is we who have dashed down the carved work with axes and hammers, and bid the mountain-grass bloom upon the pavement, and the sea-winds chant in the galleries.

You will perhaps think all this was somehow necessary for the development of the human race. I cannot stay now to dispute that, though I would willingly ; but do you think it is *still* necessary for that development ? Do you think that in this nineteenth century it is still necessary for the European nations to turn all the places where their principal art-treasures are into battle-fields ? For that is what they are doing even while I speak ; the great firm of the world is managing its business at this moment, just as it has done in past time.—*Political Economy of Art*, II. (*J. E.*, § 73–75).

202. CIVILISATION. — The great mechanical impulses of the age, of which most of us are so proud, are a mere passing fever, half-speculative,

half-childish. People will discover at last that royal roads to anything can no more be laid in iron than they can in dust; that there are, in fact, no royal roads to anywhere worth going to; that if there were, it would that instant cease to be worth going to—I mean, so far as the things to be obtained are in any way estimable in terms of *price*. For there are two classes of precious things in the world: those that God gives us for nothing—sun, air, and life (both mortal life and immortal); and the secondarily precious things which He gives us for a price; these secondarily precious things, worldly wine and milk, can only be bought for definite money; they never can be cheapened. No cheating nor bargaining will ever get a single thing out of nature's "establishment" at half-price. Do we want to be strong?—we must work. To be hungry?—we must starve. To be happy?—we must be kind. To be wise?—we must look and think. No changing of place at a hundred miles an hour, nor making of stuffs a thousand yards a minute, will make us one whit stronger, happier, or wiser. There was always more in the world than men could see, walked they ever so slowly; they will see it no better for going fast. And they will at last, and soon too, find out that their grand inventions for conquering (as they think) space and time, do, in reality, conquer nothing; for space and time are, in their own essence, unconquerable, and besides did not want any sort of conquering; they wanted *using*. A fool always wants to shorten space and time: a wise man wants to lengthen both. A fool wants to kill space and kill time: a wise man, first to gain them, then to animate them. Your railroad, when you come to understand it, is only a device for making the world smaller: and as for being able to talk from place to place, that is, indeed, well and convenient; but suppose you have, originally, nothing to say! We shall be obliged at last to confess, what we should long ago have known, that the really precious things are thought and sight, not pace. It does a bullet no good to go fast; and a man, if he be truly a man, no harm to go slow; for his glory is not at all in going, but in being.

"Well; but railroads and telegraphs are so useful for communicating knowledge to savage nations." Yes, if you have any to give them. If you know nothing *but* railroads, and can communicate nothing but aqueous vapour and gunpowder,—what then? But if you have any other thing than those to give, then the railroad is of use only because it communicates that other thing; and the question is—what that other thing may be. Is it religion? I believe if we had really wanted to communicate that, we could have done it in less than 1800 years, without steam. Most of the good religious communication that I remember, has been done on foot; and it

cannot be easily done faster than at foot pace.
Is it science ? But what science—of motion,
meat, and medicine ? Well; when you have
moved your savage, and dressed your savage,
fed him with white bread, and shown him how
to set a limb,—what next ? Follow out that
question. Suppose every obstacle overcome;
give your savage every advantage of civilisation
to the full ; suppose that you have put the Red
Indian in tight shoes ; taught the Chinese how
to make Wedgwood's ware, and to paint it with
colours that will rub off; and persuaded all
Hindoo women that it is more pious to torment
their husbands into graves than to burn themselves at the burial,—what next ? Gradually,
thinking on from point to point, we shall come
to perceive that all true happiness and nobleness
are near us, and yet neglected by us; and that
till we have learned how to be happy and noble
we have not much to tell, even to Red Indians.
The delights of horse-racing and hunting, of
assemblies in the night instead of the day, of
costly and wearisome music, of costly and burden-
some dress, of chagrined contention for place or
power, or wealth, or the eyes of the multitude;
and all the endless occupation without purpose,
and idleness without rest, of our vulgar world,
are not, it seems to me, enjoyments we need be
ambitious to communicate. And all real and
wholesome enjoyments possible to man have

been just as possible to him, since first he was made of the earth, as they are now; and they are possible to him chiefly in peace. To watch the corn grow, and the blossoms set; to draw hard breath over ploughshare or spade; to read, to think, to love, to hope, to pray,—these are the things that make men happy; they have always had the power of doing these, they never *will* have power to do more. The world's prosperity or adversity depends upon our knowing and teaching these few things: but upon iron, or glass, or electricity, or steam, in no wise.

And I am Utopian and enthusiastic enough to believe, that the time will come when the world will discover this. It has now made its experiments in every possible direction but the right one: and it seems that it must, at last, try the right one, in a mathematical necessity. It has tried fighting, and preaching, and fasting, buying and selling, pomp and parsimony, pride and humiliation,—every possible manner of existence in which it could conjecture there was any happiness or dignity: and all the while, as it bought, sold, and fought, and fasted, and wearied itself with policies, and ambitions, and self-denials, God had placed its real happiness in the keeping of the little mosses of the wayside, and of the clouds of the firmament. Now and then a wearied king, or a tormented slave, found out where the true kingdoms of the world were, and possessed himself, in a furrow or two of garden ground, of a truly infinite dominion. But the world would not believe their report, and went on trampling down the mosses, and forgetting the clouds, and seeking happiness in its own way, until, at last, blundering and late, came natural science; and in natural science not only the observation of things, but the finding out of new uses for them. Of course the world, having a choice left to it, went wrong as usual, and thought that these mere material uses were to be the sources of its happiness. It got the clouds packed into iron cylinders, and made them carry its wise self at their own cloud pace. It got weavable fibres out of the mosses, and made clothes for itself, cheap and fine,—here was happiness at last. To go as fast as the clouds, and manufacture everything out of anything,—here was paradise, indeed!

And now, when, in a little while, it is unparadised again, if there were any other mistake that the world could make, it would of course make it. But I see not that there is any other; and, standing fairly at its wits' end, having found that going fast, when it is used to it, is no more paradisiacal than going slow; and that all the prints and cottons in Manchester cannot make it comfortable in its mind, I do verily believe it will come, finally, to understand that God paints the clouds and shapes the moss-fibres, that men may

be happy in seeing Him at His work, and that
in resting quietly beside Him, and watching His
working, and—according to the power He has
communicated to ourselves, and the guidance He
grants,—in carrying out His purposes of peace
and charity among all His creatures, are the
only real happinesses that ever were, or will
be, possible to mankind.—*M. P.*, III. IV. 17,
§ 35–38.

203. THE WHOLE DUTY OF MAN.—Man's use
and function (and let him who will not grant
me this follow me no farther, for this I purpose always to assume,) are, to be the witness
of the glory of God, and to advance that
glory by his reasonable obedience and resultant
happiness.

Whatever enables us to fulfil this function is,
in the pure and first sense of the word, Useful
to us: pre-eminently, therefore, whatever sets
the glory of God more brightly before us. But
things that only help us to exist are, in a
secondary and mean sense, useful; or rather,
if they be looked for alone, they are useless, and
worse, for it would be better that we should not
exist, than that we should guiltily disappoint the
purposes of existence.

And yet people speak in this working age,
when they speak from their hearts, as if houses
and lands, and food and raiment were alone

useful, and as if Sight, Thought, and Admiration *
were all profitless, so that men insolently call
themselves Utilitarians, who would turn, if they
had their way, themselves and their race into
vegetables; men who think, as far as such can
be said to think, that the meat is more than the
life, and the raiment than the body, who look
to the earth as a stable, and to its fruit as
fodder; vine-dressers and husbandmen, who love
the corn they grind, and the grapes they crush,
better than the gardens of the angels upon the
slopes of Eden; hewers of wood and drawers of
water, who think that it is to give them wood
to hew and water to draw, that the pine-forests
cover the mountains like the shadow of God, and
the great rivers move like His eternity. And so
comes upon us that Woe of the preacher, that
though God "hath made everything beautiful in
his time, also He hath set the world in their
heart, so that no man can find out the work that
God maketh from the beginning to the end."

This Nebuchadnezzar curse, that sends men to
grass like oxen, seems to follow but too closely
on the excess or continuance of national power
and peace. In the perplexities of nations, in
their struggles for existence, in their infancy,
their impotence, or even their disorganisation,
they have higher hopes and nobler passions.

* "We live by admiration, hope, and love."
      —*Excursion*, Book IV.

Out of the suffering comes the serious mind;
out of the salvation, the grateful heart; out of
endurance, fortitude; out of deliverance, faith;
but when they have learned to live under providence of laws and with decency and justice of
regard for each other, and when they have done
away with violent and external sources of suffering, worse evils seem to arise out of their rest;
evils that vex less and mortify more, that suck
the blood though they do not shed it, and ossify
the heart though they do not torture it.   And
deep though the causes of thankfulness must be
to every people at peace with others and at unity
in itself, there are causes of fear, also, a fear
greater than of sword and sedition: that dependence on God may be forgotten, because the
bread is given and the water sure; that gratitude
to Him may cease, because His constancy of
protection has taken the semblance of a natural
law; that heavenly hope may grow faint amidst
the full fruition of the world; that selfishness
may take place of undemanded devotion, compassion be lost in vainglory, and love in dis-
simulation; that enervation may succeed to
strength, apathy to patience, and the noise of
jesting words and foulness of dark thoughts, to
the earnest purity of the girded loins and the
burning lamp.   About the river of human life
there is a wintry wind, though a heavenly sunshine; the iris colours its agitation, the frost

fixes upon its repose. Let us beware that our
rest become not the rest of stones, which, so long
as they are torrent-tossed and thunder-stricken,
maintain their majesty, but when the stream
is silent, and the storm passed, suffer the grass
to cover them and the lichen to feed on them,
and are ploughed down into dust.

And though I believe that we have salt enough
of ardent and holy mind amongst us to keep us
in some measure from this moral decay, yet the
signs of it must be watched with anxiety, in all
matters however trivial, in all directions however
distant. And at this time, when the iron roads
are tearing up the surface of Europe, as grapeshot
do the sea ; when their great net is drawing and
twitching the ancient frame and strength together,
contracting all its various life, its rocky arms and
rural heart, into a narrow, finite, calculating
metropolis of manufactures ; when there is not
a monument throughout the cities of Europe
that speaks of old years and mighty people, but
it is being swept away to build cafés and gaming-
houses ; when the honour of God is thought to
consist in the poverty of His temple, and the
column is shortened and the pinnacle shattered,
the colour denied to the casement and the marble
to the altar, while exchequers are exhausted in
luxury of boudoirs and pride of reception-rooms ;
when we ravage without a pause all the loveliness of creation which God in giving pronounced

Good, and destroy without a thought all those labours which men have given their lives and their sons' sons' lives to complete, and have left for a legacy to all their kind, a legacy of more than their hearts' blood, for it is of their souls' travail;—there is need, bitter need, to bring back into men's minds, that to live is nothing, unless to live be to know Him by whom we live; and that He is not to be known by marring His fair works, and blotting out the evidence of His influences upon His creatures; nor amidst the hurry of crowds and crash of innovation, but in solitary places, and out of the glowing intelligences which He gave to men of old. He did not teach them how to build for glory and for beauty, He did not give them the fearless, faithful, inherited energies that worked on and down from death to death, generation after generation, that we might give the work of their poured-out spirit to the axe and the hammer; He has not cloven the earth with rivers, that their white wild waves might turn wheels and push paddles, nor turned it up under as it were fire, that it might heat wells and cure diseases; He brings not up His quails by the east wind, only to let them fall in flesh about the camp of men; He has not heaped the rocks of the mountain only for the quarry, nor clothed the grass of the field only for the oven.—*M. P.*, II. III. i. 1, § 4–7.

204. IDEAS OF BEAUTY DEPEND ON PURITY OF MIND.—It is necessary to the existence of an idea of beauty, that the sensual pleasure which may be its basis should be accompanied first with joy, then with love of the object, then with the perception of kindness in a superior intelligence, finally, with thankfulness and veneration towards that intelligence itself; and as no idea can be at all considered as in any way an idea of beauty, until it be made up of these emotions, any more than we can be said to have an idea of a letter of which we perceive the perfume and the fair writing, without understanding the contents of it, or intent of it; and as these emotions are in no way resultant from, nor obtainable by, any operation of the Intellect; it is evident that the sensation of beauty is not sensual on the one hand, nor is it intellectual on the other, but is dependent on a pure, right, and open state of the heart, both for its truth and for its intensity, insomuch that even the right afteraction of the Intellect upon facts of beauty so apprehended, is dependent on the acuteness of the heart-feeling about them. And thus the Apostolic words come true, in this minor respect, as in all others, that men are alienated from the life of God through the ignorance that is in them, having the *Understanding* darkened because of the hardness of their *hearts*, and so, being past feeling, give themselves up to lasciviousness.

For we do indeed see constantly that men having naturally acute perceptions of the beautiful, yet not receiving it with a pure heart, nor into their hearts at all, never comprehend it, nor receive good from it ; but make it a mere minister to their desires, and accompaniment and seasoning of lower sensual pleasures, until all their emotions take the same earthly stamp, and the sense of beauty sinks into the servant of lust.

Nor is what the world commonly understands by the cultivation of "taste," anything more or better than this ; at least in times of corrupt and over-pampered civilisation, when men build palaces and plant groves and gather luxuries, that they and their devices may hang in the corners of the world like fine-spun cobwebs, with greedy, puffed-up, spider-like lusts in the middle. And this, which in Christian times is the abuse and corruption of the sense of beauty, was in that Pagan life of which St. Paul speaks, little less than the essence of it, and the best they had. I do not know that of the expressions of affection towards external nature to be found among Heathen writers, there are any of which the leading thought leans not towards the sensual parts of her. Her beneficence they sought, and her power they shunned ; her teaching through both they understood never. The pleasant influences of soft winds, and ringing streamlets, and shady coverts, of the violet couch and plane-tree shade, they received, perhaps, in a more noble way than we; but they found not anything, except fear, upon the bare mountain, or in the ghostly glen. The Hybla heather they loved more for its sweet hives than its purple hues. But the Christian Theoria seeks not, though it accepts and touches with its own purity, what the Epicurean sought; but finds its food and the objects of its love everywhere, in what is harsh and fearful as well as in what is kind: nay, even in all that seems coarse and commonplace, seizing that which is good; and sometimes delighting more at finding its table spread in strange places, and in the presence of its enemies, and its honey coming out of the rock, than if all were harmonised into a less wondrous pleasure; hating only what is self-sighted and insolent of men's work, despising all that is not of God, unless reminding it of God, yet able to find evidence of Him still where all seems forgetful of Him, and to turn that into a witness of His working which was meant to obscure it; and so with clear and unoffended sight beholding Him for ever, according to the written promise, " Blessed are the pure in *heart*, for they shall see God."—*M. P.*, II. III. 1, 2, § 8–10.

205. DISREGARD OF GOD'S GIFTS.—There is no subject of thought more melancholy, more wonderful, than the way in which God permits

so often His best gifts to be trodden under foot of men, His richest treasures to be wasted by the moth, and the mightiest influences of His Spirit, given but once in the world's history, to be quenched and shortened by miseries of chance and guilt. I do not wonder at what men Suffer, but I wonder often at what they Lose. We may see how good rises out of pain and evil; but the dead, naked, eyeless loss, what good comes of that? The fruit struck to the earth before its ripeness; the glowing life and goodly purpose dissolved away in sudden death; the words, half-spoken, choked upon the lips with clay for ever; or, stranger than all, the whole majesty of humanity raised to his fulness, and every gift and power necessary for a given purpose, at a given moment, centred in one man, and all this perfected blessing permitted to be refused, perverted, crushed, cast aside by those who need it most,—the city which is Not set on a hill, the candle that giveth light to None that are in the house;—these are the heaviest mysteries of this strange world, and, it seems to me, those which mark its curse the most. And it is true that the power with which this Venice had been entrusted, was perverted, when at its highest, in a thousand miserable ways: still, it was possessed by her alone; to her all hearts have turned which could be moved by its manifestation, and none without being made stronger and nobler by what her hand had wrought. That mighty Landscape, of dark mountains that guard the horizon with their purple towers, and solemn forests, that gather their weight of leaves, bronzed with sunshine, not with age, into those gloomy masses fixed in heaven, which storm and frost have power no more to shake, or shed ;—that mighty Humanity, so perfect and so proud, that hides no weakness beneath the mantle, and gains no greatness from the diadem ; the majesty of thoughtful form, on which the dust of gold and flame of jewels are dashed as the sea-spray upon the rock, and still the great Manhood seems to stand bare against the blue sky ;—that mighty Mythology, which fills the daily walks of men with spiritual companionship, and beholds the protecting angels break with their burning presence through the arrow-flights of battle :—measure the compass of that field of creation, weigh the value of the inheritance that Venice thus left to the nations of Europe, and then judge if so vast, so beneficent a power could indeed have been rooted in dissipation or decay. It was when she wore the ephod of the priest, not the motley of the masquer, that the fire fell upon her from heaven ; and she saw the first rays of it through the rain of her own tears, when, as the barbaric deluge ebbed from the hills of Italy, the circuit of her palaces, and the orb of her fortunes, rose together, like the Iris, painted upon the Cloud.—*S. V.*, II. v., § 36.

206. THE MYSTERY OF EVIL.—It seems one of the most cunning and frequent of self-deceptions to turn the heart away from this warning, and refuse to acknowledge anything in the fair scenes of the natural creation but beneficence. Men in general lean towards the light, so far as they contemplate such things at all, most of them passing "by on the other side," either in mere plodding pursuit of their own work, irrespective of what good or evil is around them, or else in selfish gloom, or selfish delight, resulting from their own circumstances at the moment. Of those who give themselves to any true contemplation, the plurality, being humble, gentle, and kindly hearted, look only in nature for what is lovely and kind; partly, also, God gives the disposition to every healthy human mind in some degree to pass over or even harden itself against evil things, else the suffering would be too great to be borne; and humble people, with a quiet trust that everything is for the best, do not fairly represent the facts to themselves, thinking them none of their business. So, what between hard-hearted people, thoughtless people, busy people, humble people, and cheerfully minded people,— giddiness of youth, and pre-occupations of age,— philosophies of faith, and cruelties of folly,—priest and Levite, masquer and merchantman, all agreeing to keep their own side of the way,—the evil that God sends to warn us gets to be forgotten,

and the evil that He sends to be mended by us gets left unmended. And then, because people shut their eyes to the dark indisputableness of the facts in front of them, their Faith, such as it is, is shaken or uprooted by every darkness in what is revealed to them. In the present day it is not easy to find a well-meaning man among our more earnest thinkers, who will not take upon himself to dispute the whole system of redemption, because he cannot unravel the mystery of the punishment of sin. But can he unravel the mystery of the punishment of NO sin? Can he entirely account for all that happens to a cab-horse? Has he ever looked fairly at the fate of one of those beasts as it is dying,—measured the work it has done, and the reward it has got,—put his hand upon the bloody wounds through which its bones are piercing, and so looked up to Heaven with an entire understanding of Heaven's ways about the horse? Yet the horse is a fact—no dream—no revelation among the myrtle trees by night; and the dust it dies upon, and the dogs that eat it, are facts;—and yonder happy person, whose the horse was till its knees were broken over the hurdles, who had an immortal soul to begin with, and wealth and peace to help forward his immortality; who has also devoted the powers of his soul, and body, and wealth, and peace, to the spoiling of houses, the corruption of the innocent, and the oppression of the poor; and has, at

this actual moment of his prosperous life, as many
curses waiting round about him in calm shadow,
with their death's eyes fixed upon him, biding
their time, as ever the poor cab-horse had launched
at him in meaningless blasphemies, when his
failing feet stumbled at the stones,—this happy
person shall have no stripes,—shall have only
the horse's fate of annihilation ; or, if other things
are indeed reserved for him, Heaven's kindness
or omnipotence is to be doubted therefore.

We cannot reason of these things.   But this I
know—and this may by all men be known—that
no good or lovely thing exists in this world without its correspondent darkness ; and that the
universe presents itself continually to mankind
under the stern aspect of warning, or of choice,
the good and the evil set on the right hand and
the left.—*M. P.*, IV. v. 19, § 32, 33.

207. FAITH.—The right faith of man is not
intended to give him repose, but to enable him
to do his work.   It is not intended that he should
look away from the place he lives in now, and
cheer himself with thoughts of the place he is
to live in next, but that he should look stoutly
into this world, in faith that if he does his work
thoroughly here, some good to others or himself,
with which however he is not at present concerned, will come of it hereafter.   And this kind
of brave, but not very hopeful or cheerful faith,

I perceive to be always rewarded by clear practical success and splendid intellectual power; while the faith which dwells on the future fades away into rosy mist, and emptiness of musical air. That result indeed follows naturally enough on its habit of assuming that things must be right, or must come right, when, probably, the fact is, that so far as we are concerned, they are entirely wrong; and going wrong : and also on its weak and false way of looking on what these religious persons call " the bright side of things," that is to say, on one side of them only, when God has given them two sides, and intended us to see both.—*M. P.*, V. IX. 2, § 10.

208. OBEDIENCE.—That principle to which Polity owes its stability, Life its happiness, Faith its acceptance, and Creation its continuance, is Obedience.

Nor is it the least among the sources of more serious satisfaction which I have found in the pursuit of a subject that at first appeared to bear but slightly on the grave interests of mankind, that the conditions of material perfection which it leads me in conclusion to consider, furnish a strange proof how false is the conception, how frantic the pursuit, of that treacherous phantom which men call Liberty : most treacherous, indeed, of all phantoms ; for the feeblest ray of reason might surely show us, that not only its attainment, but its being, was impossible. There is no such thing in the universe. There can never be. The stars have it not; the earth has it not; the sea has it not; and we men have the mockery and semblance of it only for our heaviest punishment.

In one of the noblest poems * for its imagery and its music belonging to the recent school of our literature, the writer has sought in the aspect of inanimate nature the expression of that Liberty which, having once loved, he had seen among men in its true dyes of darkness. But with what strange fallacy of interpretation! since in one noble line of his invocation he has contradicted the assumptions of the rest, and acknowledged the presence of a subjection, surely not less severe because eternal? How could he otherwise? since if there be any one principle more widely than another confessed by every utterance, or more sternly than another imprinted on every atom of the visible creation, that principle is not Liberty, but Law.

The enthusiast would reply that by Liberty he meant the Law of Liberty. Then why use the single and misunderstood word? If by liberty

---

* "Ye clouds! that far above me float and pause,
    Whose pathless march no mortal may control!
    Ye ocean-waves! that wheresoe'er ye roll
  Yield homage only to eternal laws!"
                —Coleridge's *Ode to France.*

you mean chastisement of the passions, discipline of the intellect, subjection of the will; if you mean the fear of inflicting, the shame of committing, a wrong; if you mean respect for all who are in authority, and consideration for all who are in dependence; veneration for the good, mercy to the evil, sympathy with the weak; if you mean watchfulness over all thoughts, temperance in all pleasures, and perseverance in all toils; if you mean, in a word, that Service which is defined in the liturgy of the English church to be perfect Freedom, why do you name this by the same word by which the luxurious mean licence, and the reckless mean change; by which the rogue means rapine, and the fool, equality; by which the proud mean anarchy, and the malignant mean violence? Call it by any name rather than this, but its best and truest is Obedience. Obedience is, indeed, founded on a kind of freedom, else it would become mere subjugation, but that freedom is only granted that obedience may be more perfect; and thus, while a measure of licence is necessary to exhibit the individual energies of things, the fairness and pleasantness and perfection of them all consist in their Restraint. Compare a river that has burst its banks with one that is bound by them, and the clouds that are scattered over the face of the whole heaven with those that are marshalled into ranks and orders by its winds. So that though restraint, utter and unrelaxing, can never be comely, this is not because it is in itself an evil, but only because, when too great, it overpowers the nature of the thing restrained, and so counteracts the other laws of which that nature is itself composed.—*S. L. A.*, VII., § 1, 2.

209. UNWILLING SERVANTS.—It is neither by us ascertainable what moments of pure feeling or aspiration may occur to men of minds apparently cold and lost, nor by us to be pronounced through what instruments, and in what strangely occurrent voices, God may choose to communicate good to men. It seems to me that much of what is great, and to all men beneficial, has been wrought by those who neither intended nor knew the good they did; and that many mighty harmonies have been discoursed by instruments that had been dumb or discordant, but that God knew their stops. The Spirit of Prophecy consisted with the avarice of Balaam, and the disobedience of Saul. Could we spare from its page that parable, which he said, who saw the vision of the Almighty, falling into a trance, but having his eyes open; though we know that the sword of his punishment was then sharp in its sheath beneath him in the plains of Moab? or shall we not lament with David over the shield, cast away on the Gilboa mountains, of him to whom God gave *another heart* that day, when he turned his back

to go from Samuel ? It is not our part to look
hardly, nor to look always, to the character or
the deeds of men, but to accept from all of them,
and to hold fast, that which we can prove good,
and feel to be ordained for us. We know that
whatever good there is in them is itself divine ;
and wherever we see the virtue of ardent labour
and self-surrendering to a single purpose, wherever
we find constant reference made to the written
scripture of natural beauty, this at least we know
is great and good ; this we know is not granted
by the counsel of God without purpose, nor maintained without result : their interpretation we may
accept, into their labour we may enter, but they
themselves must look to it, if what they do has
no intent of good, nor any reference to the Giver
of all gifts. Selfish in their industry, unchastened
in their wills, ungrateful for the Spirit that is
upon them, they may yet be helmed by that Spirit
whithersoever the Governor listeth ; involuntary
instruments they may become of others' good ;
unwillingly they may bless Israel, doubtingly
discomfit Amalek ; but short coming there will
be of their glory, and sure, of their punishment.
—*M. P.*, II. III. 1, 15, § 8.

210. EVERY-DAY RELIGION.—In the pressing
or recommending of any act or manner of acting,
we have choice of two separate lines of argument :
one based on representation of the expediency or

inherent value of the work, which is often small and always disputable ; the other based on proofs of its relations to the higher orders of human virtue, and of its acceptableness, so far as it goes, to Him who is the origin of virtue. The former is commonly the more persuasive method, the latter assuredly the more conclusive; only it is liable to give offence, as if there were irreverence in adducing considerations so weighty in treating subjects of small temporal importance. I believe, however, that no error is more thoughtless than this. We treat God with irreverence by banishing Him from our thoughts, not by referring to His will on slight occasions. His is not the finite authority or intelligence which cannot be troubled with small things. There is nothing so small but that we may honour God by asking His guidance of it, or insult Him by taking it into our own hands ; and what is true of the Deity is equally true of His Revelation. We use it most reverently when most habitually : our insolence is in ever acting without reference to it, our true honouring of it is in its universal application. I have been blamed for the familiar introduction of its sacred words. I am grieved to have given pain by so doing ; but my excuse must be my wish that those words were made the ground of every argument and the test of every action. We have them not often enough on our lips, nor deeply enough in our memories, nor loyally enough in our lives. The snow, the vapour, and the stormy wind fulfil His word. Are our acts and thoughts lighter and wilder than these—that we should forget it?—*S. L. A.*, *Introduction*.

211. RELIGION AND SCIENCE.—Much as I reverence physical science as a means of mental education, I reverence it, at this moment, more as the source of utmost human practical power, and the means by which the far-distant races of the world, who now sit in darkness and the shadow of death, are to be reached and regenerated. At home, or far away, the call is equally instant:—here, for want of more extended physical science, there is plague in our streets, famine in our fields; the pest strikes root and fruit over a hemisphere of the earth, we know not why; the voices of our children fade away into silence of venomous death, we know not why; the population of this most civilised country resists every effort to lead it into purity of habit and habitation,—to give it genuineness of nourishment and wholesomeness of air,—as a new interference with its liberty, and insists vociferously on its right to helpless death. All this is terrible; but it is more terrible yet that dim, phosphorescent, frightful superstitions still hold their own over two-thirds of the inhabited globe, and that all the phenomena of nature which were intended by their Creator to enforce His eternal laws of love and

judgment, and which, rightly understood, enforce them more strongly by their patient beneficence and their salutary destructiveness, than the miraculous dew on Gideon's fleece, or the restrained lightnings of Horeb—that all these legends of God's daily dealing with His creatures remain unread, or are read backwards, into blind, hundred-armed horror of idol cosmogony.

How strange it seems that physical science should ever have been thought adverse to religion! The pride of physical science is, indeed, adverse—like every other pride—both to religion and truth; but the sincerity of science, so far from being hostile, is the path-maker among the mountains for the feet of those who publish peace.—*The Oxford Museum*, 1859 (*A. C.*, I., p. 192–195).

212. SEEK, AND YE SHALL FIND.—These I hold for two fundamental principles of religion,— that, without seeking, truth cannot be known at all; and that, by seeking, it may be discovered by the simplest. I say, without seeking it cannot be known at all. It can neither be declared from pulpits, nor set down in Articles, nor in anywise "prepared and sold" in packages, ready for use. Truth must be ground for every man by himself out of its husk, with such help as he can get, indeed, but not without stern labour of his own. In what science is knowledge to be had cheap?

or truth to be told over a velvet cushion, in half an hour's talk every seventh day ?   Can you learn chemistry so ?—zoology ?—anatomy ? and do you expect to penetrate the secret of all secrets, and to know that whose price is above rubies, and of which the depth saith,—It is not in me,—in so easy fashion ?   There are doubts in this matter which evil spirits darken with their wings, and that is true of all such doubts which we were told long ago ; they can " be ended by action alone."

As surely as we live, this truth of truths can only so be discerned ; to those who act on what they know, more shall be revealed ; and thus, if any man will do His will, he shall know the doctrine whether it be of God.   Any man, not the man who has most means of knowing, who has the subtlest brains, or sits under the most orthodox preacher, or has his library fullest of most orthodox books,—but the man who strives to know, who takes God at His word, and sets himself to dig up the heavenly mystery, roots and all, before sunset, and the night come, when no man can work.   Beside such a man, God stands in more and more visible presence as he toils, and teaches him that which no preacher can teach —no earthly authority gainsay.   By such a man, the preacher must himself be judged.—*Notes on the Construction of Sheepfolds* (*O. R.*, II., § 201, 202).

213. THE MIRROR OF THE SOUL.—Here is
a short piece of precious word revelation, for
instance. "God is love." Love! yes. But what
is *that*? The revelation does not tell you that,
I think. Look into the mirror, and you will see.
Out of your own heart you may know what love
is. In no other possible way,—by no other help
or sign. All the words and sounds ever uttered,
all the revelations of cloud, or flame, or crystal,
are utterly powerless. They cannot tell you, in
the smallest point, what love means. Only the
broken mirror can.

Here is more revelation. "God is just!" Just!
What is that? The revelation cannot help you
to discover. You say it is dealing equitably or
equally. But how do you discern the equality?
Not by inequality of mind; not by a mind incapable of weighing, judging, or distributing. If the
lengths seem unequal in the broken mirror, for
you they are unequal; but if they seem equal,
then the mirror is true. So far as you recognise
equality, and your conscience tells you what is
just, so far your mind is the image of God's: and
so far as you do *not* discern this nature of justice
or equality, the words, "God is just," bring no
revelation to you.

"But His thoughts are not as our thoughts."
No: the sea is not as the standing pool by the
wayside. Yet when the breeze crisps the pool,
you may see the image of the breakers, and a

likeness of the foam. Nay, in some sort, the same foam. If the sea is for ever invisible to you, something you may learn of it from the pool. Nothing, assuredly, any otherwise.

"But this poor miserable Me! Is *this*, then, all the book I have got to read about God in?" Yes, truly so. No other book, nor fragment of book, than that, will you ever find;—no velvet-bound missal, nor frankincensed manuscript;— nothing hieroglyphic nor cuneiform; papyrus and pyramid are alike silent on this matter; nothing in the clouds above, nor in the earth beneath. That flesh-bound volume is the only revelation that is, that was, or that can be. In that is the image of God painted; in that is the law of God written; in that is the promise of God revealed. Know thyself; for through thyself only thou canst know God.—*M. P.*, V. IX. 1, § 10.

214. "THY KINGDOM COME," we are bid to ask then! But how shall it come? With power and great glory, it is written; and yet not with observation, it is also written. Strange kingdom! Yet its strangeness is renewed to us with every dawn.

When the time comes for us to wake out of the world's sleep, why should it be otherwise than out of the dreams of the night? Singing of birds, first, broken and low, as, not to dying eyes, but eyes that wake to life, "the casement slowly grows a glimmering square;" and then the gray, and then the rose of dawn; and last the light, whose going forth is to the ends of heaven.

This kingdom it is not in our power to bring; but it is, to receive. Nay, it is come already, in part; but not received, because men love chaos best; and the Night, with her daughters. That is still the only question for us, as in the old Elias days, "If ye will receive it." With pains it may be shut out still from many a dark place of cruelty; by sloth it may be still unseen for many a glorious hour. But the pain of shutting it out must grow greater and greater:—harder, every day, that struggle of man with man in the abyss, and shorter wages for the fiend's work. But it is still at our choice; the simoom-dragon may still be served if we will, in the fiery desert, or else God walking in the garden, at cool of day. Coolness now, not of Hesperus over Atlas, stooped endurer of toil; but of Heosphorus over Sion, the joy of the earth. The choice is no vague nor doubtful one. High on the desert mountain, full descried, sits throned the tempter, with his old promise—the kingdoms of this world, and the glory of them. He still calls you to your labour, as Christ to your rest;—labour and sorrow, base desire, and cruel hope. So far as you desire to possess, rather than to give; so far as you look for power to command, instead of to bless; so far as your own prosperity seems to you to issue out of contest or rivalry, of any kind, with other men, or other nations; so long as the hope before you is for supremacy instead of love; and your desire is to be greatest, instead of least;—first, instead of last;—so long you are serving the Lord of all that is last, and least;—the last enemy that shall be destroyed—Death; and you shall have death's crown, with the worm coiled in it; and death's wages, with the worm feeding on them; kindred of the earth shall you yourself become; saying to the grave, "Thou art my father;" and to the worm, "Thou art my mother, and my sister."

I leave you to judge, and to choose, between this labour, and the bequeathed peace; these wages, and the gift of the Morning Star; this obedience, and the doing of the will which shall enable you to claim another kindred than of the earth, and to hear another voice than that of the grave, saying, "My brother, and sister, and mother."—*M. P.*, V. IX. 12, § 20.

INDEX.

(The figures refer to *pages* of this volume.)

I.   2 K

THE END.

Printed by BALLANTYNE, HANSON & CO.
Edinburgh & London

THE END.

Printed by BALLANTYNE, HANSON & CO.
Edinburgh & London